ESKIMO LIFE

LECTOR HOUSE PUBLIC DOMAIN WORKS

ESKIMO LIFE

FRIDTJOF NANSEN,
WILLIAM ARCHER

ISBN: 978-93-90314-39-3

Published: 1893

LECTOR HOUSE LLP
E-MAIL: lectorpublishing@gmail.com

A HUNTER, HIS WIFE, AND A YOUNG GIRL (WEST COAST OF
GREENLAND)

ESKIMO LIFE

BY

FRIDTJOF NANSEN

AUTHOR OF 'THE FIRST CROSSING OF GREENLAND'

TRANSLATED BY
WILLIAM ARCHER

WITH ILLUSTRATIONS

1893

TRANSLATOR'S PREFACE.

Before placing his 'Eskimoliv' in my hands for translation, Dr. Nansen very carefully revised the text, and made numerous excisions and additions. Thus the following pages will be found to differ in several particulars from the Norwegian original. I also requested and received Dr. Nansen's permission to suppress one or two especially nauseous details of Eskimo manners, which seemed to have no particular ethnological significance. The excisions made on this score, however, probably do not amount to half a page in all.

Dr. Nansen suggested that I should follow the example of Dr. Rink in his 'Tales and Traditions of the Eskimo,' and treat the word 'Eskimo' as indeclinable. I have ventured, however, to overrule his suggestion. There is precedent for both 'Eskimo' and 'Eskimos' as the plural form; and where there is any choice at all, it seems only rational to prefer the regular declension.

In Chapters XIII. and XIV. Dr. Nansen naturally makes numerous references to that great storehouse of Greenland folk-lore, Dr. Rink's 'Eskimo Sagn og Eventyr,' which has been translated and condensed by the author himself, under the above-mentioned title. Where it was possible, I have given the reference to the English edition; but in cases where the text has been very freely condensed or expurgated, I have referred to the Danish original as well. Even where I have not done so, students of folk-lore may be advised to go back to the original text, which is often fuller and more characteristic than the English version.

W. A.

AUTHOR'S PREFACE.

For one whole winter we were cut off from the world and immured among the Greenlanders. I dwelt in their huts, took part in their hunting, and tried, as well as I could, to live their life and learn their language. But one winter, unfortunately, is far too short a time in which to attain a thorough knowledge of so peculiar a people, its civilisation, and its ways of thought—that would require years of patient study. Nevertheless, I have tried in this book to record the impressions made upon me by the Eskimo and his polity, and have sought, as far as possible, to support them by quotations from former authors. There may even be things which a newcomer sees more clearly than an observer of many years' standing, who lives in their midst.

On many points, perhaps, the reader may not think as I do. I cannot, it is true, find that whatever is is very good; I am weak enough to feel compassion for a declining race, which is perhaps beyond all help, since it is already stung with the venom of our civilisation. But I comfort myself with the thought that at least no words of mine can make the lot of this people worse than it is, and I hope that the reader will accept my observations in the spirit in which they are written. *Amicus Plato, amicus Socrates, magis amica veritas*—the truth before everything. And if in some points I should appear unreasonable, I must plead as my excuse that it is scarcely possible to live for any time among these people without conceiving an affection for them—for that, one winter is more than enough.

During the long, dark evenings, as I sat in the low earth-huts and gazed at the flame of the train-oil lamps, I had ample time for reflection. It often seemed to me that I could see these hardy children of Nature pressing westward, stage by stage, in their dog-sledges and in their wonderful skin-canoes, along the barren ice-coasts; I saw how they fought their way onward, and, little by little, perfected their ingenious implements and attained their masterly skill in the chase. Hundreds, nay thousands, of years passed, tribe after tribe succumbed, while other and stronger stocks survived—and I was filled with admiration for a people which had emerged victorious from the struggle with such inhospitable natural surroundings.

But in melancholy contrast to this inspiriting picture of the past, the present and the future rose before my eyes—a sad, a hopeless mist.

In Greenland the Eskimos fell in with Europeans. First it was our Norwegian forefathers of the olden times; them they gradually overcame. But we returned to the charge, this time bringing with us Christianity and the products of civilisation; then they succumbed, and are sinking ever lower and lower. The world passes on with a pitying shrug of the shoulders.

> 'What more can one say? Who's a penny the worse
> Though a beggar be dead?'

But this people, too, has its feelings, like others; it, too, rejoices in life and Nature, and bleeds under our iron heel. If anyone doubts this, let him observe their sympathy with one another, and their love for their children; or let him read their legends.

Whenever I saw instances of the suffering and misery which we have brought upon them, that remnant of a sense of justice which is still to be found in most of us stirred me to indignation, and I was filled with a burning desire to send the truth reverberating over the whole world. Were it once brought home to them, I thought, people could not but awaken from their indifference, and at once make good the wrong they had done.

Poor dreamer! You have nothing to say which has not been better said before. The hapless lot of the Greenlanders, as well as of other 'native' races, has been set forth on many hands, and always without avail.

But, none the less, I felt I must unburden my conscience; it seemed to me a sacred duty to add my protest to the rest. My pen, unhappily, is all too feeble: what I feel most deeply I have failed to express: never have I longed more intensely for a poet's gifts. I know very well that my voice, too, will be as a cry sent forth over a flat expanse of desert, without even mountains to echo it back. My only hope is to awaken here and there a feeling of sympathy with the Eskimos and of sorrow for their destiny.

FRIDTJOF NANSEN.

GODTHAAB, LYSAKER:
November 1891.

CONTENTS

LIST OF ILLUSTRATIONS

ESKIMO LIFE

CHAPTER I

GREENLAND AND THE ESKIMO

Greenland is in a peculiar manner associated with Norway and with the Norwegians. Our forefathers were the first Europeans who found their way to its shores. In their open vessels the old Vikings made their daring voyages, through tempests and drift-ice, to this distant land of snows, settled there throughout several centuries, and added it to the domain of the Norwegian crown.

After the memory of its existence had practically passed away, it was again one of our countrymen[1] who, on behalf of a Norwegian company, founded the second European settlement of the country.

It is poor, this land of the Eskimo, which we have taken from him; it has neither timber nor gold to offer us—it is naked, lonely, like no other land inhabited of man. But in all its naked poverty, how beautiful it is! If Norway is glorious, Greenland is in truth no less so. When one has once seen it, how dear to him is its recollection! I do not know if others feel as I do, but for me it is touched with all the dream-like beauty of the fairyland of my childish imagination. It seems as though I there found our own Norwegian scenery repeated in still nobler, purer forms.

It is strong and wild, this Nature, like a saga of antiquity carven in ice and stone, yet with moods of lyric delicacy and refinement. It is like cold steel with the shimmering colours of a sunlit cloud playing through it.

When I see glaciers and ice-mountains, my thoughts fly to Greenland where the glaciers are vaster than anywhere else, where the ice-mountains jut into a sea covered with icebergs and drift-ice. When I hear loud encomiums on the progress of our society, its great men and their great deeds, my thoughts revert to the boundless snow-fields stretching white and serene in an unbroken sweep from sea to sea, high over what have once been fruitful valleys and mountains. Some day, perhaps, a similar snow-field will cover us all.

Everything in Greenland is simple and great—white snow, blue ice, naked, black rocks and peaks, and dark stormy sea. When I see the sun sink glowing into the waves, it recalls to me the Greenland sunsets, with the islets and rocks floating, as it were, on the burnished surface of the smooth, softly-heaving sea, while inland the peaks rise row on row, flushing in the evening light. And sometimes when I see the sæter-life[2] at home and watch the sæter-girls and the grazing cows, I think

---

[1] Hans Egede. *Trans.*
[2] Sæter==mountain châlet. *Trans.*

of the tent-life and the reindeer-herds on the Greenland fiords and uplands; I think of the screaming ptarmigan, the moors and willow-copses, the lakes and valleys in among the mountains where the Eskimo lives through his brief summer.

'THE BOUNDLESS SNOW-FIELDS STRETCHING CALM AND WHITE FROM SEA TO SEA'

But like nothing else is the Greenland winter-night with its flaming northern lights; it is Nature's own mystic spirit-dance.

Strange is the power which this land exercises over the mind; but the race that inhabits it is not less remarkable than the land itself.

The Eskimo, more than anyone else, belongs to the coast and the sea. He dwells by the sea, upon it he seeks his subsistence, it gives him all the necessaries of his life, over it he makes all his journeys, whether in his skin-canoes in summer, or in his dog-sledges when it is ice-bound in winter. The sea is thus the strongest influence in the life of the Eskimo; what wonder, then, if his soul reflects its moods? His mind changes with the sea—grave in the storm; in sunshine and calm full of unfettered glee. He is a child of the sea, thoughtlessly gay like the playful wavelet, but sometimes dark as the foaming tempest. One feeling chases another from his childlike mind as rapidly as, when the storm has died down, the billows sink to rest, and the very memory of it has passed away.

The good things of life are very unequally divided in this world. To some existence is so easy that they need only plant a bread-fruit tree in their youth, and their whole life is provided for. Others, again, seem to be denied everything except the strength to battle for life; they must laboriously wring from hostile Nature every mouthful of their sustenance. They are sent forth to the outposts, these people; they form the wings of the great army of humanity in its constant struggle for the subjugation of nature.

Such a people are the Eskimos, and among the most remarkable in existence. They are a living proof of the rare faculty of the human being for adapting himself to circumstances and spreading over the face of the earth.

The Eskimo forms the extreme outpost towards the infinite stillness of the regions of ice, and as far, almost, as we have forced our way to the northward, we find traces left behind them by this hardy race.

The tracts which all others despise he has made his own. By dint of constant struggle and slow development, he learnt some things that none have learnt better. Where for others the conditions which make life possible came to an end, there life began for him. He has come to love these regions; they are to him a world in which he himself embodies the whole of the human race.[3] Outside their limits he could not exist.

It is to this people that the following pages are devoted.

The mutual resemblance of the different tribes of Eskimos is no less striking than their difference from all other races in features, figure, implements and weapons, and general manner of life.

A pure-bred Eskimo from Bering Straits is so like a Greenlander that one cannot for a moment doubt that they belong to the same race. Their language, too, is so far alike that an Alaska Eskimo and a Greenlander would probably, after some little time, be able to converse without much difficulty. Captain Adrian Jacobsen, who has travelled both in Greenland and in Alaska, told me that in Alaska he could

[3] The Eskimos call themselves *inuit*—that is to say, 'human beings'; all other men they conceive as belonging to a different genus of animals.

manage to get along with the few words of Eskimo he had learnt in Greenland. These two peoples are divided by a distance of about 3,000 miles—something like the distance between London and Afghanistan. Such unity of speech among races so widely separated is probably unique in the history of mankind.

The likeness between all the different tribes of Eskimos, as well as their secluded position with respect to other peoples, and the perfection of their implements, might be taken to indicate that they are of a very old race, in which everything has stiffened into definite forms, which can now be but slowly altered. Other indications, however, seem to conflict with such a hypothesis, and render it more probable that the race was originally a small one, which did not until a comparatively late period develop to the point at which we now find it, and spread over the countries which it at present inhabits.

If it should seem difficult to understand, at first sight, how they could have spread in a comparatively short time over these wide tracts of country without moving in great masses, as in the case of larger migrations, we need only reflect that their present inhospitable abiding-places can scarcely have been inhabited, at any rate permanently, before they took possession of them, and that therefore they had nothing to contend with except nature itself.

The region now inhabited by the Eskimos stretches from the west coast of Bering Straits over Alaska, the north coast of North America, the North American groups of Arctic Islands, the west coast, and, finally, the east coast, of Greenland.

By reason of his absolutely secluded position, the Eskimo has given the anthropologists much trouble, and the most contradictory opinions have been advanced with reference to his origin.

Dr. H. Rink, who has made Greenland and its people the study of his life, and is beyond comparison the greatest authority on the subject, holds that the Eskimo implements and weapons—at any rate, for the greater part—may be traced to America. He regards it as probable that the Eskimos were once a race dwelling in the interior of Alaska, where there are still a considerable number of inland Eskimos, and that they have migrated thence to the coasts of the ice-sea. He further maintains that their speech is most closely connected with the primitive dialects of America, and that their legends and customs recall those of the Indians.

One point among others, however, in which the Eskimos differ from the Indians is the use of dog-sledges. With the exception of the Incas of Peru, who used the llama as a beast of burden, no American aborigines employed animals either for drawing or for carrying. In this, then, the Eskimos more resemble the races of the Asiatic polar regions.

But it would lead us too far afield if we were to follow up this difficult scientific question, on which the evidence is as yet by no means thoroughly sifted. So much alone can we declare with any assurance, that the Eskimos dwelt in comparatively recent times on the coasts around Bering Straits and Bering Sea—probably on the American side—and have thence, stage by stage, spread eastward over Arctic America to Greenland.

It is in my judgment impossible to determine at what time they reached Greenland and permanently settled there. From what has already been said it appears probable that the period was comparatively late, but it does not seem to me established, as has been asserted in several quarters, that we can conclude from the Icelandic sagas that they first made their appearance on the west coast of Greenland in the fourteenth century. It certainly appears as though the Norwegian colonies of Österbygd and Vesterbygd (*i.e.* Easter- and Wester-district or settlement) were not until that period exposed to serious attacks on the part of the 'Skrellings' or Eskimos, coming in bands from the north; but this does not preclude the supposition that they had occupied certain tracts of the west coast of Greenland long before that time and long before the Norwegians discovered the country. They do not seem to have been settled upon the southern part of the coast during the first four hundred years of the Norwegian occupation, since they are not mentioned in the sagas; but it is expressly stated that the first Norwegians (Erik the Red and others) who came to the country, found both in the Easter- and the Wester-districts ruins of human habitations, fragments of boats, and stone implements, which in their opinion must have belonged to a feeble folk, whom they therefore called 'Skrellings' (or 'weaklings'). We must accordingly conclude that the 'Skrellings' had been there previously; and as such remains were found in both districts, it seems that they could scarcely have paid mere passing visits to them. It is not impossible that the Eskimos might simply have taken to their heels when the Norwegian viking-ships appeared in the offing; we, too, found them do so upon the east coast; but it does not seem at all probable that they could vanish so rapidly as to let the Norwegians catch no glimpse of them. The probability is, on the whole, that at that time the permanent settlements of the Eskimos were further north on the coast, above the 68th degree of north latitude, where seals and whales abound, and where they would first arrive on their course from the northward[4] (see p. 13). From these permanent settlements they probably, in Eskimo fashion, made frequent excursions of more or less duration to the more southerly part of the west coast, and there left behind them the traces which were first found. When the Norwegian settlers began to range northwards they at last came in contact with the Eskimos. Professor G. Storm[5] is of opinion that this must first have happened in the twelfth century.[6] We read in the 'Historia Norvegiæ' that the hunters in the unsettled districts of north Greenland came upon an undersized people whom they called 'Skrellings,' and who used stone knives and arrow-points of whalebone. As their more northern settlements became over-populated, the Eskimos no doubt began to migrate southwards in earnest; and as the Norwegians often dealt hardly with them when they met, they may eventually have taken revenge in the fourteenth century by first (after 1341) attacking and devastating (?) the West-

---

[4] North of the 68th degree they could kill seals and whales in plenty from the ice all the winter through; and this is a method of hunting which they must have learnt further north, where it would be the most important of all for them.

[5] Gustav Storm: *Studies on the Vineland Voyages,* Extracts from *Mémoires de la Société Royale des Antiquaires du Nord,* 1888, p. 53.

[6] The Eskimos themselves have several legends as to their encounters with the old Norsemen. See Rink: *Tales and Traditions of the Eskimo,* pp. 308-321.

er-district, and later (1379) making an expedition against the Easter-district, which seems in the following century to have been entirely destroyed.[7] It was about this time, accordingly, that the Eskimos probably effected their first permanent settlements in the southern parts of the country.

There is evidence in the Eskimo legends as well of the battles between them and the old Norsemen. But from the same legends we also learn that there was sometimes friendly intercourse between them; indeed the Norsemen are several times mentioned with esteem. This appears to show that there was no rooted hatred between the two races; and the theory that the Eskimos carried on an actual war of extermination against the settlers seems, moreover, in total conflict with their character as we now know it. Thus it can scarcely have been such a war alone that caused the downfall of the colony. We may, perhaps, attribute it partly to natural decline due to seclusion from the world, partly to absorption of the race, brought about by the crossing of the two stocks; for the Europeans of that age were probably no more inaccessible than those of to-day to the seductions of Eskimo loveliness.

As to the route by which the Eskimos made their way to the west coast of Greenland there has been a good deal of difference of opinion. Dr. Rink maintains that after passing Smith's Sound the Eskimos did not proceed southwards along the west coast, which would seem their most natural course, but turned northwards, rounded the northernmost point of the country, and came down along the east coast. In this way they must ultimately have approached the west coast from the southward, after making their way round the southern extremity of Greenland. This opinion is mainly founded upon the belief that Thorgils Orrabeinsfostre fell in with Eskimos upon the east coast, and that this was the Norsemen's first encounter with them. I have already, in a note on the preceding page, remarked on the untrustworthiness of this evidence; and such a theory as to the route of the Eskimo immigration stands, as we know, in direct conflict with the accounts given in the sagas, from which it appears (as above) that the Eskimos came from the north and not from the south, the Wester-district having been destroyed before the Easter-district. It appears, moreover, that we can draw the same conclusion from an Eskimo tradition in which their first encounter with the old Norsemen is described. In former days, we are told, when the coast was still very thinly populated, a boatful of explorers came into Godthaab-fiord and saw there a large house whose inhabitants were strange to them, not being Kaladlit—that is, Eskimo. They had suddenly come upon the old Norsemen. These, on their side, saw the Kaladlit for the first time, and treated them in the most friendly fashion. This happened, it will be observed, in Godthaab-fiord, which was in the ancient Wester-district—

---

[7] Some writers have concluded from the mention of 'troll-women' in the 'Flóamannasaga' that so early as the year 1000, or thereabouts, Thorgils Orrabeinsfostre must have encountered Eskimos on the south-east coast of Greenland. But, as Professor Storm has pointed out, the romantic character of this saga forbids us to base any such inference upon it. It must also be remembered that the extant manuscript dates from no earlier than about 1400, long after the time when the Norsemen had come in contact with the Eskimos on the west coast. Even if the Eskimos are meant in the passage about the troll-women, which is extremely doubtful, it may very well be a late interpolation.

that is to say, the more northern colony. There is another circumstance which, to my thinking, renders improbable the route conjectured by Dr. Rink, and that is that if they made their way around the northern extremity of the country, they must, while in these high latitudes, have lived as the so-called Arctic Highlanders—that is, the Eskimos of Cape York and northwards—now do; in other words, they must have subsisted chiefly by hunting upon the ice, must have travelled in dog-sledges, and, while in the far north, must have used neither kaiaks nor woman-boats, since the sea, being usually ice-bound, offers little or no opportunity for kaiak-hunting or boating of any sort. It may not be in itself impossible that, when they came further south and reached more ice-free waters again, they may have recovered the art of building woman-boats and kaiaks, of which some tradition would in any case survive; but it seems improbable, not to say impossible, that after having lost the habit of kaiak-hunting they should be able to master it afresh, and to develop it, and all the appliances belonging to it, to a higher point of perfection than had elsewhere been attained.

The most natural account of the matter, in my opinion, is that the Eskimos, after crossing Smith's Sound (so far there can be no doubt about their route), made their way southwards along the coast, and subsequently passed from the west coast, around the southern extremity of the country, up the east coast. It is impossible to determine whether they had reached the east coast and settled there before the Norsemen came to Greenland. On their southward journey from Smith's Sound they must, indeed, have met with a great obstacle in the Melville glacier (at about 77° north latitude), which stands right out into the sea at a point at which the coast is for a long distance unprotected by islands. But, in the first place, they may have been able to make their way onward in the lee of the drift-ice; and, in the second place, this difficulty is at worst not so great as those they must have encountered in passing round the northern extremity of Greenland. Moreover, the passage in an open boat from Smith's Sound southward along the west coast of Greenland to the Danish colonies has been several times accomplished in recent years without any particular difficulty. In opposition to this theory it may, no doubt, be alleged that the East Greenlanders possess dog-sledges, which are not used on the southern part of the west coast, where there is not enough ice for them. But if we remember with what rapidity, comparatively speaking, the Eskimos travel in their women-boats, and how fond they were in former times of roaming up and down along the coast—and when we take into account the fact that from time immemorial dogs have been kept along the whole of the west coast—this objection seems to lose its weight.

The Eskimos are at present spread over the whole west coast of Greenland, right from Smith's Sound to Cape Farewell. On the Danish part of the west coast they number very nearly 10,000. On the east coast, as we learn from the account of the Danish woman-boat expedition of 1884-85, under Captain Holm, there are Eskimos as far north as the Angmagsalik district (66° north latitude), their numbers in the autumn of 1884 being in all 548. Further north, as the Eskimos told Captain Holm, there were no permanent settlements so far as they knew. They often, however, made excursions to the northward, possibly as far as to the 68th or 69th degree of latitude; and a year or two before two woman-boats had sailed in that direction, and had never been heard of again. It is uncertain whether there may not be Eskimos upon the east coast further north than the 70th degree of latitude. Clavering is known to have found one or two families of them in 1823 at about 74° north latitude; but since that time none have been seen; and the German expedition which explored that coast in 1869-70, and wintered there, found houses and other remains, but no people, and therefore assumed that they must have died out. The Danish expedition of 1890 to Scoresby Sound, under Lieutenant Ryder, reports the same experience. It therefore seems probable that they have either died out or have abandoned this part of Greenland. This does not seem to me absolutely certain, however. There may be small and confined Eskimo colonies in these northern districts, or there may be a few nomadic families whom no one has as yet come across. This portion of the east coast must, in my opinion, be quite specially adapted for Eskimo habitation, as it is very rich in game. It therefore seems to me strange that when once the Eskimos had arrived there they should have gone away again; nor does it seem probable that they would die out in so excellent a hunting-ground. If there are Eskimos upon this north-east coast, their secluded position, debarring them from all intercourse, direct or indirect, with the outer world, must render them, from an ethnological point of view, among the most interesting people in existence.

CHAPTER II
APPEARANCE AND DRESS

As I now sit down to describe these people, at such a distance from them and from the scenery amid which we lived together, how vividly my first meeting with them, upon the east coast of Greenland, stands before my mind's eye! I see two brown laughing countenances, surrounded by long, coal-black hair, beaming, even amid the ice, with bright contentment both with themselves and the world, and full of the friendliest good-humour, mingled with unaffected astonishment at the appearance of the marvellous strangers.

The pure-bred Eskimo would at first glance seem to most of us Europeans anything but beautiful.

He has a round, broad face, with large, coarse features; small, dark, sometimes rather oblique eyes; a flat nose, narrow between the eyes and broad at the base; round cheeks, bursting with fat; a broad mouth; heavy, broad jaws; which, together with the round cheeks, give the lower part of the face a great preponderance in the physiognomy. When the mouth is drawn up in an oleaginous smile, two rows of strong white teeth reveal themselves. One receives the impression, upon the whole, of an admirable chewing apparatus, conveying pleasant suggestions of much and good eating. But, at the same time, one traces in these features, especially in those of the women, a certain touch of ingratiating petted softness.

To our way of thinking, such a face could scarcely be described as beautiful; but how much prejudice there is in our ideas of beauty! I soon came to find these brown faces, gleaming with health and fat, really pleasing. They reflected the free life of nature, and suggested to my mind pictures of blue sea, white glaciers, and glittering sunshine.

It was, however, chiefly the young that produced this impression; and they soon grow old. The shrunken, blear-eyed, hairless old women, reminding one of frost-bitten apples, were certainly not beautiful; and yet there was a certain style in them, too. Toil had left its traces upon their wrinkled countenances, but also a life of rude plenty and a habit of good-humoured, hopeless resignation. There was nothing of that vitreous hardness or desiccated dignity which the school of life so often imprints upon aged countenances in other parts of the world.

The half-caste race which has arisen upon the west coast, of mingled European and Eskimo blood, is apt to be, according to our ideas, handsomer than the pure-bred Eskimos. They have, as a rule, a somewhat southern appearance, with their dark hair, dark eyebrows and eyes, and brown complexion. A remarkably Jewish cast of countenance sometimes appears among them. Types of real beauty are by no means rare—male as well as female. Yet there is apt to be something feeble about these half-breeds. The pure-bred Eskimos undoubtedly seem more genuine and healthy.

It is a common error among us in Europe to think of the Eskimos as a diminutive race. Though no doubt smaller than the Scandinavian peoples, they must be reckoned among the middle-sized races, and I even found among those of purest breeding men of nearly six feet in height. Their frame produces, on the whole, an impression of strength, especially the upper part of the body. The men have broad shoulders, strong, muscular arms, and a good chest; but, on the other hand, one notices that their thighs are comparatively narrow, and their legs not particularly strong. When they get up in years, therefore, they are apt to have an uncertain gait, with knees slightly bent. This defective development of the lower extremities must be ascribed, for the most part, to the daily confinement in the cramped kaiak.

A noticeable physical characteristic of the women appeared to me to be their comparatively narrow hips, which we are apt to regard as inconsistent with the type of feminine beauty. They certainly seemed to me considerably narrower than those of European women; but it is hard to say how much of this effect is to be ascribed to difference of dress. The Eskimo women, however, are remarkable for their very small and well-formed hands and feet. Their physique, as a whole, strikes one as sympathetic and pleasing.

The complexion of the pure-bred Greenlander is of a brownish or greyish yellow, and even among the half-breeds a certain tinge of brownish yellow is unmistakable. This natural darkness of the skin, however, is generally much intensified, especially in the case of men and old women, by a total lack of cleanliness. As an indication of their habits in this particular, it will be sufficient if I quote the concise description given by our very reverend countryman, Hans Egede, of the method of washing practised by the men in particular: 'They scrape the sweat off their faces with a knife.'

The skin of new-born children is fair, and that not merely because they have not yet had time to grow dirty. Hans Egede Saabye noted long ago in his Journal[8] that children have on the small of their back a bluish-black patch, about the size of a sixpenny piece, from which the dark colour of the skin seems to spread as they grow older. Holm makes a note to the same effect in his account of the east coast.[9] I cannot speak on the subject from personal observation. It is perhaps worth noting that something similar is related of Japanese children.

Most of my readers have probably formed some idea of the Eskimo costume from pictures (see Frontispiece). They are probably aware that its most noteworthy peculiarity lies in the fact that the women dress almost like the men. Their costume is certainly very much prettier and more sensible than our ugly and awkward female fashions.

---

[8] Saabye: *Greenland; being extracts from a Journal kept in that country in the years 1770 to 1778*. London: 1818.

[9] *Meddelelser om Grönland*. Pt. 10, p. 58. Copenhagen: 1889.

In South Greenland the men wear upon their body what is called a *timiak*. It is made of bird-skins, with the feathers or down turned inwards, is shaped very much like our woollen jerseys, and, like them, is drawn over the head. The timiak is provided with a hood, used as a head-covering in the open air; at other times it is thrown back, and forms, with its upstanding selvage of black dog-skin, a sort of collar round the neck. At the wrists, too, the timiak is edged with black dog-skin, like a showy fur overcoat among us. Above the timiak, an outer vest (*anorak*) is worn, now for the most part made of cotton. Trousers of seal-skin, or of European cloth, are worn upon the legs; on the feet a peculiar sort of shoes, *kamiks*, made of seal-skin. These consist of two layers, an interior sock of skin with the fur turned inwards, and an exterior shoe of hairless, water-tight hide. In the sole, between the sock and the outer shoe, is placed a layer of straw or of bladder-sedge.[10] Into these kamiks the naked foot is thrust.

The costume of the women closely resembles that of the men. In South Greenland a bird-skin jacket is worn upon the body, which has, however, no hood to cover the head, but instead of it a high upstanding collar edged with black dog-skin, which is made to glisten as much as possible; and outside this collar a broad necklace of glass beads is often worn, radiant with all the colours of the rainbow. The wrists, too, are edged with black dog-skin. The cotton vest above this garment is of course as brightly coloured as possible, red, blue, green, yellow, and round its lower edge there generally runs a broad variegated band of cotton, or, if possible, of silk. Trousers are worn on the legs, generally of mottled seal-skin, but sometimes of reindeer-skin. They are considerably shorter than the men's trousers, coming only to a little way above the knee, but are richly decorated in front with bright-coloured embroideries in leather, and white stripes of reindeer-skin or dog-skin. The kamiks are longer than those of the men, and come up to above the knees; they are generally painted red, but sometimes blue, violet, or white. Down the front of them is sewn a band of many-coloured embroidery.

Besides the garments above-mentioned, there is another, used by women who are nursing children. It is called an *amaut*, and resembles an ordinary anorak, except that at the back there is a great enlargement or pouch, in which they carry the child all day long, whatever work they may be about. As the amaut is lined both inside and out with reindeer- or seal-skin, this pouch makes a nice warm nest for the child.

As no fashion-paper is published in Greenland, fashions are not so variable among the Eskimos as they are with us. Even in this respect, however, they are no mere barbarians, as the following example will show:

In former times, the women's anoraks and jackets were as long as the men's; but after the Europeans had imported the extravagant luxury of wearing white linen, they felt that such a wonderful tissue was far too beautiful and effective to be concealed. Instead, however, of cutting away their bodices from above, like our beauties at home, they began below, and made their anoraks so short that between them and the trouser-band, which was allowed to slip right down on the hips, there appeared a gap of a hand's breadth or more, in which the fabric in question

[10] Norwegian, *sennegræs*. *Trans.*

became visible. A somewhat original style of 'low dress,' this.

The Eskimos of the east coast wear costumes practically similar to those here described, only that they almost always use seal-skins instead of bird-skins for their jackets. In North Greenland, too, seal-skin and reindeer-skin are greatly used for these garments, and the same was the case in earlier times all along the west coast.

On the east coast, a surprising habit prevails; to wit, that in their houses and tents, men, women, and children go about entirely naked—or so, at least, it seemed to me. Balto, however, no doubt after closer examination, assured me that the grown men and women had all a narrow band around their loins, a detail which my bashfulness had prevented me from discovering. This remarkable observation of our friend Balto is corroborated by the majority of travellers who have undertaken researches on the subject, so I am bound to believe them. This band, which the travellers are pleased to designate under-drawers—how far it deserves such a name I will leave to the reader to judge from the accompanying illustration—is, I am told, called *nâtit* by the Greenlanders.

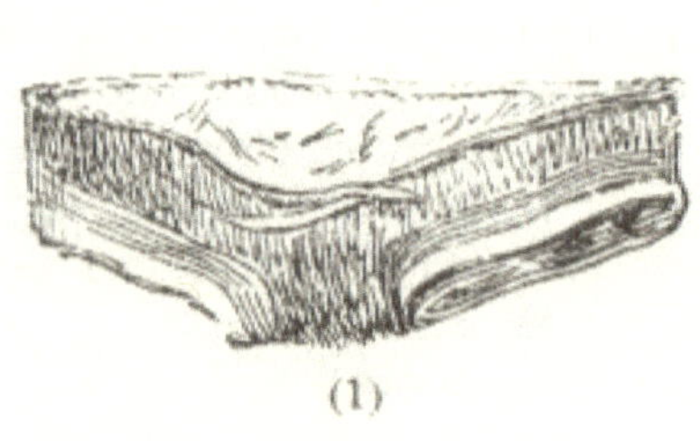

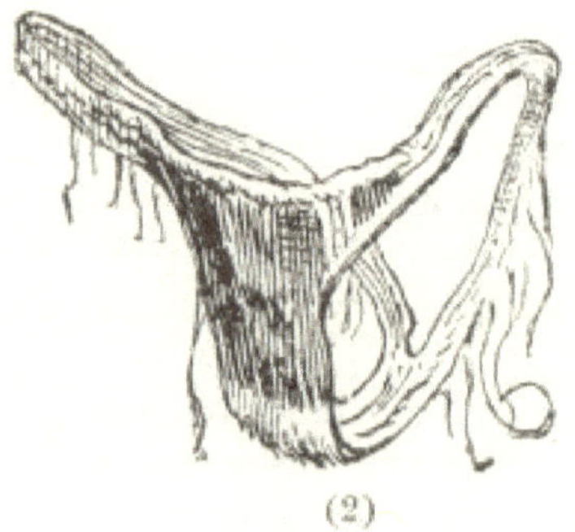

GREENLAND INDOOR DRESS (EAST COAST). (1) MALE COS-TUME. (2) FEMALE COSTUME.

In former days this simple indoor garb was worn all over Greenland, right up to the northernmost settlements on Smith's Sound, where, indeed, it is still in use.

This light raiment is, of course, very wholesome; for the many layers of skins in the outdoor dress greatly impede transpiration, and it is therefore a natural impulse which leads the Eskimo to throw them off in the warm rooms, where they would be particularly insanitary. When the Europeans came to the country, however, this free-and-easy custom offended their sense of propriety, and the missionaries preached against it. Thus it happens that the national indoor dress has been abolished on the west coast. Whether this has led to an improvement in morality, I cannot say—I have my doubts. That it has not been conducive to sanitation, I can unhesitatingly declare.

The Eskimos, however, are still very unsophisticated with respect to the exposure of their person. Many women, it is true, make some attempt to conceal their nudities when a European enters their houses; but I greatly fear that this is rather an affectation which they think will please us, than a result of real modesty; and when they discover that we are not greatly impressed by their attempts, they very soon give them up. In regard to their own countrymen they show very little sense of modesty.

The hair of the Eskimos is coal-black, coarse and straight, like horsehair, and is allowed by the men to grow wild. On the east coast they usually do not cut it at all, even regarding it as dangerous to lose any of it; they keep it back from the face by means of a band or thong. Sometimes they take it into their heads to cut the hair of children, and the children so treated must continue all through their lives to cut their hair, and must also observe certain fixed formalities in the matter; for instance, they must cut the ears and tails of their dogs while they are puppies. Iron must on no account come in contact with the hair, which is, therefore, sawn off with the jawbone of a Greenland shark.

The women knot their hair in a tuft upon the crown of the head. This they do by gathering it tightly together from all sides and tying it up, on the east coast with a thong, on the west coast with ribbons of various colours. Unmarried women wear a red ribbon, which they exchange for green if they have had a child. Married women wear a blue, and widows a black ribbon. If a widow wants to marry again she will probably mingle a little red with the black; elderly widows, who have given up all thought of marriage, often wear a white ribbon. If a widow gives birth to a child, she too must assume the green ribbon.

Her top-knot is the pride of the Greenland woman, and it must stand as stiff and straight up in the air as possible. This is, of course, held especially important by the young marriageable women, and as they are scarcely less vain than their European sisters, they draw the hair so tightly together that it is gradually torn away from the forehead, the temples and the neck, whence they often become more or less bald while still comparatively young. This does not add greatly to their attractiveness, but is, nevertheless, a speaking proof of the vanity of human nature.

In order to get the hair thoroughly well knotted together, and at the same time to give it the glistening appearance which is prized as a beauty, they have furthermore the habit of steeping it in urine before doing it up, thus making it moist and easier to tighten.

Mothers lick their children instead of washing them, or at least did so in former days; and as to the insects they come across in the process, their principle is, 'They bite, therefore they must be bitten.'

If any should be offended by these peculiarities in the manners and customs of the Greenlanders, they ought to reflect that their own forefathers, not so many generations ago, conducted themselves not so very differently. Let them read the accounts of the domestic life of the Teutonic peoples some centuries ago, and they will learn many things that will surprise them.

CHAPTER III
THE 'KAIAK' AND ITS APPURTENANCES

A superficial examination of certain details in the outward life of the Eskimo might easily lead to the erroneous conclusion that he stands at a low grade of civilisation. When we take the trouble to look a little more closely at him, we soon see him in another light.

Many people nowadays are vastly impressed with the greatness of our age, with all the inventions and the progress of which we daily hear, and which appear indisputably to exalt the highly gifted white race far over all others. These people would learn much by paying close attention to the development of the Eskimos, and to the tools and inventions by aid of which they obtain the necessaries of life among natural surroundings which place such pitifully small means at their disposal.

Picture a people placed upon a coast so desert and inhospitable as that of Greenland, cut off from the outer world, without iron, without firearms, without any resources except those provided by Nature upon the spot. These consist solely of stone, a little drift-wood, skins, and bone; but in order to obtain the latter they must first kill the animals from which to take them. We, in their place, would inevitably go to the wall, if we did not get help from home; but the Eskimo not only manages to live, but lives in contentment and happiness, while intercourse with the rest of the world has, to him, meant nothing but ruin.

In order that the reader may realise more vividly upon what an accumulation of experiences the civilisation of this people rests, I shall try to give a sketch of the way in which we must conceive it to have arisen.

Let us, then, assume that the ancestors of the Eskimos, according to Dr. Rink's opinion, lived in long bygone ages somewhere in the interior of Alaska. They must at all events have been inlanders somewhere and at some time, either in America or in Asia. Besides being hunters upon land, these Eskimos must also have gone a-fishing upon the lakes and rivers in birch-bark canoes, as the inland Eskimos of Alaska and the Indians of the North-West do to this day. In course of time, however, some of these inland Eskimos must either have been allured by the riches of the sea or must have been pressed upon by hostile and more warlike Indian tribes, so that they must have migrated in their canoes down the river-courses toward the western and northern coasts. The nearer they drew to the sea, the more scanty became the supply of wood, and they had to hit upon some other material than birch-bark with which to cover their canoes. It is not at all improbable that before leaving the rivers they had made experiments with the skins of aquatic animals; for we still see examples of this among several Indian tribes.

It was not, however, until the Eskimo encountered the rough sea at the mouths of the rivers that he thought of giving his boat a deck, and at last of closing it in entirely and joining his own skin-jacket to it so that the whole became water-tight. The kaiak was now complete. But even these inventions, which seem so simple and straightforward now that we see them perfected—what huge strides of progress must they not have meant in their day, and how much labour and how many failures must they not have cost!

COVERING A KAIAK

Arrived at the sea-coast, these Eskimos of the past soon discovered that their existence depended almost entirely upon the capture of seals. To this, then, they directed all their cunning, and the kaiak guided them to the discovery of the many remarkable and admirable seal-hunting instruments, which they brought to higher and ever-higher perfection, and which prove, indeed, in the most striking fashion, what ingenious animals many of us human beings really are.

The bow and arrow, which they used on land, they could not handle in their constrained position in the kaiak; therefore, they had to fall back upon throwing-weapons.

The idea of these, too, they borrowed from America, making use in the first instance of the Indian darts with steering-feathers, which they had themselves used in hunting upon land. Small harpoons or javelins of this sort are still in use among Eskimos of the southern part of the west coast of Alaska.

BLADDER-DART

As one passes northward along this coast, however, the feathers soon disappear, and are replaced by a little bladder fastened to the shaft of the javelin. This device has been found necessary in order to prevent the harpooned seals from diving and swimming. Further, it has been found necessary so to arrange the point of the javelin that it cannot be broken by the seal's violent efforts to get rid of it, but detaches itself instead (at *c* on accompanying engraving) and remains hanging to a line (from *c* to *b*) fastened (at b^1) to the middle of the javelin-shaft, which is thus made to take a transverse position, and still further to impede the movements of the seal when it rushes away with it. Such was the origin of the so-called *bladder-dart*, known to all Eskimo tribes who live by the sea.

The bladder is made of a seagull's or cormorant's gullet, inflated and dried. It is fastened to the javelin-shaft by means of a piece of bone with a hole bored through it for the purpose of blowing up the bladder. This hole is closed with a little wooden plug.

From this bladder-dart the Eskimo's principal hunting-weapon—the ingenious harpoon with bladder and line—has probably developed. In order to cope with the larger marine animals, the size of the bladder was doubtless gradually increased; but the disadvantage of this—the fact that it offered too much resistance to the air to be thrown far and with force—must soon have been felt. The bladder was then separated from the javelin, and only attached to its point by means of a long and strong line, the harpoon-line. The harpoon, which was now made larger and heavier than the original javelin, was henceforward thrown by itself, but drawing the line after it. The bladder, fastened to the other end of the line, remained in the kaiak until the animal had been pierced, when it was thrown overboard.

This harpoon, with all its ingenuity of structure, ranks, along with the kaiak, as the highest achievement of the Eskimo mind.[11]

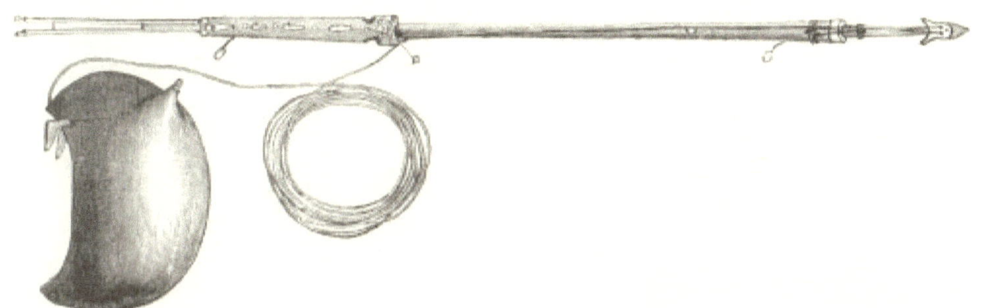

HARPOON

Its shaft is made in Greenland of red drift-wood—a sort of fir from Siberia, drifted by the polar current across the Polar Sea—which is heavier than the white drift-wood used in making smaller and lighter projectiles. The upper end of the shaft is fitted with a thick and strong plate of bone, on the top of which is fixed a long bone foreshaft—commonly made of walrus or narwhal tusk—which is fastened to the shaft by means of a joint of thongs, so that a strong pressure or blow from the side, instead of shattering the foreshaft, causes it to break off at the joint. This foreshaft fits exactly into a hole in the harpoon-head proper, which is made of bone, generally of walrus or narwhal tusk. It is now always provided with a point, or rather a sharp blade, of iron; in earlier days they used flint or simply bone. The harpoon-head is fastened to the harpoon-line by means of a hole bored through it, and is provided with barbs or hooks so that it sticks fast wherever it penetrates. It is, moreover, so adjusted that it works itself transversely into the flesh as the wounded seal tugs at the line. It is attached to the harpoon-shaft by being fitted to the before-mentioned foreshaft, whereupon the line is hooked on to a peg, placed some distance up the harpoon-shaft (at *a*), by means of a perforated piece of bone fixed at the proper distance. Thus the head and the shaft are held firmly together.

When the harpoon strikes and the seal begins to plunge, the bone foreshaft instantly breaks off at the joint (see illustration), and the harpoon-head, with the line attached to it, is thus loosened from the shaft, which floats up to the surface and is picked up by its owner, while the seal dashes away, dragging the line and bladder after it. It must be admitted, I think, that it is difficult to conceive a more ingenious appliance, composed of such materials as bone, seal-skin, and drift-wood; and we may be sure that it has cost the labour of many generations.

Two forms of this harpoon are in use in Greenland. The one is called *unâk*; its butt-end is finished off with nothing more than a bone knob, and it is longer and slighter than the other. This is called *ernangnak*, and has at its butt-end two flanges

[11] The Indians of the North-West and the Tchuktchi—and even, if I am not mistaken, the Koriaks and the Kamtchatkans—use the same harpoon, with a line and large bladder, in hunting sea animals, throwing the harpoon from the bow of their large open canoes or skin-boats. It seems probable, however, that they have learned the use of these instruments from the Eskimos.

or wings of bone, now commonly made of whale-rib, designed to increase the weight of the harpoon and to guide it through the air. It is one of these which is represented on p. 36.[12]

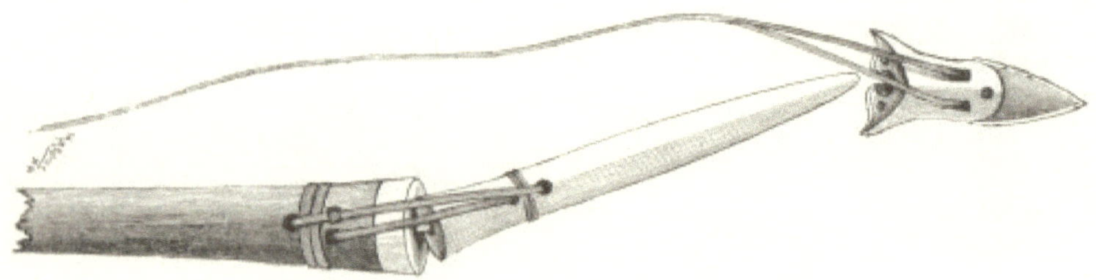

THE HEAD OF THE HARPOON

At Godthaab the ernangnak was most in use; but I heard old hunters complaining that, in a wind, it was more difficult to throw than the unâk, since a side gust was apt to take too strong hold of the bone flanges and to make the harpoon twist.

The harpoon-line is made of the hide either of the bearded seal (*Phoca barbata*) or of the young walrus. It is generally from 15 to 18 yards long, and a good quarter of an inch (about 7 millimetres) thick.

For the bladder they use the hide of a young ringed seal (*Phoca fœtida*). The skin is slipped off, as nearly as possible whole, the hair is removed, the apertures at the head, the fore limbs, and the hind limbs are tied up so as to be air-tight, and the whole is dried.

The line is coiled upon the kaiak-stand, which is fixed in front of the man. It serves to keep the coil well above the sea, which is always washing over the deck; and thus the line is always ready to run out without fouling when the harpoon is thrown.

The harpooned seal is killed by means of a lance (*anguvigak*). This consists of a wooden shaft (commonly made of the light white drift-wood, in order that it may carry well), a long bone foreshaft, and an iron-bladed tip. In former days flint was used instead of iron. The foreshaft is generally made of reindeer-horn or else of narwhal tusk. In order that the seal may not break it off, it is fastened to the shaft by a joint similar to that which fastens the foreshaft to the harpoon.

LANCE

The Eskimos have also the so-called bird-dart (*nufit*). Its shaft is likewise of

---

[12] In North Greenland there is yet a third and larger form of the harpoon, which is used in walrus-hunting, and is hurled without a throwing-stick; it has instead two bone knobs, one for the thumb and one for the fore-finger.

white drift-wood. Its point consists of a long narrow spike, now made of iron, but in earlier times of bone; and besides this there are fastened to the middle of the shaft three forward-slanting spikes, made of reindeer-horn and provided with large barbs. The idea is that if the end of the dart does not pierce the bird, the shaft shall glide along it, and one of these outstanding spikes must strike and penetrate it; and it is thus, in fact, that the bird is generally brought down. Another invention, this, which no one need blush to own.

All these projectiles can, as I have shown above, be traced back to the Indian feather-dart.

But in order to throw their weapons further and with greater force, the Eskimos have invented an appliance which distinguishes them from all surrounding races, whether American or Asiatic. This invention is the *throwing-stick*. Oddly enough, this admirable device, which by its sling-like action greatly augments the length and strength of the arm, is known in very few parts of the world—probably only in three. It is found in Australia in a very primitive form, among the Conibos and Purus on the Upper Amazon, where it is scarcely more developed than in Australia, and finally among the Eskimos, where it has reached its highest perfection.[13] We can scarcely conjecture that the throwing-stick, appearing in places so remote from each other, springs from any common origin, and we must thus accept the Eskimo form of it as an original invention of that particular race. It is generally made in Greenland of red drift-wood, and is about half a yard long (fourteen sticks in my possession range from 42 to 52 centimetres in length). At its lower and broader end it is about 3 inches (7 or 8 centimetres) in width, and is flat, with a thickness of rather more than half an inch (about 1½ centimetre). The sides, at the lower and broader end, have indentations in them for convenience in grasping—on one side for the thumb, on the other for the fore-finger; while on the upper flat side there runs a long groove along the whole length of the stick, to receive the dart or harpoon.[14] The throwing-stick is found in two forms. The one is most used for the bladder-dart and the bird-dart; it has at the upper narrow end a knob which fits into an indentation in a plate of bone fixed to the butt-end of the dart. (Compare illustrations on pp. 40 and 42). The other form is used for harpoons and lances; it has a hole in the upper narrow end, into which fits a backward-slanting spur in the side of the harpoon or lance-shaft, and it has besides another hole further down and near the grip, into which fits another slanting spur. (Compare illustration, p. 43). Throwing-sticks of this sort are used in the North, for example in Sukkertoppen, for the bird-dart as well.

A third form of the throwing-stick is used in the most southern part of Greenland and on the east coast for the ernangnak or flange harpoon. This form has in its upper narrow end a small knob, as in the bird-dart throwing-stick, and this knob

---

[13] As to the different forms of the throwing-stick among the Eskimos, see Mason's paper upon them in the Annual Report, &c. of the Smithsonian Institution for 1884, Part II. p. 279.

[14] In some places—for example, in the most southern part of Greenland and on the East Coast—there is only a hollow for the thumb, while the other side is smooth or edged with a piece of bone in which are notches to prevent the hand from slipping.

fits into an indentation in the butt-end of the harpoon between the bone flanges; in the lower end of the shaft, on the other hand, near the grip, there are one or even two holes into which fit bone knobs in the side of the harpoon-shaft, as above described.

When the harpoon or the dart is to be hurled, the throwing-stick, of whatever form it may be, is seized by the grip and held backward, together with the weapon, in a horizontal position. (See illustration, page 40); being then jerked forward with force, its lower end comes away from the dart or harpoon, while, with the upper end, still fitted to its knob or peg (see illustrations on this and the next page), the thrower hurls the weapon away to a considerable distance and with great accuracy. This is an extremely simple and effective invention.

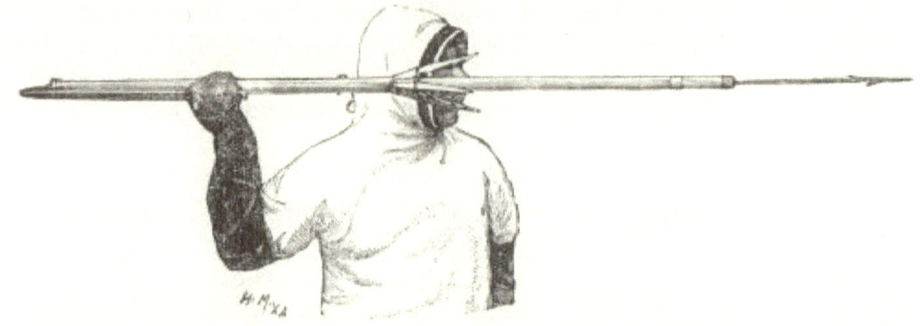

THROWING-STICK WITH BIRD-DART

Besides the weapons above-mentioned, the Eskimo has behind him in his kaiak, when he goes out hunting, a knife with a handle about 4 feet long (1·20 metre) and a pointed blade measuring some 8 inches (20 centimetres). This is used for giving the seal or other game its finishing stroke. He has, moreover, a smaller knife lying before him in the kaiak; it is used, amongst other things, for piercing holes in the seal through which to pass the bone knobs of the towing-line, wherewith the seal is made fast to the kaiak and towed to land. To this end, too, he always carries with him one or more towing-bladders, which he inflates and fastens to the seal in order to keep it afloat. These bladders are made of the pouch of small whales (*e.g.* the grampus).

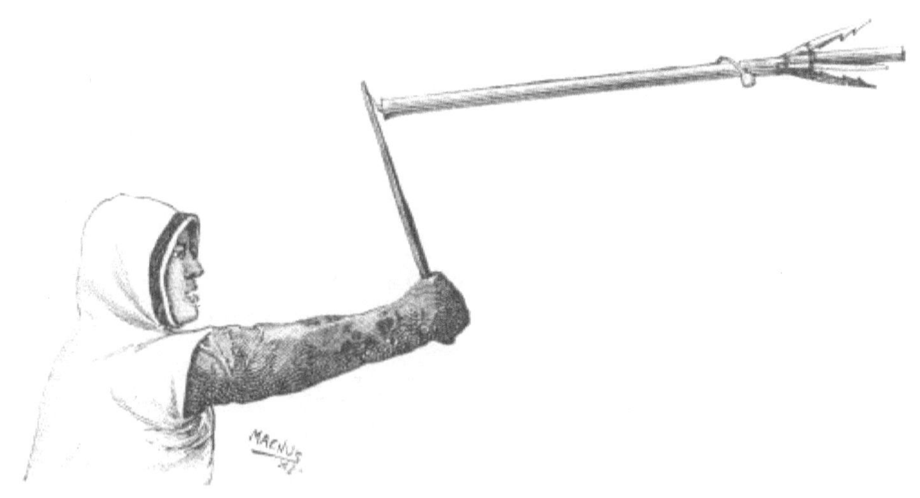

THE BIRD-DART THROWN

To complete this description, I should also mention the bone-knife which forms part of the kaiak-man's outfit, especially in winter, and which is principally used for scraping the ice off the kaiak.

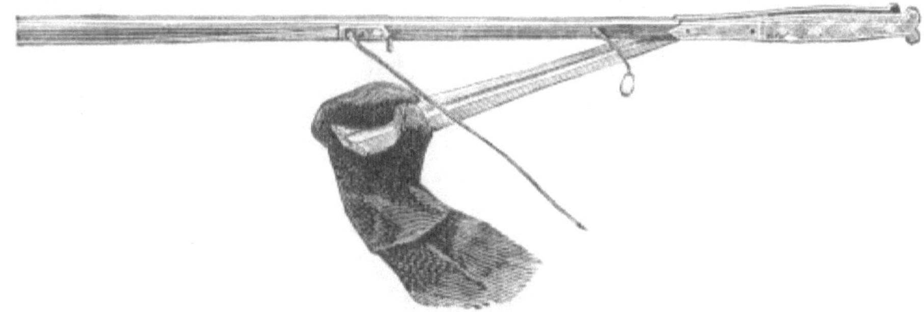

THROWING-STICK WITH HARPOON

From the accompanying drawing, the reader will be able to form an idea of how all these weapons are fitted to the kaiak when it is in full hunting trim: a is the kaiak-opening; b, the harpoon-bladder; c, the kaiak-stand with coiled harpoon-line (e); d, the harpoon hanging in its place; f, the lance; g, the kaiak-knife; h, the bladder-dart; i, the bird-dart; k, its throwing-stick.

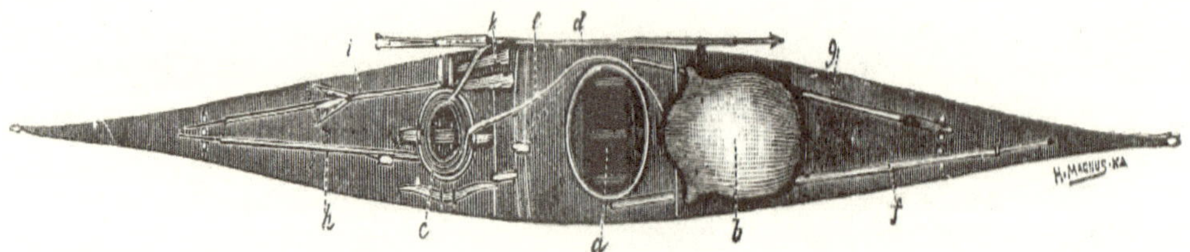

KAIAK, SEEN FROM ABOVE

KAIAK-FRAME

But the most important thing of all yet remains, and that is a description of the kaiak itself.

It has an internal framework of wood. This, of which the reader can, I hope, form some conception from the accompanying drawing, was formerly always made of drift-wood, usually of the white wood, which is lightest. For the ribs, osiers were sometimes used, from willow bushes which are found growing far up the fiords. In later days they have got into the habit of buying European boards of spruce or Scotch fir in the west coast colonies, although drift-wood is still considered preferable, especially on account of its lightness.

This framework is covered externally with skins, as a rule with the skin of the saddleback seal (*Phoca grœnlandica*), or of the bladder-nose or hood seal (*Cystophora cristata*). The latter is not so durable or so water-tight as the former; but the skin of a young bladder-nose, in which the pores are not yet very large, is considered good enough. Those who can afford it use the skin of the bearded seal (*Phoca barbata*), which is reckoned the best and strongest; but, as it is also used for harpoon lines, it is, as a rule, only on the south and east coast that it is found in such quantities that it can be commonly used for covering the kaiak. The skin of the great ringed seal (*Phoca fœtida*) is also used, but not so frequently.

The preparation of the kaiak-skins will be described subsequently, in Chapter VIII. They are generally fitted at once to the kaiak in a raw state; but if they have been already dried they must be carefully softened for several days before they can be used. The point is to get them as moist and pliant as possible, so that they can be thoroughly well stretched, and remain as tense as a drum-head when they dry. The preparation of the skins, and the sewing and stretching them on the kaiak, belongs to the women's department; it is not very easy work, and woe to them if the skin sits badly or is too slack! They feel it a great disgrace.

All, or at any rate a great many, of the women of the village are generally present when a kaiak is being covered; it is a great entertainment to them, especially as, in reward for their assistance, they are often treated to coffee by the owner of the kaiak. The cost of the entertainment ranges, according to his wealth, from three-pence or fourpence up to a shilling or more.

In the middle of the kaiak's deck there is a hole just large enough to enable a man to get his legs through it and to sit down; his thighs almost entirely fill the aperture. Thus it takes a good deal of practice before one can slip into or out of the kaiak with any sort of ease. The hole is surrounded by the kaiak-ring, which consists of a hoop of wood. It stands a little more than an inch (3 or 3½ centimetres) above the kaiak's deck, and the waterproof jacket, as we shall presently see, is drawn over it. At the spot where the rower sits, pieces of old kaiak-skin are laid in the bottom over the ribs, with a piece of bearskin or other fur to make the seat softer.

As a rule, each hunter makes his kaiak for himself, and it is fitted to the man's size just like a garment. A kaiak for a Greenlander of average size measures, in the neighbourhood of Godthaab, about 6 yards (5½ metres) in length. The greatest breadth of deck, in front of the kaiak-ring, is about 18 inches (45 centimetres), or a little more; but the boat narrows considerably towards the bottom. The breadth, of course, varies according to the width of the man's thighs, and is generally no greater than just to allow him to slip in. I should note, however, that the kaiaks in Godthaab fiords—as, for example, at Sardlok and Karnok—were longer and nar-rower than the kaiaks on the sea-coast, for example at Kangek, obviously for the reason that on the open coast they are exposed to heavier seas, and must therefore be stiffer and easier to handle. The shorter and broader kaiaks are better sea-boats, and ship less water.

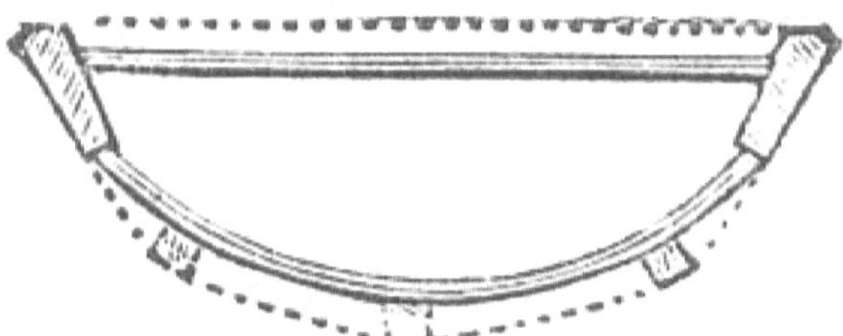

SECTION OF THE KAIAK (THE DOTTED LINE REPRESENTS THE SKIN.)

The depth of the kaiak from deck to bottom is generally from 5 to 6½ inches (12 to 15 centimetres), but in front of the kaiak-ring it is an inch or two more, in order to give room for the thighs, and to enable the rower to get more easily into his place. The bottom of the kaiak is pretty flat, sloping to a very obtuse angle (probably about 140°) in the middle. The kaiak narrows evenly in, both fore and aft, and comes to a point at both ends. It has no keel, but its underpart at both ends is generally provided with bone flanges, for the most part of whale-rib, designed to save the skin from being ripped up by drift-ice, or by stones when the kaiak is beached. Both points are commonly provided with knobs of bone, partly for ornament, partly for protection as well.

Across the deck, in front of the kaiak-ring, six thongs are usually fastened, and from three to five behind the rower. Under these thongs weapons and implements are inserted, so that they lie safe and handy for use. Pieces of bone are let into the thongs, partly to hold them together, partly to keep them a little bit up from the deck, so that weapons can the more easily and quickly be pushed under them, and partly also for the sake of ornament. To some of these thongs the booty is fastened. The heads of birds are stuck in under them; seals, whales, or halibut are attached by towing-lines to the thongs at the side of the kaiak; and smaller fish are not fastened at all, but either simply laid on the back part of the deck or pushed in under it.

PADDLE

A kaiak is so light that it can without difficulty be carried on the head, with all its appurtenances, over several miles of land.

It is propelled by a two-bladed paddle, which is held in the middle and dipped in the water on each side in turn, like the paddles we use in canoes. It has probably been developed from the Indians' one-bladed paddles. Among the Eskimos on the south-west coast of Alaska the one-bladed paddle is universal; not until we come north of the Yukon River do we find two-bladed paddles, and even there the single blade is still the more common. Further north and eastward along the American coast both forms are found, until the two blades at last come into exclusive use eastward of the Mackenzie River.

The Aleutians seem, strangely enough, to be acquainted with only the two-bladed paddle,[15] and this is also the case, so far as I can gather, with the Asiatic Eskimos.[16]

In fair weather the kaiak-man uses the so-called *half-jacket* (*akuilisak*). This is made of water-tight skin with the hair removed, and is sewn with sinews. Round its lower margin runs a draw-string, or rather a draw-thong, by means of which the edge of the jacket can be made to fit so closely to the kaiak-ring that it can only be pressed and drawn down over it with some little trouble. This done, the half-jacket forms, as it were, a water-tight extension of the kaiak. The upper margin of the jacket comes close up to the armpits of the kaiak-man, and is supported by braces or straps, which pass over the shoulders and can be lengthened or shortened by means of handy runners or buckles of bone, so simple and yet so ingenious that we, with all our metal buckles and so forth, cannot equal them.

---

[15] On this point, see even such early authors as Cook and King, *A Voyage to the Pacific Ocean, &c.*, 3rd ed., ii. p. 513, London, 1785.

[16] It is remarkable that the inhabitants of St. Lawrence Island do not seem to use the kaiak at all. They have large open skin-boats (*baidars*) of the same build as those of the Tchucktchi. (Compare Nordenskiöld, *The Voyage of the Vega*, ii. p. 254, London, 1881.)

Loose sleeves of skin are drawn over the arms, and are lashed to the over-arm and to the wrist, thus preventing the arm from becoming wet. Watertight mittens of skin are drawn over the hands.

This half-jacket is enough to keep out the smaller waves which wash over the kaiak. In a heavier sea, on the other hand, the *whole-jacket* (*tuilik*) is used. This is made in the same way as the half-jacket, and, like it, fits close to the kaiak-ring, but is longer above, has sleeves attached to it, and a hood which comes right over the head. It is laced tight round the face and wrists, so that with it on the kaiak-man can go right through the breakers and can capsize and right himself again, without getting wet and without letting a drop of water into the kaiak.

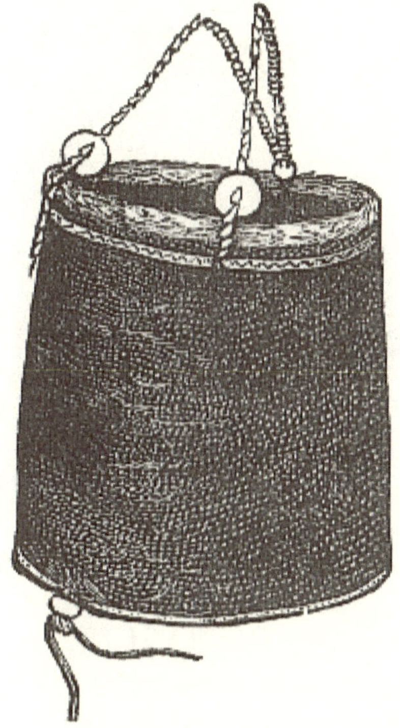

HALF-JACKET

It will readily be understood that it is not easy to sit in a vessel like the kaiak without capsizing, and that it needs a good deal of practice to master its peculiarities. I have seen a friend of mine in Norway, on making his first experiment in my kaiak, capsize four times in the space of two minutes; no sooner had we got him up on even keel and let him go, than he again stood on his head with the bottom of the kaiak in the air.

But when one has acquired by practice a mastery of the kaiak and of the two-bladed paddle, one can get through the water in all sorts of weather at an astonishing speed. The kaiak is beyond comparison the best boat for a single oarsman ever invented.

In order to become an accomplished kaiak-man, one ought to begin early. The Greenland boys often begin to practise in their father's kaiak at from six to eight years old, and when they are ten or twelve the provident Greenlander gives his sons kaiaks of their own. This was the rule, at any rate, in former times. Lars Dalager even says: 'When they are from eight to ten years old they take seriously to work in little kaiaks.'

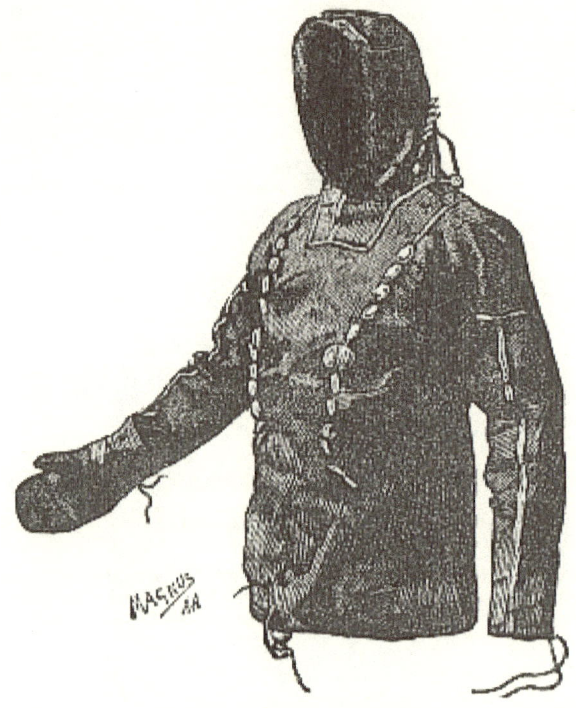

WHOLE-JACKET

From this age onwards, the young Greenlander remains a toiler of the sea. At first he generally confines himself to fishing, but before long he extends his operations to the more difficult seal-hunting.

You cannot rank as an expert kaiak-man until you have mastered the art of righting yourself after capsizing. To do this, you seize one end of the paddle in your hand, and with the other hand grasp the shaft as near the middle as possible; then you place it along the side of the kaiak with its free end pointing forward towards the bow; and thereupon, pushing the end of the paddle sharply out to the side,[17] and bending your body well forward towards the deck, you raise yourself by a strong circular sweep of the paddle. If you do not come right up, a second stroke may be necessary.

---

[17] While the paddle is being pushed out sideways, until it comes at right angles to the kaiak, it is held slightly aslant, so that the blade, in moving, forces the water under it, and acquires an upward leverage.

A thorough kaiak-man can also right himself without an oar by help of his throwing-stick, or even without it, by means of one arm. The height of accomplishment is reached when he does not even need to use the flat of his hand, but can clench it; and to show that he really does so, I have seen a man take a stone in his clenched hand before capsizing, and come up with it still in his grasp.

An Eskimo told me of another who was so extraordinarily skilful at righting himself that he could do it in every possible way: with or without an oar, with or without a throwing-stick, or with his clenched hand. The only thing he could not right himself with was—his tongue; and my informant protruded that member and made some horrible grimaces with it to illustrate what exertions it would cost to recover yourself with so inconvenient an implement.

In earlier times, on the west coast of Greenland, every at all capable kaiak-man was able to right himself; but in these later days, since the introduction of European civilisation, and the consequent degeneracy of the race, this art has declined, along with everything else. It is still quite common, however, in many places. For instance, I can assert of my own knowledge that at Kangek, near Godthaab, almost all the hunters possessed it. On the east coast, according to Captain Holm, it seems to be usual, yet not so much so as it was in former times upon the west coast. Nor is this to be wondered at, as it is far more necessary on the west coast, where there is little drift-ice and heavy seas are common.

A kaiak-man who has entirely mastered the art of righting himself can defy almost any weather. If he is capsized, he is on even keel again in a moment, and can play like a sea-bird with the waves, and cut right through them. If the sea is very heavy, he lays the broadside of his kaiak to it, holds the paddle flat out on the windward side, pressing it against the deck, bends forward, and lets the wave roll over him; or else he throws himself on his side towards it, resting on his flat paddle, and rights himself again when it has passed. The prettiest feat of seamanship I have ever heard of is that to which some fishers, I am told, have recourse among overwhelming rollers. As the sea curls down over them they voluntarily capsize, receive it on the bottom of the kaiak, and when it has passed right themselves again. I think it would be difficult to name a more intrepid method of dealing with a heavy sea.

If you cannot right yourself, and if there is no help at hand, you are lost beyond all hope as soon as you capsize. This may happen easily enough—a wave can do it, or even the fouling of the harpoon-line when a seal is struck. Just as often, too, it happens through an unguarded movement in calm weather, or at moments when there seems to be no danger.

Many Eskimos find their death every year in this manner. For example, I may state that in Danish South Greenland in 1888, out of 162 deaths (of which 90 were of males), 24, or about 15 per cent. (that is to say, more than a fourth part of the male mortality), were caused by drowning in kaiaks.

In 1889, in South Greenland, out of 272 deaths (of which 152 were of males), 24, or about 9 per cent., were due to the same cause. This in a population of 5,614, of which 2,591 were males.

CHAPTER IV

THE ESKIMO AT SEA

One often hears the Eskimo accused of cowardice. This is no doubt mainly due to the fact that his accusers have seen him only on land, or in fine weather at sea; and then he is too good-natured and easy-going to show any courage. It may be, too, they have not taken the trouble to place themselves in sympathy with his view of life; or else they may have called upon him to do things which he neither understood nor cared about.

If by courage we understand the tigerish ferocity which fights to the last drop of blood, even against superior force—that courage which, as Spencer says, is undoubtedly most common among the lowest races of men, and is especially characteristic of many species of animals—it must be admitted that of this the Eskimos do not possess any great share. They are too peaceable and good-natured, for example, to strike back when attacked; and therefore Europeans, ever since the time of Egede and the first missionaries, have been able to strike them with impunity and to call them cowardly. But this sort of courage is held in no great respect by the natives in Greenland, and I am afraid that they do not look up to us any the more because we exhibit a superabundance of it. They have from all time respected the beautiful Christian doctrine that if a man smite you on the right cheek, you should turn to him the left also.

But to conclude from this that the Eskimo is a coward would be unjust.

To estimate the worth of a human being, you must see him at his work. Follow the Eskimo to sea, observe him there—where his vocation lies—and you will soon behold him in another light; for, if we understand by courage that faculty which, in moments of danger, lays its plans with calmness and executes them with ready presence of mind, or which faces inevitable danger, and even certain death, with immovable self-possession, then we shall find in Greenland men of such courage as we but rarely find elsewhere.

Kaiak-hunting has many dangers.

Though his father may have perished at sea, and very likely his brother and his friend as well, the Eskimo nevertheless goes quietly about his daily work, in storm no less than in calm. If the weather is too terrible, he may be chary of putting to sea; experience has taught him that in such weather many perish; but when once he is out he goes ahead as though it were all the most indifferent thing in the world.

It is a gallant business, this kaiak-hunting; it is like a sportive dance with the sea and with death. There is no finer sight possible than to see the kaiak-man breasting the heavy rollers that seem utterly to engulf him. Or when, overtaken by a storm at sea, the kaiaks run for the shore, they come like black storm-birds rushing before the wind and the waves, which, like rolling mountains, sweep on in their wake. The paddles whirl through air and water, the body is bent a little forwards, the head often turned half backwards to watch the seas; all is life and spirit—while the sea around reeks like a seething cauldron. And then it may happen that when the game is at its wildest a seal pops its head up before them. Quicker than thought the harpoon is seized and rushes through the foam with deadly aim; the seal dashes away with the bladder behind it, but is presently caught and killed, and then towed onwards. Everything is done with the same masterly skill and with the same quiet demeanour. The Eskimo never dreams that he is performing feats of heroism.

Here he is great—and we? Ah, in these surroundings we are apt to seem very small.

Let us follow the Eskimo on a day's hunting.

'THE HEAD TURNED HALF BACKWARDS TO WATCH THE SEAS'

Several hours before dawn he stands upon the outlook-rock over the village, and scans the sea to ascertain whether the weather is going to be favourable. Having assured himself on this point, he comes slowly down to his house and gets out his kaiak-jacket. His breakfast in the good old days consisted of a drink of water; now that European effeminacy has reached him too, it is generally one or two cups of strong coffee. He eats nothing in the morning; he declares that it makes him uneasy in the kaiak, and that he has more endurance without it. Nor does he take any food with him—only a quid of tobacco.

When the kaiak is carried down to the beach and the hunting-weapons are ranged in their places, he slips into the kaiak-hole, makes fast his jacket over the ring, and puts out to sea. From other houses in the village his neighbours are also putting forth at the same time. It is the bladder-nose that they are after to-day, and the hunting-ground is on some banks nine miles out to the open sea.

It is calm, the smooth sea heaves in a long swell towards the rocky islets that fringe the shore, a light haze still lies over the sounds between them, and the sea-birds floating on the surface seem double their natural size. The kaiaks cut their way forwards, side by side, making only a silent ripple; the paddles swing in an even rhythm, while the men keep up an unbroken stream of conversation, and now and then burst out into merry laughter. Bird-darts are thrown in sport, now by one, now by another, in order to keep eye and hand in practice. Presently an auk comes within range of one of them; the dart speeds through the air, and the bird, transfixed, attempts, with much flapping of wings, to dive, but is held up next moment upon the point of the dart. The point is pulled out, the hunter seizes the bird's beak between his teeth, and with a strong twitch breaks its neck, then fastens it to the back part of the kaiak.

They soon leave the sounds and islets behind them and put straight out to the open sea.

After some hours' paddling, they have at last reached the hunting-ground. Great seal-heads are seen peering over the water in many directions, and the hunters scatter in search of their prey.

SEAWARD IN SEARCH OF SEALS

Boas, one of the best hunters of the village, has seen a large he-seal far off, and has paddled towards it; but it has dived, and he lies and waits for its reappearance. There! a little way before him its round black head pops up. He bends well forward, while with noiseless and wary strokes he urges the kaiak toward the seal, which lies peaceful and undisturbed, stretching its neck and rocking up and down upon the swell. But suddenly it is on the alert; it has caught a glimpse of the flashing paddle-blade, and now looks straight at him with its great round eyes. He instantly stops paddling and sits motionless, while the way on the kaiak carries it noiselessly forward. The seal discovers nothing new to be alarmed at, and resumes its former quietude. It throws its head backwards, holds its snout straight up in the air, and bathes in the morning sun which gleams upon its black, wet skin. In the meantime the kaiak is rapidly nearing; every time the seal looks in that direction, Boas sits still and moves no muscle; but as soon as it turns its head away again, he shoots forward like a flash of lightning. He is coming within range; he gets his harpoon clear, sees that the line is properly coiled upon the stand; one stroke more and it is time to throw—when the seal quietly disappears under the water. It was not frightened, and will consequently come up again at no great distance. He lies still and waits. But the minutes drag on; a seal can remain under water an incredible time, and it seems even longer to one who is waiting for his prey. But the Eskimo is gifted with admirable patience; he lies absolutely motionless except for his head, with which he keeps watch on every side. At last the seal's head once more appears over the water a little way off and to one side. He cautiously turns the kaiak, unobserved by his prey, and once more he shoots towards it over the mirror-like sea. But suddenly it catches sight of him again, looks at him sharply for a moment, and dives. He knows its habits, however, and at full speed he dashes towards the spot where it disappeared. Before many moments have passed it pops up its head again to look around. Now he is within range: the harpoon is seized and carried back over his shoulder, then with a strong movement, as if hurled from a steel spring, it rushes whistling from the throwing-stick, whirling the line behind it. The seal gives a violent plunge, but at the moment it arches its back to dive, the harpoon sinks into its side, and buries itself up to the shaft. A few convulsive strokes of its tail churn the water into foam, and away it goes, dragging the harpoon-line behind it towards the depths. In the meantime Boas has seized the throwing-stick between his teeth, and, quicker than thought, has thrown the bladder out of the kaiak behind him. It dances away over the surface of the sea, now and then seeming on the point of disappearing, as indeed it finally does. Before long, however, it again comes in sight, and he chases after it as quickly as his paddle can take him, snapping up on the way his harpoon-shaft which has floated to the surface. The lance is laid ready for use. Next moment the seal comes up; infuriated at its inability to escape, it turns upon its pursuer, attacks first the bladder, which it tears to pieces, and then goes straight for the kaiak. Again Boas is within range; the animal arches its back and hurls itself forward with gaping maw, so that the water foams around it. A miss may now cost him his life; but he calmly raises his lance and sends it speeding with terrible force through the seal's mouth and out at the back of its neck. A shudder runs through it, and its head sinks; but the next moment it raises itself perpendicularly in the water, the blood pours frothing from its mouth, it gapes wildly and utters a smothered roar, while the hood over its nose is inflated to an astounding size. It shakes its head so that the lance-shaft quivers and waves to and fro; but it does not succeed in breaking it or getting free from it. A moment more and Boas's second lance has pierced through one of its fore-flappers into its lungs; the seal collapses, and the fight is over. He paddles up to its side, and as it still moves a little, he gives it a finishing stab with his long-handled knife. Then he sets quietly about pulling out his lances and replacing them in the kaiak, takes out his towing-line and blows up his towing-bladder, which he fastens to the seal, cuts the harpoon-head out and once more makes it fast to the shaft, coils the line on the stand, and takes out a new bladder and places it behind him. Next, the seal's flappers are lashed close to its body, with the thong designed for that purpose, and the animal is attached by means of the towing-line to one side of the kaiak, so that it can easily be towed along, its head being fastened to the foremost pair of thongs on the deck, and its tail to the hindmost. Now Boas is ready to look about him for more game. He is lucky, and has not paddled far before he catches sight of another seal. In an instant he has cast loose the one already killed, which is kept afloat by the towing-bladder, while he again sets off in pursuit. This one, too, he kills, after some wary stalking and eager waiting; he takes it in tow and returns for his first prey. The two great animals are fastened one on each side of the kaiak. He has now a good cargo, and cannot get very quickly through the water; but that does not prevent him from increasing his bag. As soon as another seal comes in sight those already secured are cast loose, and when the next one is killed it is fastened behind the others. In this way one man will sometimes come towing as many as four seals, or even more at a pinch.

SEAL-HUNTING

Tobias, in the meantime, another of the best hunters of the village, has not been quite so fortunate as Boas. He began by chasing a seal which dived and did not come up again within sight. Then he set off after another; but as he is skimming over the sea towards it the huge head of a hooded seal[18] suddenly pops up right in front of the kaiak, and is harpooned in an instant. It makes a frightful wallowing and dives, the harpoon-line whirls out, but suddenly gets fouled under the bird-dart throwing-stick; the bow of the kaiak is drawn under with an irresistible rush, and before Tobias knows where he is, the water is up to his armpits, and nothing can be seen of him but his head and shoulders and the stern of the kaiak, which sticks right up into the air. It looks as if it were all over with him; those who are near him paddle with all their might to his assistance, but with scant hope of arriving in time to save him. Tobias, however, is a first-rate kaiak-man. In spite of his difficult position, he keeps upon even keel while he is dragged through the water by the seal, which does all it can to get him entirely under. At last it comes up again, and in a moment he has seized his lance and, with a deadly aim, has pierced it right through the head. A feeble movement, and it is dead. The others come up in time to find Tobias busy making his booty fast and to get their pieces of blubber from it.[19] They cannot restrain their admiration for his coolness and skill, and speak of it long afterwards. Tobias and Boas, however, are the best hunters of the village. It is related of them that, in their younger days, they were such masters of their craft that they even disdained the use of bladders. They made fast the harpoon-line round their own waist or round the kaiak-ring, and when the harpooned seal was not killed at the first stroke, they let it drag themselves and the kaiak after it instead of the bladder. This is looked upon by the Greenlanders as the summit of possible achievement, but there are very few who attain such mastery.

Hitherto the weather has been fine, the glassy surface of the sea has been heaving softly under the rising sun. But in the course of the last hour or two, black and threatening banks of clouds have begun to draw up over the southern horizon. Just as Tobias has made fast his seal, a distant roar is heard and a sort of steam can be seen rising over the sea to the southward. It is a storm approaching, and the steam is the flying spray which it drives before it. Of all winds, the Greenlanders fear the south wind (*nigek*) most, for it is always violent and sets up a heavy sea.

The thing is now to get under the land as quickly as possible. Those who have no seals in tow have the best of it, yet they try to keep with the others. One relieves Boas of one of his seals. They have not paddled far before the storm is upon them; it thrashes the water to foam as it approaches, and the kaiak-men feel it on their backs, like a giant lifting and hurling them forward. The sport has now turned to earnest; the seas soon tower into mountains of water and break and welter down upon them. They are making for the land with the wind nearly abeam; but they are still far off, they can see nothing around them for the spray, and almost every wave buries them so that only a few heads, arms, and ends of paddles can be seen above the combs of froth.

---

[18] *Hættesæl*, the full-grown male of the *Klapmyts* (bladder-nose). It has a hood over its nose, which it can inflate enormously.

[19] When a seal is killed, each of the kaiak-men in the neighbourhood receives a piece of its blubber, which he generally devours forthwith.

BEFORE THE WIND

Here comes a gigantic roller—they can see it shining black and white in the far distance. It towers aloft so that the sky is almost hidden. In a moment they have stuck their paddles under the thongs on the windward side and bent their bodies forward so that the crest of the wave breaks upon their backs. For a second almost everything has disappeared; those who are further a-lee await their turn in anxiety; then the billow passes, and once more the kaiaks skim forward as before. But such a sea does not come singly; the next will be worse. They hold their paddles flat to the deck and projecting to windward, bend their bodies forward, and at the moment when the white cataract thunders down upon them they hurl themselves into its very jaws, thus somewhat breaking its force. For a moment they have again disappeared—then one kaiak comes up on even keel, and presently another appears bottom upwards. It is Pedersuak (*i.e.* the big Peter) who has capsized. His comrade speeds to his side, but at the same moment the third wave breaks over them and he must look out for himself. It is too late—the two kaiaks lie heaving bottom upwards. The second manages to right himself, and his first thought is for his comrade, to whose assistance he once more hastens. He runs his kaiak alongside of the other, lays his paddle across both, bends down so that he gets hold under the water of his comrade's arm, and with a jerk drags him up upon his side, so that he too can get hold of the paddle and in an instant raise himself upon even keel. The water-tight jacket has come a little loose from the ring on one side and some water has got in; not so much, however, but that he can still keep afloat. The others have in the meantime come up; they get hold of the lost paddle, and all can again push forward.

A KAIAK-MAN RESCUING A COMRADE

It grows worse and worse for those who have seals in tow; they lag far behind, and the great beasts lie heaving and jarring against the sides of the kaiaks. They think of sacrificing their prey, but one difficult sea passes after another, and they will still try to hang on for a while. The proudest moments in a hunter's life are those in which he comes home towing his prey, and sees his wife's, his daughter's, and his handmaiden's happy faces beaming upon him from the shore. Far out at sea he already sees them in his mind's eye, and rejoices like a child. No wonder that he will not cast loose his prey save at the direst pinch of need.

After passing through many ugly rollers, they have at last got under the land. Here they are somewhat protected by a group of islands lying far to the southward. The seas become less violent, and, as they gradually get further in, they push on more quickly for home over the smoother water.

In the meantime the women at home have been in the greatest anxiety. When the storm arose they ran up to the outlook-rock or out upon the headlands, and stood there in groups gazing eagerly over the angry sea for their sons, husbands, fathers, and brothers. So they stand watching and shivering, until, with eyes rendered keener by anxiety, they at last discern what seem like black specks approaching from the horizon, and the whole village echoes to one glad shout: 'They are coming! They are coming!' They begin to count how many there are; two are missing! No, there is one of them! No, they are all there! They are all there!

They soon begin to recognise individuals, partly by their method of paddling, partly by the kaiaks, although as yet they are little more than tiny dots. Suddenly there sounds a wild shout of joy: 'Boase kaligpok!' ('Boas is towing')—him they easily identify by his size. This joyful intelligence passes from house to house, the children rush around and shout it in through the windows, and the groups upon the rocks dance for joy. Then comes a new shout: 'Ama Tobiase kaligpok!' ('Tobias too is towing'); and this news likewise passes from house to house. Next is heard: 'Ama Simo kaligpok!' 'Ama David kaligpok!' And now again comes another swarm of women out of the houses and up to the rocks to look out over the sea breaking white against the islets and cliffs, where eleven black dots can now and then be seen far out amid the rolling masses of water, moving slowly nearer.

At last the leading kaiaks shoot into the little bight in front of the village. They are those who have no seals. Lightly and with assured aim one after the other dashes up on the flat beach, carried high upon the crest of the waves. The women stand ready to receive them and to draw them further up.

Then come those who have seals in tow; they must proceed somewhat more cautiously. First, they cast loose their prey and see that it comes to the hands of the women on shore. Then they themselves make for the land. When once they have got out of the kaiak, they, like the first comers, pay no heed to anything but themselves and their weapons, which they carry to their places above high-water mark. They do not even look at their prey as it lies on the shore. From this time forward all work in connection with the 'take' falls to the share of the women.

The men go to their homes, take off their wet clothes and put on their indoor dress, which, as we have seen, was in the heathen times exceedingly airy, but has now become more visible.

Then at last comes the first meal of the day; but it does not begin in earnest till the day's 'take' is boiled and served up in a huge dish placed in the middle of the floor. Then there disappear incredible quantities of flesh and raw blubber.

When hunger is appeased, the women always set themselves to some household work, sewing or the like, whilst the men give themselves up to well-earned laziness, or attend a little to their weapons, hang up the harpoon-line to dry, and so forth.

Then the hunters begin to relate the events of the day, the family listening eagerly, especially the boys. The narrative is sober, with none of that boasting or striving to impress the hearers with an exaggerated idea of the difficulties overcome, in which we Europeans, under similar circumstances, would often indulge.

But at the same time it is lively and picturesque, with a peculiar breadth of colouring. Experiences are described with illustrative gestures, and, as Dalager says: "When they have come so far in the story that the cast has to be depicted, they swing the right arm in the air while the left is held straight out to represent the animal. Then the demonstration goes on as follows: 'When the time came for using the harpoon, I looked to it, I took it, I seized it, I gripped it, I had it fast in my hand, I balanced it' — and so forth. This alone may go on for several minutes, until at last the hand sinks to represent the throw; and after that they do not forget to make note of the last twitches given by the seal."

At other times the most remarkable events are dismissed in a few words. But as often as an opportunity presents itself, a broad humour enters into the narration, and is unfailingly rewarded by shrieks of laughter from the eager listeners. No more perfect picture could be imagined of happy family life.

So the days pass for the Eskimo. Although there is nothing unusual in experiences such as these, they have for him a distinct attraction. His best thoughts are wedded to the sea, the hard life upon it is for him the kernel of existence—and when he is forced to remain at home, his heart is heavy. But when he grows old—ah, then the saga is over. There is always a melancholy in old age, and nowhere more than here. These kindly old men have also in their day known strength and youth—times when they were the pillars of their little society. Now they have only the memories of that life left to them, and they must let themselves be fed by others. But when the young people come home from sea with their booty, they, too, hobble down to the beach to receive them; even if it were but a poor foreigner like me, they were glad to be able to help me ashore with my kaiak. And then when evening comes they set themselves to story-telling; adventure follows adventure, the past comes to life again, and the young people are spurred on to action.

The hunting is often more dangerous than that described above. It will easily be understood that from his constrained position in the kaiak, which does not permit of much turning, the hunter cannot throw backwards or to the right. If, then, a wounded seal suddenly attacks him from these quarters, it requires both skill and presence of mind to elude it or to turn so quickly as to aim a fatal throw at it before it has time to do him damage. It is just as bad when he is attacked from below, or when the animal suddenly shoots up close at his side, for it is lightning-like in its movements and lacks neither courage nor strength. If it once gets up on the kaiak and capsizes it, there is little hope of rescue. It will often attack the hunter under water, or throw itself upon the bottom of the kaiak and tear holes in it. In such a predicament, it needs very unusual self-mastery to preserve the coolness necessary for recovering oneself upon even keel and renewing the fight with the furious adversary. And yet it sometimes happens that after being thus capsized the kaiak-man brings the seal home in triumph.

A still more terrible adversary is the walrus; therefore there are generally several in company when they go walrus-hunting, so that one can stand by another if anything should happen. But often enough, too, a single hunter will attack and overcome this monster.

The walrus, I need scarcely say, is a huge animal of as much as 16 feet (5 metres) in length, with a thick and tough hide, a deep layer of blubber, a terribly hard skull, and a powerful body. There needs, then, a sure and strong arm to kill it. The walrus has the habit, as soon as it is attacked, of turning upon its assailant, and will often, with its ugly tusks, make itself exceedingly unpleasant. If there are several walruses in a flock, they will very likely surround him and attack him all at once.

Even the Norwegian hunters, who go after the walrus in large, strong boats, each containing many men, armed with guns, lances, and axes—even they stand much in awe of it.

How much more courage and skill does it require for the Eskimo to attack it in his frail skin canoe, with his light ingenious projectiles—and alone!

A KAIAK-MAN ATTACKED BY A WALRUS

But this is no unusual occurrence for the Eskimo. He fights out his fight with his dangerous adversary; calmly, with his lance ready poised for throwing, he awaits its attack, and, coolly seizing his advantage, he at the right moment plunges the weapon into its body.

Coolness is more than ever essential in walrus-hunting, for the most unforeseen difficulties may arise; and catastrophes are by no means rare. At Kangamiut, some years ago, a kaiak was attacked from below, and a long walrus-tusk was suddenly thrust through its bottom, through the man's thigh, and right up through the deck. His comrades at once rushed to his assistance, and the man was rescued and helped ashore.

Besides these animals, the Eskimo also attacks whales from his little kaiak. There is one species in particular which is more dangerous than any other—the grampus, or, as he calls it, *ardluk*. With its strength, its swiftness, and its horrible teeth, if it happens to take the offensive, it can make an end of a kaiak in an instant. Even the Eskimo fears it; but that does not prevent him from attacking it when opportunity offers.

In former times they hunted the larger whales as well, using, however, the great woman-boats, with many people in them, both men and women. For this sort of whale-hunting, says Hans Egede, 'they get themselves up in their greatest finery as if for a marriage, for otherwise the whale will avoid them; he cannot endure uncleanliness.' The whale was harpooned, or rather pierced with a big lance, from the bow, and it sometimes happened that with a whisk of its tail it would crush the boat or capsize it. The men were often so daring as to jump on the whale's back, when it began to be exhausted, in order to give it a finishing stroke. This method of hunting is now unusual.

It is not only the larger animals that expose the Eskimo to danger. Even in ordinary fishing—for example, for halibut—disasters may happen. If one has not taken care to keep the line clear, and it gets fouled in one place or another, while the strong fish is making a sudden dash for the bottom, the crank kaiak is easily enough capsized. Many have met their end in this way.

HALIBUT-FISHING

But we must not dwell too long on the shady sides of life. I hope I have succeeded in giving the reader a slight impression of the life of the Eskimo at sea, and of some of the dangers which are his daily lot—enough, perhaps, to have convinced him that this race is not lacking in courage when it comes to the pinch, nor in endurance and cool self-command.

But the Eskimo has more than this; when disaster overtakes him, he will often show the rarest endurance and hardihood. In spite of the many dangers and sufferings inseparable from his industry, he devotes himself to it with joy. If the history of the Eskimos had ever been written, it would have been one long series of feats of courage and fortitude; and how much moving self-sacrifice and devotion to others would have had to be recorded! How many deeds of heroism have been irrecoverably forgotten! And this is the people whom we Europeans have called worthless and cowardly, and have thought ourselves entitled to despise.

CHAPTER V

WINTER-HOUSES, TENTS, WOMAN-BOATS, AND EXCURSIONS

In winter the Greenlanders live in houses built of stones and turf. They rise only from four to six feet (one and a half to two metres) above the level of the ground, and the floor is sunk somewhat beneath it. The roof is flat or slightly arched. From outside, the whole structure generally looks like an insignificant mound of earth.

There is only one room in these houses, and in it several families generally live together—men and women, young and old. The roof is so low that a man of any stature can scarcely stand upright. The room forms an oblong quadrangle. Along the whole of the longer wall, opposite the door, runs the chief sleeping-bench, about six feet six inches in width, upon which sleep the married people, with grown-up unmarried daughters and young boys and girls. Here they lie in a row, side by side, with their feet towards the wall and their heads out into the room.

Hans Egede Saabye says, in his before-mentioned Journal, that they make their marriage-bed under the sleeping-bench. I saw nothing to indicate that any such practice now exists anywhere in the Godthaab district.

Unmarried men generally lie upon smaller benches under the windows, which are in the opposite long wall, and of which there are one, two, or three, according to the size of the house. The windows were formerly filled with gut-skin, or some similar material; but nowadays, on the west coast, glass is commonly used. Against the side walls, too—the shorter walls—there are generally benches. These, or the window-benches, are, as a rule, assigned to strangers as their sleeping-places.

When several families, as is generally the case, dwell in one house, the chief sleeping-bench is divided into stalls—one for each family. The stalls are marked off by wooden posts, placed against the outer edge of the bench, and reaching to the roof, from which low partitions extend to the back wall. It is incredible how little room they are content with. Captain Holm describes a house on the east coast which measured about twenty-seven feet by fourteen and a half, and in which dwelt eight families, consisting in all of thirty-eight persons. In one stall, four feet broad, dwelt a man with two wives and seven children. This does not give much space to each.

They use seal-skins or reindeer-skins to lie upon, and also, in former days, as bedclothes, going to bed entirely naked, with the exception of the before-mentioned indoor dress. Nowadays, on the west coast, down quilts are commonly used as bedclothes.

Internally, the walls of the house were in former times always lined with skins. The floor was formed by the naked earth, partly paved with flags. Nowadays, since the introduction of so much European luxury, they have begun, on the west coast, to line the walls with boards and to lay wooden floors. They have even, to a certain extent, adopted the habit of washing the floors—so much as several times a year.

The house is entered through a long and narrow passage, partly dug out beneath the level of the ground, and, like the houses, walled with stones and turf. You descend into it from the level of the ground through a hole. It is, as a rule, so low and narrow that one has to crouch one's way through it, and a large man finds it difficult enough to effect an entrance. I was told at Sardlok of a fat storekeeper from Godthaab who stuck fast at a difficult point in the passage leading to Terkel's house. There he stuck, struggling and roaring, but could not advance, and still less retreat. In the end, he had to get four small boys to help him, two shoving behind and two, from within the house, dragging him in front by the arms. They laboured and toiled in the sweat of their brows, but the man was jammed as fast as a wad in a gun-barrel, and there was some thought of pulling down the walls of the passage in order to liberate him, before he at last managed to squeeze through. If I remember rightly, a window had to be torn down in order to let him out of the house again.

From the passage, you enter the house through a little square opening, usually in the front long wall, which is closed by a door or trap-door.

The purpose of this passage is to prevent the cold air from coming in and the warm light air from escaping. It is to this end that it is made to lie lower than the house; by which means, too, a little ventilation is obtained, since the heavy bad air can, to some extent, sink down into it and escape.

In Greenland houses of the old style there are no fireplaces; they are warmed, as well as lighted, by train-oil lamps, which burn day and night. They are left burning all night through, not merely for the sake of warmth, but also because the Eskimos are exceedingly superstitious, and therefore afraid of even sleeping in darkness. You may hear them relate, as a proof of extreme poverty, that this family or that, poor things, have to sleep at night with no lamp burning.

The lamps are large, flat open saucers of soapstone. They are of semi-circular form, and along the straight side lies the wick, which is formed of dry moss, or, nowadays, of cotton. These lamps rest on a wooden stand, and are placed on a little table or raised place in front of the sleeping-bench. There is generally one of these lamp-tables to each family. If several families dwell in one house, there are many lamps, for each family has at least one burning, and, as a rule, more.

In former days, food used to be cooked over these lamps in soapstone pots, which hung from the roof. The preparation of food, like every other business of life, of course went on in the common room.

So it is to this day on the east coast. On the west coast, modern civilisation has effected a change, in so far that food is now generally cooked in a special room with a fireplace, built on to the side of the passage leading into the house. Peat is used as fuel in these fireplaces, and also lumps of dried seagulls' dung. Iron saucepans, too, bought at the stores in the colonies, are now used instead of soapstone pots.

Many West Greenlanders have, moreover, become so highly sophisticated as to have bought stoves, which they use instead of the train-oil lamps for heating their houses. The fuel used is the same as that mentioned above. At the same time, however, the indispensable lamps are kept burning, for the sake of light, if for no other reason.

In former days the houses were generally large, and several families lived in each. By this means they were able to economise in fuel, and they lived warmly and comfortably, while in many other ways the habitation in common was found advantageous. In this point the influence of the Europeans has been unfortunate. They have encouraged the distribution of the families into separate small houses, and have even offered prizes for house-building; it was thought to be such a grand thing that each family should have its own home for itself. The result was that the houses became poorer and colder, more material in proportion was needed for warming and lighting — material which was not always forthcoming — and the advantages of the old system of partial communism were sacrificed; so that the separation tended to the greater discomfort of the greater number.

In winter, when everything is frozen hard, these houses are all well enough; but in summer, when the moisture exudes from the thawing walls and the roof leaks and sometimes falls in, they are anything but wholesome dwelling-places. As soon as spring arrives, therefore, with the month of April, the Greenlanders used always in former days to quit their houses, often unroofing them themselves, in order that they might be thoroughly ventilated and washed out by the autumn rains — an exceedingly simple method of house-cleaning.

The whole summer through, and a good way into the autumn (until September or October), the Greenlanders dwelt in tents, each family, as a rule, having its own. These tents are of a peculiar semi-circular form, with the entrance-door in the high flat side. Internally, they are arranged very like the houses, with the sleeping-bench running along the curved back wall opposite to the door, which is closed with a curtain of semi-transparent gut-skin. The walls of the tent consist of an outer layer of water-tight skin with the hair taken off (old boat-skins being used as a rule), and an inner layer of reindeer- or seal-skin with the fur turned inwards. These tents are tolerably warm, and in them, as in their houses, they go without clothes.

The woman-boat is inseparably connected with this summer tent-life. These boats, which are from 30 to 40 feet long (10 to 12 metres), have received their name from the Europeans, because, unlike the kaiaks, they are rowed by women.

AN ESKIMO CAMP

They are entirely open boats, consisting of a wooden framework covered with seal-skin, and are narrow in proportion to their length, and flat-bottomed. They are easy to row, but their shape renders them defective and inconvenient sea-boats, so that as soon as there is any wind the Greenlanders make for the land with them. They have generally a small sail which can be set in the bow, for running before a fair wind; but it will be readily understood that they are not good sailing-boats. Sailing is, on the whole, a pursuit of which the Eskimo understands little, and for which he has no great liking.

In these boats there is room for all a family's worldly goods—tents, household implements, dogs, children, women, &c. They are rowed by as many as half a score of oarswomen, and when they are so well 'manned,' they attain a good speed. A run of fifty English miles a day is not at all uncommon. They are generally steered by the paterfamilias, while the other males of the family follow in their kaiaks.

In their woman-boats, the Greenlanders used to move from one hunting-ground to another all through the summer. For one or two months they always went far up the fiords in search of reindeer, and there they lived on the fat of the land.

In those days they often undertook long journeys up and down the west coast, as they do to this day on the east coast. To show how long these journeys sometimes are, I may mention that on the east coast families travel from the Angmagsalik district, in 65½° north latitude, the whole way to the trading-settlements west of Cape Farewell, and back again—a distance of about 500 miles. They do not generally travel quickly; one of two woman-boats which we met on the east coast at Cape Bille in 1888, on their way southwards, did not reach Pamiagdluk, west of Cape Farewell, until two years later, in 1890—and this is only a distance of some 180 miles, which we with our boats could no doubt have covered in a week or two. But as soon as the Eskimos come to a place where there are plenty of seals, they go ashore, pitch their camp, take to hunting, and live at their ease. When the autumn and winter approach, they choose a good site and build a winter-house, continuing their journey in the spring or summer as soon as the ice permits. The woman-boat in question had in this manner spent three years on the passage from Umivik, and would no doubt take pretty nearly as long to return. The other woman-boat that was passing southwards from Cape Bille got as far as Nanusek, about 65 miles from the trading-settlements west of Cape Farewell, and there went into winter quarters; but then the father of the family died, and they faced round and set about the long journey back to Angmagsalik, without ever having reached their goal, the trading-settlements, or accomplished their errand.

A SUMMER JOURNEY

Journeys along the west coast were of course easier and more rapid, as the drift-ice did not there present impediments.

By means of this habit of wandering they escaped the evil effects of too great seclusion in separate villages; they met together and kept up intercourse with other people, so that there was all through the summer a certain life and traffic from which they reaped many benefits. Their minds were enlivened, interest in hunting was stimulated, and skill was developed in many different ways, to say nothing of the fact that the frequent changing of hunting-grounds brought much more game within their reach.

This summer life in the comparatively clean, airy tents, besides being exceedingly pleasant, was, as we may easily understand, very much healthier than confinement in the close, evil-smelling earth cabins. No wonder, then, that the Greenlanders' fairest dreams of happiness were associated with the woman-boat and the tent.

Here again, alas! we Europeans have brought about melancholy changes. Hans Egede, indeed, complained bitterly of the difficulty of getting the Greenlanders to leave off their perpetual wanderings and settle down peaceably in one place, so that he could preach Christianity to them at his ease; he even proposed that they should be forcibly bound down to a less migratory life. If this pious man, who thought of nothing but the advancement of the Kingdom of God, had been living now, he might in so far have been happy; for the Christian Greenlanders of to-day scarcely travel at all. By reason of the great impoverishment which we have brought upon them, there are every day fewer and fewer hunters who can procure enough skins to make a woman-boat and a tent, both of which are of course necessary for travelling. They are more and more forced to pass the whole year round in the unwholesome winter houses, which are, of course, mere hot-beds for bacteria and all sorts of contagious diseases, while the men are thus unable to change their hunting-grounds, and must keep to the same spots year out year in. By this means the 'take' is of course greatly diminished, food is consequently much less plentiful, and the indispensable seal-skins become fewer and fewer. As soon as the whole Greenland community has sunk to the level of Egede's ideal and has entirely abandoned its migratory habits, it will be almost, if not quite, beyond salvation. The decline in this direction has of late years been very alarming.

CHAPTER VI
COOKERY AND DAINTIES

One feature of the Greenlanders' daily life, which to us seems strange enough, is that they have no fixed meal-times; they simply eat when they are hungry, if there is anything to be had. As already mentioned, the hunters often go the whole day without anything to eat. They have a remarkable power of doing without food, but to make up for this they can consume at a sitting astonishing quantities of meat, blubber, fish, &c.

Their cookery is simple and easy to learn.

Meat and fish are eaten sometimes raw or frozen, sometimes boiled, sometimes dried; and sometimes meat is allowed to undergo a sort of decomposition or fermentation, when it is called *mikiak*, and is eaten without further preparation. A dish of this sort, which is very highly esteemed, is rotten seals'-heads.

The blubber of seals and whales is generally eaten raw. My dainty readers will of course shudder at the very thought of eating raw blubber; but I can assure them that, especially when quite fresh, it is very good. It has a sweetish, perhaps rather mawkish, taste, reminding one of cream, with nothing of what we should call an oily or fishy flavour; this does not make itself felt until the blubber has been boiled or roasted, or when it has grown rancid. There are still people, no doubt, who believe that the Eskimos are in the habit of drinking train-oil, although even Hans Egede has pointed out that this is a mistake. That they do not always refuse it, however, when it comes in their way, I was able to assure myself at Godthaab; for I always saw our old maid-servant Rosina take a sip or two out of our lamp when she was cleaning it in the morning, and, as she usually did, had filled the vessel a little too full. It did not seem at all to disagree with her.

They also preserve the stalks of angelica in train-oil, preparing them, according to Saabye's account, in the following peculiar fashion; 'A woman takes a mouthful of blubber, chews it, and spits it out, and so continues until she thinks she has enough. When the angelica-stalks have steeped for a certain time in this liquid, they are taken out and eaten as dessert with much appetite.'

Of vegetable food, the primitive Greenlanders used several sorts; in addition to angelica, I may mention dandelions, sorrel, crowberries, bilberries, and different kinds of seaweed. One of their greatest delicacies is the contents of a reindeer's stomach. If a Greenlander kills a reindeer, and is unable to convey much of it home with him, he will, I believe, secure the stomach first of all; and the last thing an Eskimo lady enjoins upon her lover, when he sets off reindeer-hunting, is that he must reserve for her the stomach of his prey. It is no doubt because they stand in need of vegetable food that they prize this so highly, and also because it is in reality a very choice collection of the finest moss and grasses which that *gourmet*, the reindeer, picks out for himself. It has undergone a sort of stewing in the process of semi-digestion, while the gastric juice provides a somewhat sharp and aromatic sauce. Many will no doubt make a wry face at the thought of this dish, but they really need not do so. I have tasted it, and found it not uneatable, though somewhat sour, like fermented milk. As a dish for very special occasions, it is served up with pieces of blubber and crowberries.

Another dish, which will doubtless shock many Europeans, is the entrails of ptarmigans. In this case they do not confine themselves to the stomachs, but devour in a twinkling the viscera with their contents. The remainder of the ptarmigan they sell to the traders for a penny or less (5 to 8 öre). This is the reason why, in Greenland, one never sees ptarmigan whole, except those one has shot oneself.

One time when we went on a hunting expedition up the Ameralik fiord, and had the Greenlander Joel with us, he devoted a day to tearing the entrails out of all our ptarmigan; but as they numbered a good many more than a hundred, he could not devour the whole on the spot, and gathered up the remains in a large sack. Upon its delicious contents, which must have become a sort of gruel before he reached home, he no doubt intended to feast in company with his well-beloved Anna Cornelia. I hope the reader will pardon my inability to inform him how this dish tastes; it was the one Greenland delicacy which I could not make up my mind to essay.

Among other dainties I must mention the skin (*matak*) of different sorts of whales, especially of white whale and porpoise, which is regarded as the acme of deliciousness. The skin is taken off with the layer of blubber next to it, and is eaten raw without further ceremony. I must offer the Eskimos my sincerest congratulations on the invention of this dish. I can assure the reader that now, as I write of it, my mouth waters at the very thought of matak with its indescribably delicate taste of nuts and oysters mingled. And then it has this advantage over oysters, that the skin is as tough as india-rubber to masticate, so that the enjoyment can be protracted to any extent. Even the Danes in Greenland are greatly addicted to this delicacy when it is to be had; they cook it, however, as a rule, thus making it of a jellyish consistency and easy of mastication. The taste of nuts and oysters disappears entirely.

A delicate dish, which does not, however, rival matak, is raw halibut-skin. It has the same advantage that, by reason of its toughness, it goes such a long way. I can confidently recommend it as exceedingly palatable, especially in winter.

The Greenlander is also very fond of raw seal-skin with the blubber. Its taste was very tolerable, but I could not quite reconcile myself to the hairs, and therefore took the liberty of spitting them out again, after having made several vain attempts to swallow them.

They eat the flesh of seals, whales, reindeer, birds, hares, bears, even of dogs and foxes. The only things, so far as I know, that they despise, are ravens; as these birds feed to some extent upon the dung-heaps, they are regarded, like the plants that grow there, as unclean.

Lean meat they do not care about at all; therefore they prefer, for example, sea-birds to ptarmigan. It happened once that in one of the colonies in South Greenland, a clergyman, who had just arrived in the country, invited some of his flock to a party, and his wife treated them to the greatest delicacy she knew, namely, roast ptarmigan. The Greenlanders ate very sparingly of it, though their hostess pressed it hospitably upon them. At last she asked whether they did not like ptarmigan. Oh yes, they answered, they ate it sometimes—when there was a famine.

What I have said above will doubtless be enough to prove that the Eskimos are by no means so easily contented in their diet as is generally supposed. In famine times, however, they will eat almost anything. Dalager assures us that they will, for example, 'cut their tent skins to pieces and make soup with them,' and it is not uncommon to hear of someone who has made soup of his old skin trousers.

The method of serving the food differs considerably from that which obtains in Europe. There are no tables in the Greenland house; therefore the dish is placed in the middle of the floor, and the people sit on the benches around, and dip into it with the forks provided by Nature. It seldom occurs to them to place the dish upon a box or any other raised place; it seems almost a necessity for them to stoop. An example of this may be found in an anecdote of a young Danish lady who, soon after her arrival in Greenland, got some Eskimo women into her house to do washing. Coming into the wash-house, she found them bending over the wash-tubs, which stood upon the floor, and, thinking this an awkward position, she brought them some stools to place the tubs upon. Shortly afterwards she went in again to see how they were getting on, and found them, to her astonishment, standing upon the stools and, of course, stooping still more awkwardly over the tubs, which remained upon the floor. *Se non è vero è ben trovato.*

Of all the many delicacies to which we have introduced them, the Christian Greenlanders are most addicted to coffee, and the indulgence in it has on the west coast become almost a vice. They brew it strong, and seldom drink less than two large bowls at a time; and it is not at all unusual for them to take coffee four or five times a day—it tastes so nice and puts them in such excellent spirits. They are not insensible to its deleterious effects, however, and therefore young men are allowed little or none of it, lest it should spoil them for hunting. A dizziness from which the older men sometimes suffer, and which makes them unsteady in the kaiak, they attribute in large part to coffee. This harmonises curiously with the results of recent physiological experiments, which have shown that the most dangerous poisons contained in coffee—cafeonet, &c.—attack precisely that part of the nervous system on which equilibrium depends.

Next to coffee they are devoted to tobacco and bread. On the west coast, tobacco is for the most part smoked or chewed; while snuff is the East Greenlanders' weakness. The women on the west coast, too, are given to snuffing, and it is often an unpleasant surprise to observe an attractive young woman blackening her nostrils and upper lip with a copious pinch. They grind their own snuff with flat stones, out of undamped roll-tobacco, which they cut up small and dry over the lamp. To make it go further it is sometimes mixed with powdered stone; and it is kept in horns of different sizes. On the east coast, snuff performs a definite social function. The Eskimos have no words for 'good-day' or 'welcome,' and fill up the gap by offering their snuff-horns to any stranger who is acceptable in their sight, whereupon the newcomer responds by offering his horn in exchange. When they part, the same ceremony is repeated.

The West Greenlanders prepare their chewing tobacco in a way which to us seems somewhat surprising. A deep Danish porcelain pipe is half-filled with smoking-tobacco, which is then thoroughly drenched with water, after which the pipe is filled to the brim with dry tobacco; then it is smoked till the fire reaches the wet tobacco and is extinguished. The ashes are then knocked out, and as much oil as possible is scraped together from the oil-cell, the pipe-stem, the old accretions in the pipe-bowl, &c., and is added to the already well impregnated mass in the bottom of the bowl, which is then considered ready for chewing. This particularly strong preparation is specially prized for use on board the kaiak.

The Government has, fortunately, prohibited the sale of brandy to the Greenlanders. Europeans, however, are allowed to order it from home, and may treat the Greenlanders with it. It is very common to let them have a dram when they are serving as rowers on board the boats of Europeans travelling in the summer-time, and after any bargain has been concluded with them. It has furthermore been wisely ordained that the *kifaks*, or those who are in the employ of the Danish Company, get each his dram every morning; while the hunters, who ought to be more capable and better men than the kifaks, cannot obtain any without either entering into the service of the Europeans or selling something to them.

They are passionately fond of brandy—women as well as men—not, as they often confided to me, because they like the taste of it, but because it is so delightful to be drunk; and they get drunk whenever an opportunity offers, which is, happily, not very often. That the intoxication is really the main object in view appears also from the fact that the kifaks do not greatly value their morning dram, because it is not enough to make them drunk. Several of them, therefore, agreed to bring their portions into a common stock, one of them drinking the whole to-day, the next to-morrow, and so on by turns. Thus they could get comfortably drunk at certain fixed intervals. When the authorities discovered this practice, however, they took means to stop it.

Unlike their sisters here in Europe, the Eskimo wives, as a rule, find their husbands charming in their cups, and take great pleasure in the sight of them. I must confess, indeed, that the Eskimos, both men and women, seemed to me, with few exceptions, considerably less repulsive, and, of course, considerably more peaceable, in a state of intoxication than Europeans are apt to be under similar conditions.

When the Europeans first came to the country, the natives could not at all understand the effects of brandy. When Christmas approached, they came and asked Niels Egede when his people were going to be 'mad'; for they thought that 'madness' was an inseparable accompaniment of the feast, and the recurring paroxysm had become to them a landmark in the almanack. They afterwards ascertained that it was due to this liquor, which they therefore called *silaerúnartok*—that is to say, the thing which makes men lose their wits; but now they usually call it *snapsemik*.

CHAPTER VII

CHARACTER AND SOCIAL CONDITIONS

When I see all the wrangling and all the coarse abuse of opponents which form the staple of the different party newspapers at home, I now and then wonder what these worthy politicians would say if they knew anything of the Eskimo community, and whether they would not blush before the people whom that man of God, Hans Egede, characterises as follows:—'These ignorant, cold-blooded creatures, living without order or discipline, with no knowledge of any sort of worship, in brutish stupidity.' With what good right would these 'savages' look down upon us, if they knew that here, even in the public press, we apply to each other the lowest terms of contumely, as for example 'liar,' 'traitor,' 'perjurer,' 'lout,' 'rowdy,' &c., while they never utter a syllable of abuse, their very language being unprovided with words of this class, in which ours is so rich.

This contrast typifies a radical difference of character. The Greenlander is of all God's creatures gifted with the best disposition. Good-humour, peaceableness, and evenness of temper are the most prominent features in his character. He is eager to stand on as good a footing as possible with his fellow-men, and therefore refrains from offending them and much more from using coarse terms of abuse. He is very loth to contradict another even should he be saying what he knows to be false; if he does so, he takes care to word his remonstrance in the mildest possible form, and it would be very hard indeed for him to say right out that the other was lying. He is chary of telling other people truths which he thinks will be unpleasant to them; in such cases he chooses the vaguest expressions, even with reference to such indifferent things as, for example, wind and weather. His peaceableness even goes so far that when anything is stolen from him, which seldom happens, he does not as a rule reclaim it even if he knows who has taken it. 'Give to every man that asketh of thee; and of him that taketh away thy goods ask them not again' (Luke vi. 30).

The result is that there is seldom or never any quarrelling among them. The Greenlanders cannot afford to waste time in wrangling amongst themselves; the struggle to wring from nature the necessities of life, that great problem of humanity, is there harder than anywhere else, and therefore this little people has agreed to carry it on without needless dissensions.

On the whole, the Greenlander is a happy being, his soul being light and cheerful as a child's. If sorrow overtakes him, he may perhaps suffer bitterly for the moment; but it is soon forgotten, and he is once more as radiantly contented with existence as he used to be.

This happy levity of his saves him from brooding much upon the future. If he has enough to eat for the moment, he eats it and is happy, even if he has afterwards to suffer want—which is now, unfortunately, often the case, and becomes so oftener year by year.

His carelessness has frequently been made a subject of bitter reproach to him. The missionaries declare, no doubt rightly, that it makes him inaccessible to civilisation, and have tried to exhort him to greater providence and frugality. They quite overlook the fact that it is written, 'Take ye no thought for the morrow.... Behold the fowls of the air: for they sow not, neither do they reap, nor gather into barns; yet your heavenly Father feedeth them.'

This levity of mind has also its bright side; it is even, in a way, the Eskimo's chief strength.

Poverty and want have, with us, two consequences. The most immediate is, of course, the physical suffering; but together with it and after it comes mental suffering, 'the cares of bread,' the unceasing anxiety which pursues one night and day, even in sleep, and embitters every hour of life. In the majority of cases, this is probably what tells most upon our poor people; but for this, the bodily sufferings, which, after all, are generally transitory, would be easily supported. But it is precisely from this phase of suffering that the Eskimo's elastic spirit saves him. Even a long period of starvation and endurance is at once forgotten so soon as he is fed; and the memory of bygone sufferings can no more destroy his enjoyment and happiness, than can the fear of those which to-morrow or the next day may bring. The only thing that really makes him unhappy is to see others in want, and therefore he shares with them whenever he has anything to share.

What chiefly cuts the Eskimos to the heart is to see their children starving; 'and therefore,' says Dalager, 'they give food to their children even if they themselves are ready to die of hunger; for they live every day in the hope of a happy change of fortune—a hope which really sustains life in many of them.'

In order to obtain a clearer conception of the radical difference between the Eskimo character and ours, we ought to study the Eskimos in their social relations.

It is not unusual to hear people express the opinion that the Eskimo community is devoid of law and order. This is a mistake.

Originally, on the contrary, it was singularly well ordered. It had its customs and its fixed rules for every possible circumstance, and these customs and rules were handed down from generation to generation, and were almost always observed; for the people are really incredibly well-disposed, as even Egede himself, who has, as we have seen, written so harshly of them, cannot help admitting in such a passage as, for example, the following; 'It is wonderful in what peace and unity they live with each other; for quarrelling and strife, hatred and covetousness, are seldom heard of among them.[20] And even if one of them happens to bear an

---

[20] 'When they have seen our dissolute sailors quarrelling and fighting, they regard such behaviour as inhuman, and say: "They do not treat each other as human beings." In

ill-will to another, he does not let it be seen, nor, on account of their great tenderness for each other, does he take upon himself to attack him openly with violence or abuse, their language being indeed devoid of the necessary words.' Observe that this is said by a missionary of heathens, who, therefore, could not have developed this peaceful temper through the influence of Christianity.

Then came the Europeans. Without knowing or understanding the people or its requirements, they started from the assumption that it stood in need of improvement in every possible way, and consequently set to work to disturb and overturn the whole social order. They tried to force upon the Eskimos a totally new character, gave them, all in a moment, a new religion, and broke down their respect for their old customs and traditions, of course without being able to give them new ones in their place. The missionaries thought that they could make this wild, free people of hunters into a civilised Christian nation, without for a moment suspecting that at heart these people were in many respects more Christian than themselves, and, among other things, like so many primitive people, had put into practice the Christian doctrine of love (charity) very much more fully than any Christian nation. The Europeans, in short, conducted themselves in Greenland exactly as they are in the habit of doing wherever they come forward in the name of the Christian religion to 'make the poor heathen partakers in the blessings of eternal truth.'

Very characteristic of this view is the following utterance of Egede's, of which I have already spoken: 'The inborn stupidity and dulness of the Greenlanders, their slothful and brutish upbringing, their wandering and unstable way of life, certainly offer great hindrances to their conversion, and ought as much as possible to be obviated and remedied.' What a lack of comprehension! Only think, to want to obviate and remedy the nomadic life of a tribe of hunters! What would remain to them? I may add that he at another time proposes to attain this end by means of 'chastisement and discipline.'

The Eskimos at first listened in astonishment to the strangers. They had hitherto been very well content with themselves and their whole way of living; they did not know that man and his life on earth were so miserable as the missionaries again and again assured them they were. They had not, as Egede says, 'any just realisation of their own profound corruption,' and had great difficulty in understanding a religion so cruel as to condemn people to everlasting fire. They could quite well recognise 'original sin' as a common characteristic of the *kavdlunaks* (Europeans), for it was clear enough that many of them were bad; but the *kaladlit* (Eskimos) were good people, and ought without any trouble to get into heaven.

When in 1728 a number of Danish men and women came to Godthaab to colonise the country, many of them gave great offence to the heathens by their evil ways, so that they 'often asked how it was that so many of our people were so bad. Women (that is, Greenland women), they said, are naturally quiet and modest; but these (the Europeans) were boisterous, brazen, and lacking in all womanly propriety. Yet they surely all knew God's will.' And the Greenlanders looked down

the same way, if one of the officers strikes a subordinate, they at once exclaim: "He behaves to his fellow-men as if they were dogs."'

upon and laughed at the stupid, self-satisfied Europeans who preached so finely but practised so little what they preached, and who, besides, knew nothing about hunting or about all the things which the Eskimos regarded as the most important in life.

The power which comes of a higher development gradually gave the Europeans the upper hand, so that in the course of time they have brought about a complete disturbance of the primitive social order, and replaced it by an indeterminate mixture of Eskimo and modern European habits and civilisation; while they have also effected a deplorable mixture of breeds, and produced, without the help of the clergy, an exceedingly mongrel population.

But, as the Eskimos are a very conservative people, we can still find many important traces of their primitive condition.

The Greenlanders, like all nations of hunters, have a very restricted sense of property; but it is a mistake to suppose it entirely non-existent.

As regards the great majority of things, a certain communism prevails; but this is always limited to wider or narrower circles according to the nature of the thing in question. Ascending from the individual, we find in the family the narrowest social circle; then come housemates and the nearest kinsfolk, and then all the families of the village. Private property is most fully recognised in the kaiak, the kaiak-dress and the hunting-weapons, which belong to the hunter alone, and which no one must touch. With them he supports himself and his family, and he must therefore always be sure of finding them where he last laid them; it is seldom that they are even lent to others. In former times, good hunters would often own two kaiaks, but that is seldom the case now. Snow-shoes may almost be regarded as belonging to implements of the chase; but as they were introduced by the Europeans, they are not considered matters of private property in the same degree; so that while an Eskimo seldom or never touches another's weapons he will scarcely think twice about using another's snow-shoes without asking leave.

Next to clothes and hunting implements come the tools which are used in the houses, such as knives, axes, saws, skin-cutters, &c. Many of these, and especially the women's sewing materials, are regarded as altogether private property.

Other household implements are the common property of the family or even of all the occupants of the house. The woman-boat and the tent belong to the father of the family or to the family as a whole. The house belongs to the family, and if several families live together they own it in common.

The Eskimo knows nothing of private property in land; yet there seems to be a recognised rule that no one shall pitch a tent or build a house at a place where people are already settled without obtaining their consent.

As an example of their consideration for each other in this respect I may cite a custom which was thus described by Lars Dalager more than a hundred years ago: 'In the summer, when they take their tents and baggage with them, and think of settling down at a place where other Greenlanders are living, they row very slowly towards the shore, and when they come to within a gunshot of it they stop and lie upon their oars without saying a word. If those on shore are equally silent and give no sign, the newcomers think they are not wanted and therefore row away as fast as possible to some unoccupied place. But if those on shore, as generally happens, meet them with compliments, such as: "Look here! here are good places for your tents, a good beach for your woman-boats—come and rest after the labours of the day!" they, after a little consideration, lay in to the shore where the others stand ready to receive them and to help with the landing of the baggage. But when they are starting again, the people of the place confine themselves to helping in the launch of the woman-boat, and let the strangers themselves see to the rest, unless they happen to be very good friends or near relations, in which case they are despatched with the same marks of honour with which they were received, and with some such phrases as this: "Your visit will be a pleasant memory to us."'[21]

We may perhaps find the rudiments of the conception of private property in land in the fact that where dams have been built in a salmon river to gather the fish together, it is not regarded as the right thing if strangers come and interfere with the dams or fish with nets in the dammed-up waters, as Europeans were often in the habit of doing in earlier times. This too is mentioned by Dalager.

Driftwood belongs to whoever first finds it floating in the sea, wherever it may happen to be. In order to sustain his right to it, the finder is bound to tow it ashore and place it above the high-water line, if possible marking it in one way or another. For this form of property the Eskimo has the greatest respect, and one who has left a piece of drift-wood on the shore may be sure of finding it again even several years after, unless Europeans have come along in the meantime. Any one taking it would be regarded as a scoundrel.

As to their customs in lending and trading, I may again quote Dalager: 'If one man lends another anything, for example a boat, a harpoon, a fishing-line, or other sea-implement, and it comes to harm—if, for instance, the seal gets away with the harpoon, or the fish breaks the line, or the fish or seal does injury to the boat—the owner must bear the loss, the borrower making no reparation. But if anyone borrows darts or implements without the knowledge of the owner, and they come to harm, the borrower is bound to make good the damage. This happens very seldom; for a Greenlander must be hard pushed before he will trouble his neighbour to lend him anything, for fear of any harm occurring to it.'

'When one makes a purchase from another, and the wares do not suit him, he can return them even after a considerable time has elapsed.'

'If one buys of another such costly things as a boat or a gun, and the buyer is not in a position to satisfy the seller in ready money, he is allowed credit until he can pay up. But if the debtor dies in the meantime, the creditor never makes any claim. This,' adds Dalager, 'is an inconvenient habit for the merchants of the colony, who are always bound to give credit; whereof I have had several experiences, especially this year, many of my debtors having departed this life, and thus brought me into considerable perplexity.'

On his complaining to 'some influential and reasonable Greenlanders,' they

[21] Dalager, *Grönlandske Relationer*, Copenhagen, 1752, pp. 15-16.

advised him 'to register his claim at once, but to let the man's lice die in the grave (as they expressed it) before he proceeded to execution.'

Beyond the articles above enumerated,[22] the Greenlander, according to his primitive customs, can possess but little. Even if he had a faculty for laying up riches, which he very seldom has, his needier fellows would have the right to enforce a claim upon such of his possessions as were not necessary for himself. Thus we find in Greenland this unfortunate state of things: that the European immigrants, who are in reality supported by the natives, often become rich and live in abundance (at any rate, according to the Eskimo ideas), while the natives themselves are in want.

The Greenlander has not even unrestricted rights over the game he himself secures. There have been fixed rules from time immemorial according to which it is divided, and there are only a few sorts of animals which he can keep pretty well to himself and to his family. To these belong the *atak* or Greenland seal; but even in its case he must give a portion of blubber to each of the kaiak-men who are present when he takes it, and in the same way the children of the village, when he comes home, receive a little scrap of blubber apiece. There are fixed rules for other sorts of game, in accordance with which the whole animal is divided among those who were present when it was killed or even among all the houses of the village. This is especially the case with regard to the walrus and several sorts of whales, as, for example, the white whale; of this the hunter receives only a comparatively small portion, even when he has killed it without help from others. When a whale of any size is brought to shore, it is said to be quite a horrible sight to see all the inhabitants of the village, armed with knives, flinging themselves upon it to secure each his share, while it is still in the water.

The scene is so sanguinary that Dalager declares that he has 'never seen or heard of a whale being cut up without someone or other being mutilated, or at least badly wounded, so great is the careless eagerness with which several hundred people will rush upon the fish, each one doing his best for himself, and, therefore, paying very little heed as to where he slashes with his knife.' It is characteristic of their amiability, however, that 'when one of them has thus come to harm, he does not bear any grudge against the man who injured him, but regards it as an accident.'

It is not only with respect to the larger animals that such rules hold good; they also apply in the case of certain fishes. Thus if a halibut is caught, the fisher is bound to give the other kaiak-men upon the hunting-ground a piece of the skin for division among themselves; and in addition to this, when he comes home, he generally gives some of the animal to his housemates and neighbours.[23]

---

[22] Dogs, however, must be added to the list, and, in the case of the North and East Greenlanders, dog-sledges.

[23] When several are hunting in company, there are fixed rules to determine to whom the game belongs. If two or more shoot at a reindeer, the animal belongs to him who first hit it, even if he only wounded it slightly. As to the rules for seal-hunting, Dalager says: 'If a Greenlander strikes a seal or other marine animal with his light dart, and it is not killed, but gets away with the dart, and if another then comes and kills it with his darts, it nevertheless belongs to the first; but if he has used the ordinary harpoon, and the line breaks, and

FISHING

Even when a Greenlander has fulfilled all the aforesaid laws, he cannot always keep to himself his own share of his booty. For instance, if he makes a catch at a time when there is scarcity or famine in the village, it is regarded as his duty either to give a feast or to divide his prey among other families, who may perhaps have had to go for long without fresh meat.

After a good haul, they make a feast, and eat as long as they can. If everything is not eaten up, and there is plenty in the other houses as well, what remains is stored against the winter; but in times of scarcity it is regarded as the duty of those who have anything to help those who have nothing, even to the last remnant of food. After that, they starve in company, and sometimes starve to death. That some people should live in profusion while others suffer need, as we see it occurring daily in European communities, is an unheard of thing in Greenland; except that the European settlers, with the habitual providence of our race, have often stores of food while the Greenlanders are starving.

It will be understood from what has been said that the tendency of the law is, as much as possible, to let the whole village benefit by the captured prey, so that no family shall be entirely dependent upon the daily 'take' of those who provide another comes and kills the animal, the first has lost his right to it. If, however, they both throw at the same time and both harpoons strike, the animal is cut lengthwise in two, and divided between them, skin and all.' 'If two throw at a bird simultaneously, it is divided between them.' 'If a dead seal is found with a harpoon fixed in it, if the owner of the harpoon is known in the neighbourhood, he gets his weapon back, but the finder keeps the seal.' Similar rules seem also to be in force upon the east coast.

for it. These are laws which have developed through the experience of long ages, and have become established by the habit of many generations.

The Greenlander is, on the whole, like a sympathetic child with respect to the needs of others; *his first social law is to help his neighbour.* Upon it, and upon their habit of clinging together through good and ill, depends the existence of the little Greenland community. A hard life has taught the Eskimo that however capable he may be, and able as a rule to look after himself, there may come times when without the help of his fellow-men he would have to go to the wall; therefore, it is best to help others. 'Therefore, all things whatsoever ye would that men should do to you, do ye even so to them'—this commandment, one of the first and most important of Christianity, Nature itself has instilled into the Greenlander, and he always acts up to it, which can scarcely be affirmed of Christian nations. It is unfortunate that, as he advances in civilisation, this commandment seems to lose its power over him.

Hospitality to strangers is a no less binding law among the Eskimos than helpfulness to neighbours. The traveller enters the first hut he comes to, and remains there as long as convenient. He is kindly received and entertained with what the house can offer, even if he be an enemy. When he proceeds on his way, he often takes a store of food along with him; I have seen kaiak-men leave houses where they had remained weatherbound for several days, loaded with halibut flesh, which had been presented to them on their departure. No payment is ever made for the entertainment. A European, too, is everywhere hospitably received, although the Greenlanders would not think of making similar claims upon his hospitality. Europeans, however, often make some sort of recompense by treating their entertainers to coffee and such other delicacies as they may have with them.

That hospitality is considered a very binding duty upon the east coast of Greenland appears from several remarkable instances related by Captain Holm. I may refer the reader to what he tells of the murderer Maratuk, who had killed his stepfather. He was a bad man, and no one liked him; yet when he presented himself at the house of the murdered man's nearest relatives, he was received and entertained for a long time—but they spoke ill of him when he had gone.

Hospitality is of course forced upon them by their natural surroundings; for it often happens that they are overtaken by storms when far from home, so that they are compelled to take refuge in the nearest dwelling-place.

It seems, unhappily, as though hospitality had declined of late years on the west coast. Doubtless it is once more the Europeans who have given the example. And the fact that the people are by no means so well-to-do as in earlier times, and are therefore less able to entertain strangers, has no doubt tended in the same direction.

Many of my readers are probably of opinion that I am unjust to us Europeans; but that is far from my intention. If the Europeans have not had the best influence, the fact cannot always be directly laid to their charge; circumstances have rendered it inevitable, in spite of excellent intentions on their part. For example, they have conscientiously laboured to foster the sense of property among the Greenlanders, encouraging them to save up portions of their booty, instead of lavishing it abroad in their usual free-handed way, and so forth; the principle being that a more highly developed sense of property is the first condition of civilisation. Whether this is a benefit may seem doubtful to many; for my part I have no doubt about the matter. I must admit, of course, that civilisation presupposes a much greater faculty for the acquisition of worldly goods than the Eskimo is possessed of; but what I cannot understand is what these poor people have to do with civilisation. It assuredly makes them no happier, it ruins what is fine and admirable in their character, makes them weaker in the struggle for existence, and inevitably leads them to poverty and misery. But more of this at a later opportunity.

The laws upon which the heathen community in Greenland rests are, as we have seen, as nearly as possible socialism carried into practice. In this respect, accordingly, they are more Christian than those of any Christian community. The social reformers of to-day might learn much in these high latitudes.

Spencer has in one of his books pointed out that mankind has two religions. The first and most natural is the instinct of self-preservation, which impels the individual to protect himself against all outward opposition or hostile interference. This he calls the religion of enmity. The other is the instinct of association, which impels men to join fellowship with their neighbours; and to it we trace the Christian doctrine that you should love your neighbour as yourself, and should even love your enemies. This he calls the religion of friendship. The former is the religion of the past, the latter that of the future.

Precisely this religion of the future the Eskimo seems to have made his own to a peculiar degree.

The men of some tribes or races are driven to combine with each other by the pressure of human enemies, others by inhospitable natural surroundings. The latter has been the case with the Eskimos. Where the instinct of association and mutual help has been most strongly developed, there has the community's power of maintaining itself been greatest, and it has increased in numbers and in well-being; while other small communities, with less of this instinct, have declined or even succumbed altogether.

In so far as we believe with Spencer that the religion of friendship is that of the future, that self-sacrifice for the benefit of the community is the point towards which development is tending, we must assign to the Eskimo a high place in the scale of nations.

It is a question, however, whether our forefathers also, in long bygone ages, did not act upon a similar principle. It may be that social development proceeds in a spiral with ever wider and wider convolutions.

CHAPTER VIII
THE POSITION AND WORK OF WOMEN

Many leading thinkers have remarked that the social position occupied by its women affords the best criterion of a people's place in the scale of civilisation. I am not entirely convinced that this is always the case; but if it is, I think we have here another indication that the Eskimo must be allowed to have reached a pretty high level of development. For the Eskimo woman plays no insignificant part in the life of the community.

It is true that, according to the primitive Eskimo conception, she is practically regarded as the property of her husband, who has either carried her off, or sometimes bought her, from her father. He can therefore send her away when he pleases, or lend her, or exchange her for another; and, when he can afford it, he can have more wives than one. But as a rule she is well treated, and we find this conception of her as the husband's chattel more clearly marked among many other races; there is even a good deal of it in our own society, only under a somewhat different disguise.

There are some who maintain that our women have plenty to do, but that the great mistake is that their employments are not exactly the same as those of the men. These people will be no better contented with the state of affairs in Greenland, for there, too, the employments of the two sexes are entirely distinct.

It is true that both sexes wear trousers, and have done so from time immemorial; but nevertheless they have not yet attained to the conception that there is little or no difference between men and women.

They hold that there are, among other things, certain essential physical differences, and imagine that women are not as a rule so strong, active, and courageous as men, and that they therefore are not so well fitted for hunting and fishing. On the other hand, they do not think that men are best fitted to have the care of children, to give them suck, and so forth.

This is no doubt the reason for the very clear line of demarcation between the employments proper to the two sexes in Greenland.

To the man's share falls the laborious life at sea, as hunter and food-provider; but when he reaches the shore with his booty, he has fulfilled the most important part of his social function. He is received by his women-folk, who help him ashore; and while he has nothing to do but to look after his kaiak and his weapons, it is the part of the women to drag the booty up to the house. In earlier times, at any rate, it was beneath the dignity of any hunter to lend a hand in this work, and so it still is with the majority.

The women flay the seal and cut it up according to fixed rules, and the mother of the family presides at the division of it. Further, it is the women's duty to cook the food, to prepare the skins, to cover the kaiaks and woman-boats, to make clothes, and to attend to all other domestic tasks. In addition to this they build the houses, pitch the tents, and row the woman-boats.

To row in a woman-boat was formerly, at any rate, quite beneath a hunter's dignity, but it was the part of the father of the family to steer it. Now we often see men sitting and rowing, especially if they are hired by travelling Europeans. When you have become thoroughly accustomed to their way of life, this makes an unpleasant impression; the kaiak is and must be the indispensable condition of their existence, and one feels that they ought to neglect no opportunity for exercising themselves in its use. Even now no hunter of the first rank will condescend to enter a woman-boat, except as steersman.

When the family is out reindeer-hunting, it is of course the men who shoot the reindeer, while it often falls to the share of the women to drag the game to the tent; and this is a laborious business, calling for a great deal of endurance.

The only sort of fishery with which the women as a rule concern themselves is caplin-fishing. The season for this is the early summer, when the caplin appear on the coast in such dense shoals that they can be drawn up in bucketsful into the woman-boats. The fishing continues until a sufficient store is laid up against the winter; when once that is done they care no more about them, however abundant they may be. The fish are dried by being spread out on the rocks and stones; it is the women's business to look after them, and, when they are dried, to pack them together.

Sometimes they take part in seal-fishing, when a sort of battue is made, the seals being hunted into narrow sounds and fiords and driven ashore.

Only a few cases are on record in which women have tried their hand at kaiak-fishing.

Captain Holm mentions two girls at Imarsivik on the east coast who had taken to the kaiak. The proportion between men and women in the village was unfortunate, there being only five men out of a population of twenty-one. We are unhappily not informed whether these women had attained as great skill in hunting as their male comrades.

They had entirely adopted the masculine manner of living, dressed like men and wore their hair like men. When they were allowed to select what they wanted from among Holm's articles of barter, they did not choose needles or other feminine implements, but preferred spear-heads for their weapons. It must have been difficult to distinguish them from men; I must doubtless have seen them when I was on the east coast in 1888, without suspecting their sex. Holm mentions that one or two other girls in the same place were also destined to be trained as hunters, but they were as yet too young.

While the men pass most of their time on the sea, the women remain at home in their houses; and there you will generally find them busily occupied with one task or another, in contrast to those fair ones on our side of the ocean who do nothing but eat, lounge about, gossip, and sleep. When they go beyond the circle of their ordinary domestic employments, it is generally to busy themselves with the weapons of the men, ornamenting them with bone-carvings, &c.; these are their chief pride.

The men generally sit at the outer edge of the sleeping-bench with their feet on the floor; but the women always sit well back on the bench, with their legs crossed, like a tailor on his table. Here they sew, embroider, cut up skins with their peculiar crooked knives, chew bird-skins, and in short attend to many of their most important occupations, while their tongues are in ceaseless activity; for they are very lively and seldom lack matter for conversation. I cannot, unhappily, quite acquit them of the proverbial feminine loquacity; and, if we may believe Dalager, they are not altogether free from graver defects. He says: 'Lying and backbiting are chiefly to be found among the women. The men, on the other hand, are much more honest, and shrink from relating anything which they are unable to substantiate.'

Oh woman, woman, are you everywhere the same!

> The very first thought to which Lokë gave birth,
> It was a lie, and he bade it descend
> In a woman's shape to the men of earth.

The preparation of skins is a very important part of the women's work, and as the methods are extremely peculiar, I shall give a short description of them, as I learnt them from the Eskimos of the Godthaab district. The processes vary according to the different sorts of skins and the purposes for which they are destined.

Kaiak-skins are dressed either black or white.[24]

The black skin (*erisâk*) is obtained by scraping the blubber from the under side of the skin while it is fresh, and then steeping it for a day or two in stale urine, until the hairs can be plucked out with a knife. These being removed, the skin is rinsed in sea water, and in summer it is then dried, but not in the sun. In winter, it is not dried, but if possible preserved by being buried in snow. Whether in summer or winter, however, it is best if, immediately after being washed, it can be stretched on the kaiak so as to dry upon the framework. These skins are dark because the grain or outer membrane of the skin of the seal is either black or dark brown.

White kaiak-skins (*únek*) are prepared in this way: While they are quite fresh, and after the blubber has been roughly removed, they are rolled up and laid in a tolerably warm place either out of doors or in. There they lie until the hairs and the outer membrane can easily be scraped away with a mussel-shell. For this purpose, however, the Greenland beauties generally prefer to use their teeth, since they can thus suck out a certain amount of blubber, which they consider delicious. Then, in summer, the skins are hung up to dry—not in the sun—upon a wooden rail, and

[24] The skins used, as before-mentioned (p. 45) are usually those of the saddleback seal or hood seal; but the skin of the bearded seal is also used, and occasionally that of the ringed seal or even of the mottled or common seal (*Phoca vitulina*).

are often turned in order that they may dry evenly all over. In winter they are preserved, like the black skins, in the snow. The dark membrane being scraped away, these skins are quite light-coloured or white when they are finished.

It must be noted that neither of these sorts of skins is stretched while drying.

Both sorts are used for woman-boats as well as for kaiaks.

For the kaiak, the white skins, which ought always to be kept well greased with seal-blubber, are considered best in summer; the black, on the other hand, which are never greased, are preferred in winter. A well-appointed hunter, therefore, ought to re-cover his kaiak twice a year: nowadays, however, he can generally do so only once, and sometimes only once in two years.

If the seal-skins are to be used for kamiks (shoes), the blubber and the inner layer of the skin itself is scraped away with a crooked knife (*ulo*) upon a board made for the purpose out of a whale's shoulder-blade. When the skin has been scraped thin it is steeped for a day or so in stale urine until the hairs can be plucked off with a knife. This done, the skin is stretched, by means of small bone pegs, upon the earth or the snow, and dried. Then it is rubbed until it is soft, and the process is complete. As this sort of skin has its outer membrane intact, it is of a dark colour.

White kamik-skins are prepared up to a certain point like the foregoing, but when the hairs have been removed they are dipped in warm water (not too warm) until the black membrane is loosened, and then steeped in sea water, as cold as possible. If all the membrane is not removed, the skin is again dipped alternately in warm water and sea water until it comes away. Then the skin is pegged out and dried like the black skin.

The white skins, not being as strong and water-tight as the black, are used almost entirely by women, who either keep them white or dye them in different ways.

Sole leather for the kamiks is prepared in the same way as the black kaiak-skin, but is pegged out while drying.

Skins for kaiak-gloves are prepared at first like the black kamik-skins, but after the hairs have been removed they are dressed with blood, and then rolled together and put away. This is repeated two or three times until they become entirely black. Then they are stretched for drying—in summer out of doors, but in winter in the houses. This skin is wonderfully water-tight.

If the seal-skin is to be prepared with its hairs on, as for example, for the inner sock of the kamiks or for jackets, it is scraped on the blubber side with a crooked knife, just like the ordinary kamik-skin. Then it is steeped in water, and washed with soft soap; whereupon it is rinsed out in clean water, stretched, and dried as above described. It is then made soft and pliant by rubbing, and is ready for use.

Reindeer-skin is simply dried and rubbed, no water being applied to it.

In preparing bird-skins, the first step is carefully to dry the feathers; then the skins are turned inside out, and the layer of fat is scraped away as thoroughly as possible with a mussel-shell or a spoon, and is eaten—it is held a great delicacy. Then the skins are hung up under the roof to dry. After a few days, the last remnants of fat are removed from them by means of chewing, then they are dried again, then washed in warm water with soda and soap three times over, then rinsed out in very cold water, pressed, and hung up for the final drying. If the feathers are to be removed so that only the down is left, as, for example, in the case of the eider-duck, they are plucked out when the skin is half dry. Then it is thoroughly dried and cut up, and so is ready for use.

The chewing above-mentioned is a remarkable process. The operator takes the dry skin, almost dripping with fat, and chews away at one spot until all the fat is sucked out and the skin is soft and white; then the chewing area is slowly widened, the skin gradually retreating further and further into the mouth, until it often disappears entirely, to be spat out again at last with every particle of fat chewed away. This industry is for the most part carried on by the women and children, and is very highly relished by reason of the quantity of fat it enables them to absorb. In times of scarcity, the men are often glad enough to be allowed to do their share. It is a strange scene that is presented when one enters a house and finds the whole of its population thus engaged in chewing, each with his skin in his mouth. The excellence of the Greenland bird-skins is due to this process. How few of those who have admired the exquisite eider-down rugs which adorn so many a luxurious European home, have any idea of the stages through which they have gone! And how many a European beauty, resplendent in costly skins, would shudder if she could see in a vision all the more or less inviting mouths through which her finery has passed, up there in the far North, before it came to deck her swan-like form!

On the whole, the Greenland women make great use of their teeth, now to stretch the skins, now to hold them while they are being scraped, and again for the actual scraping. It is rather startling to us Europeans to see them take up a skin out of the tub of fetid liquor in which it has been steeping, and straightway fix their teeth in it and begin to dress it. The mouth, in fact, is a third hand to them; and therefore the front teeth of old Eskimo women are often worn away to the merest stumps.

The sinews of seals, whales, and reindeer are used as thread in making garments out of skins. The sinews are simply dried. For sewing kaiak-jackets, kaiak-gloves, and sometimes for kamiks, the gullet of the saddleback seal, the ringed seal, the bladder-nose seal, the small mottled seal, and the cormorant is also used. The outer membranes of the gullet are cut away while it is quite fresh, and then it is drawn over a round stick prepared for the purpose, and greased with blubber. Sometimes the gullet is also scraped with mussel-shells. When it has dried upon the stick and has been cut lengthwise into narrow strips, it is ready for use. The thread thus obtained has this advantage over the sinew-thread that it does not soften in water.

The Greenland women are very capable at their work, and are especially skilful with their needle. One has only to examine the seams of a kaiak-skin, a kaiak-jacket, or a gut-skin shirt to convince oneself of this. But their skill is still more conspicuous in the admirable embroideries with which they ornament their trousers, kamiks, and other garments. On the west coast, where they have learned the use of dyes from the Europeans, they now execute these embroideries with small patches of hide of different colours, which they sew together into a sort of mosaic. They work entirely in freehand, without any pattern to go by, and display great neatness and precision, to say nothing of their sense of colour and of form.

In living with the Eskimos in their homes, one does not at all receive the impression that the women are particularly oppressed or slighted. It seemed to me, on the contrary, that the housewives of Godthaab and the surrounding district often played a very important part in the domestic economy, in some cases even ruling the roost. Judging from my own experience, then, I should say that there is a good deal of exaggeration in what Dalager says of the women, that 'even what ought to be the best hours of their life, from the time they come to maturity, are nothing but a long chain of trouble, contempt, and sorrow.'

It cannot be denied that in social life one observes a certain difference of status between men and women. Thus at meal-times or at coffee-parties, the hunters and the men of most importance are first helped, then the less important males, and finally the women and children. Dalager, in last century, makes a similar remark in his description of a banquet. The men, he says, take the leading place, and tell each other their adventures, while 'the women too have in the meantime formed a little party by themselves in another corner, where, no doubt, nothing but empty chatter is to be heard.' But, if it comes to that, such a description would apply in several other parts of the world besides Greenland.

I must admit, however, that the Eskimo men sometimes show themselves sadly deficient in politeness towards the ladies. For example, 'when the women are hard at work, building houses, drawing water, or carrying heavy burdens of one sort or another, the men stand by with their hands thrust into the breast of their jackets, and laugh at them, without offering the slightest help.' But is this so very much worse than what we often see in Norway, when a Bergen peasant, returning from market, lights his pipe, stretches himself in the stern of the boat, and lets his women row him home?

That women are not held in such high esteem as men is also unhappily evident from the fact that when a man-child is born, the father is jubilant, and the mother beams with pride, while if it be a girl, they both weep, or are at any rate very ill content.

But is this so very much to be wondered at? With all his goodness of heart, the Eskimo is, after all, no more than a man. The boy is, of course, regarded as the kaiak-man and hunter of the future, the support of the family in the old age of his parents, in short as a direct addition to the working capital; while they no doubt think that there will always be plenty of girls in the world.

The same difference is observable in the bringing-up of the children, the boys being always regarded as the food-providers of the future, who must in every way be well cared for; and if a boy's parents die, his position is never a whit the worse, for all the neighbours are quite willing to receive him into their houses and do all they can to make a man of him. With the girls it is different; if they lose their parents and have no relations, they can always, indeed, have plenty of food, but they have often to put up with the most miserable clothing, so that it is pitiful to see them. When they come to the marriageable age, however, they stand on pretty much the same level as girls who have been more fortunately situated; for no such thing as a dowry is known, and their chances simply depend upon 'beauty and solidity, which shall secure them favour in the eyes of the young men—lacking these they are despised, and will never be married, since there are always plenty to choose from.' Of this, however, they cannot complain, for the men themselves are no better off. If they are not strong enough to make good hunters, as sometimes happens, they have poor enough chances of ever finding a mate, and are looked down upon by every one.

That boys are regarded very much in the light of capital appears from the fact that although widows are not in demand in the marriage-market, it sometimes happens that they find a husband, 'especially if they have a family of boys; in that case they are pretty sure one day to make a match with a respectable widower.'

Even in death, women seem to be placed at a disadvantage, as we may conclude from the following remark of Dalager's: 'It sometimes happens that a woman of no great importance, when mortal sickness falls upon her, is buried alive. A horrible case of this sort occurred a short time ago at this very place. Several people declared that they had heard the woman, a long time after her burial, calling out from her grave and begging for something to drink. If you remonstrate with them upon such inhuman cruelty, they answer that when the patient cannot recover, it is better that she should be put away in her last resting-place, than that the survivors should go through the agony of death in observing her misery. But this reasoning will not hold good; for if any male person were thus barbarously dealt with, it would be regarded as the most brutal murder.' Yes, this was ill done; but fortunately such events are very exceptional. Their real reason, moreover, is probably to be found in the Eskimos' intense dread of touching dead bodies, which makes them clothe the dying, whether men or women, in their grave-clothes, often long before death occurs, preparing everything for the carrying out of the corpse and its burial, while the patient himself lies and looks on. For the same reason, they shrink from assisting one who has met with an accident at sea, if he seems to be already in the pinch of death, fearing lest they should happen to lay hands upon him after life has departed.

CHAPTER IX

LOVE AND MARRIAGE

Love, that power which permeates all creation, is by no means unknown in Greenland; but the Greenland variety of it is a simple impulse of nature, lacking the many tender shoots and intricate blossoms of the hot-house plant which we know by this name.

It does not make the lover sick of soul, but drives him to sea, to the chase; it strengthens his arm and sharpens his sight; for his one desire is to become an expert hunter, so that he can lead his Naia home as his bride, and support a family. And the tender young Naia stands upon the outlook-rock gazing after him; she sees with what speed and certainty he shoots ahead, how gracefully he wields the paddle, and how lightly his kaiak dances over the waves. Then he disappears in the far distance; but she still gazes over the endless blue expanse, which heaves over the grave of so many a bold kaiak-man.

At last he comes home again, towing his booty; she rushes down to the beach and helps the other women to bring his prey ashore, while he quietly puts his weapons together and goes up to his house.

But one evening he does not return, for all her waiting and gazing; all the others have come—him the sea has taken. She weeps and weeps, she can never survive the blow. But her despair does not last long; after all, there are other men in the world, and she begins to look on them with favour.

The pure-bred Eskimo generally marries as soon as he can provide for a wife. The motive is not always love; 'the right one' has perhaps not yet appeared on the scene; but he marries because he requires a woman's help to prepare his skins, make his clothes, and so forth. He often marries, it is said, before he is of an age to beget children. On the east coast, indeed, according to Holm, it is quite common for a man to have been married three or four times before that age.[25]

Marriage in Greenland was, in earlier times, a very simple matter. When a man had a mind to a girl, he went to her house or tent, seized her by the hair or wherever he could best get hold of her, and dragged her without further ceremony home to his house,[26] where her place was assigned her upon the sleeping-bench. The bridegroom would sometimes give her a lamp and a new water-bucket, or

[25] *Meddelelser om Grönland*, pt. 10, p. 94.

[26] It sometimes happened, too, that he got others to do this for him; but the affair must always take the form of a capture or abduction. Similar customs, as is well known, formerly prevailed in Europe, and have even, in certain places, survived down to our own day.

something of that sort, and that concluded the matter. In Greenland, however, as in other parts of the world, good taste demanded that the lady in question should on no account let it appear that she was a consenting party, however favourably disposed towards her wooer she might be in her heart. As a well-conducted bride among us feels it her duty to weep as she passes up the church, so the Eskimo bride was bound to struggle against her captor, and to wail and bemoan herself as much as ever she could. If she was a lady of the very highest breeding, she would weep and 'carry on' for several days, and even run away home again from her husband's house. If she went too far in her care for the proprieties, it would sometimes happen, we are told, that the husband, unless he was already tired of her, would scratch her a little on the soles of the feet, so that she could not walk; and before the sores were healed, she was generally a contented housewife.

When they first saw marriages conducted after the European fashion, they thought it very shocking that the bride, when asked if she would have the bridegroom for her husband, should answer Yes. According to their ideas, it would be much more becoming for her to answer No, for they regard it as a shameful thing for a young lady to reply to such a question in the affirmative. When assured that this was the custom among us, they were of opinion that our women-folk must be devoid of modesty.

The simple method of marriage above described is still the only one known upon the east coast of Greenland, and a good deal of violence is sometimes employed in the carrying off of the bride. The lady's relations, however, stand quite unmoved and look on. It is all a private matter between the parties, and the Greenlander's love of a good understanding with his fellows makes him chary of mixing himself up in the affairs of others.

It sometimes happens, of course, that the young lady really objects to her wooer; in that case she continues her resistance until she either learns to possess her soul in patience, or until her captor gives her up.

Graah relates a curious instance[27] proving how difficult it is for an onlooker to determine what are really the lady's sentiments. An able-bodied young rowing-woman in his boat, an East Greenlander named Kellitiuk, was one day seized and carried to the mountains by one of her countrymen named Siorakitsok, in spite of the most violent resistance on her part. As Graah believed that she really disliked him, and as her friends affirmed the same thing, he went after her and rescued her. A few days later, as he was preparing to set forth on his journey again, and the boat had just been launched, Kellitiuk jumped into it, lay down under the thwarts, and covered herself with bags and skins. It soon appeared that this was because Siorakitsok had just landed on the island, bringing his father with him to back him up. While Graah's back was turned for a moment, he jumped into the boat and dragged the fair one out of her hiding-place. Convinced that her brutal wooer was really repulsive to her, Graah thought it his duty to rescue her. When he came up, the suitor had already got her half out of the boat, and his father stood by on shore ready to lend a hand. Graah tore her from his grasp, and recommend-

[27] W. A. Graah, *Narrative of an Expedition to the East Coast of Greenland*, London, 1837, pp. 140-143.

ed him instead to try his luck with 'Black Dorothy,' another of the rowing-women, whom he would have been glad to get rid of. The baffled bridegroom listened to him quietly, 'muttered some inaudible words in his beard, and went away with wrathful and threatening looks.' The father did not take his son's fate much to heart, 'but helped us to load the boat,' says Graah, 'and then bade us a no doubt well-meant farewell.' When they were about to start, however, Kellitiuk was nowhere to be found, although they shouted and searched for her all over the little island. She had evidently hidden herself away somewhere, and they set off without her; so it appears that she had, after all, no irreconcilable antipathy to Siorakitsok.

Among the heathen Greenlanders, divorce is as simple an affair as marriage. When a man grows tired of his wife—the reverse is of rarer occurrence—he need only, says Dalager, 'lie apart from her on the sleeping-benches, without speaking a word. She at once takes the hint,' and next morning gathers all her garments together and quietly returns to her parents' house, trying, as well as she can, to appear indifferent. How many husbands at home could wish that their wives were Greenlanders!

If a man takes a fancy to another man's wife, he takes her without ceremony, if he happens to be the stronger. Papik, a highly respected and skilful hunter at Angmagsalik, on the east coast, took a fancy to the young wife of Patuak, and, towing a second kaiak behind his own, he set off for the place where Patuak lived. He went to his tent, carried off the woman, made her get into the second kaiak, and paddled away with her. Patuak, being younger than Papik, and not to be compared with him in strength and skill, had to put up with the loss of his wife.[28]

There are cases on the east coast of women who have been married to half-a-score of different men. Utukuluk, at Angmagsalik, had tried eight husbands, and the ninth time she remarried husband No. 6.[29]

Divorce is especially easy so long as there are no children. When the woman has had a child, especially if it be a boy, the bond is apt to become more lasting.

On the east coast, if a man can keep more than one wife, he takes another; most of the good hunters, therefore, have two, but never more.[30] It appears that in many cases the first wife does not like to have a rival; but sometimes it is she that suggests the second marriage, in order that she may have help in her household work. Another motive may also come into play. 'I once asked a married woman,' says Dalager, 'why her husband had taken another wife? "I asked him to myself," she replied, "for I'm tired of bearing children."'

The first wife seems always to be regarded as the head of the household, even if the husband shows a preference for the second.

Polyandry seldom occurs. Nils Egede mentions a woman who had two hus-

---

[28] Holm, *Meddelelser om Grönland*, pt. 10, p. 96.

[29] Holm, *Meddelelser om Grönland*, pt. 10, p. 103.

[30] Dalager states that, in his time, on the west coast, 'scarcely one in twenty of the Greenlanders had two wives, very few three, and still fewer four; I have, however, known a man who had eleven.'—*Grönlandske Relationer*, p. 9.

bands, but both she and they were angekoks.[31]

On the introduction of Christianity, these primitive and simple marriage customs were of course abolished on the west coast of Greenland, where people are now united with religious ceremonies as in Europe. The bride, too, is no longer required to offer so determined a resistance.

But if it was formerly easy to get oneself a wife, under the new order of things it has become difficult enough. For the ceremony must necessarily be performed by a clergyman, the native catechists, who fill the place of the pastors in the various villages, not being reckoned good enough. If, then, you happen to live at a place which the pastor visits only once a year, or perhaps once in two years, you must take care to come to an understanding with the lady of your choice just in time to seize the opportunity. If a young fellow should take it into his head to marry just after the pastor has gone away, he must wait a year, or perhaps two, before he can go through the necessary ceremony, unless, indeed, he and his bride are prepared to take a long journey in search of clerical ministrations.

Such a state of things would inevitably lead many to form less binding connections, or to marry without the help of the clergy, even if the Greenlanders were naturally less inclined towards such laxity than as a matter of fact they are. I have heard of a case in which a cleric, on coming to a certain village after a two years' absence, had to confirm a girl, marry her, and christen her child on the same day. This may be called summary procedure. Such an arrangement cannot but be hurtful, tending to undermine all respect for the ceremony whose impressiveness it is sought to enhance by making the clergy alone competent to officiate at it.

On the introduction of Christianity, polygamy was of course abolished. The missionaries even insisted that when a man who was married to two wives became a Christian, he should put away one of them. In 1745, an Eskimo at Frederikshaab had a mind to be baptised, 'but when it came to a question of putting away his second wife, he began to hesitate, for he had two sons by her, whom he would thus lose. In the end he changed his mind and went his way.'[32] For this one can scarcely blame him. Similar cases, in which it is required that a man shall put away one of his wives, with whom he has perhaps lived happily for many a year, still occur now and then, when a Greenlander from the east coast settles on the west coast (near Cape Farewell) and is baptised. The hardship which the man is thus forced to inflict upon the woman need scarcely be insisted upon. Even to Dalager, in last century, it appeared an injustice, and 'how far it conflicted with the ordinances of God that a man should have more than one wife, seemed to him a problem.'

Polygamy, however, is still occasionally to be found upon the west coast, a second wife being apparently one of the indulgences which first occur to a Greenlander's mind when he is inclined to kick over the traces.

In Greenland, as elsewhere, the position of women in marriage differs according to the circumstances of each particular case. As a rule the man is the master; but I have also seen cases, doubtless exceptional, in which the grey mare has been

[31] Angekok==medicine-man, or priest.
[32] Dalager: *Grönlandske Relationer*, p. 9.

the better horse.

Among the primitive Eskimos, the wife seems practically to have been regarded as the husband's property. It sometimes happens on the east coast that a formal bargain and sale precedes the marriage, the bridegroom paying the father a harpoon, or something of the sort, for the privilege of wedding his lovely daughter. Sometimes, on the other hand, the father will pay a hunter of credit and renown to take his daughter off his hands, and the daughter is bound to marry at her father's bidding.[33] Moreover, it often occurs on the east coast that two hunters agree to exchange wives for a longer or shorter period—sometimes for good. Temporary exchanges of wives still occur, doubtless, on the west coast as well, especially during the summer reindeer-hunting, when the people are living in tents in the interior of the country. At these times they allow themselves many liberties which cannot be controlled by the missionaries.

Married people as a rule live on very good terms with each other. I have never heard an unkind word exchanged between man and wife; and this is the general experience. Dalager declares that 'the longer a married couple live together, the more closely are they united in affection, until at last they pass their old age together like innocent children.' They are, on the whole, exceedingly considerate towards each other, and may sometimes be seen to exchange caresses. They do not kiss as we do, however, but press their noses together or snuff at each other. This process I am unfortunately unable to describe, as I lack the necessary practice.

On the east coast, too, the relation between husband and wife seems to be very good as a rule, though it appears, according to Captain Holm, that scenes of violence are not unknown.

A certain Sanimuinak one day came home to his spouse Puitek, bringing with him a second wife, the young Utukuluk (the before-mentioned lady of the nine husbands), whereupon Puitek became angry and fell to scolding her husband. This made him so furious that he seized her by the top-knot and struck her with his clenched fist on the back and in the face. At last he seized a knife and stabbed her in the knee, so that the blood spurted forth.[34] Holm also relates a case in which a man received a sound thrashing from his wife. Scenes of this sort, however, are very rare among this peaceable people.

Any very deep love between man and wife is no doubt exceptional, depth of feeling being, on the whole, uncommon among the Eskimos. If one dies the survivor is generally pretty easily consoled. 'If a man loses his wife,' says Dalager, 'not many of his own sex come to condole with him. The women-folk, on the other hand, squat along the inner edge of the sleeping-benches in his house and bewail the deceased, while he, in response, sobs and wipes his nose. After a short time, however, he begins to adorn himself as he used to in his bachelor days, polishing up his kaiak and his weapons with particular care, these being the things with which a Greenlander always makes the greatest show. When, at sea, he comes dashing up to his comrades in this brilliant array, they say to each other: "Look,

[33] Holm: *Meddelelser om Grönland*, pt. 10, p. 96.
[34] Holm: *Meddelelser om Grönland*, pt. 10, p. 102.

look—here comes a new brother-in-law." If he overhears it, he says nothing, but smiles to himself.' It is highly incumbent upon a widower's new wife to lament her own imperfections and belaud the virtues of her predecessor: 'Whence we learn that the Greenland women are as apt at acting a part, where their interest is concerned, as are others of their sex in more polite countries.'

The chief end and aim of marriage in Greenland is unquestionably the procreation of children. Therefore, as in the Old Testament times, unfruitful women are contemned, and a childless marriage is often dissolved.

On the average, the pure-bred Greenlanders are not prolific. Two, three, or four children to each marriage is the general rule, though there are instances of families of six or eight, or even more.

Twins are uncommon, and I was often asked by the women if it were true that in the land of the long beards (Norway) women gave birth to two children at a time. When I answered that they not only bore twins but also triplets and even four children at a birth, they shrieked with laughter and declared that our women were like dogs: for human beings and seals bear only one at a time.

As a rule, the Greenland women suffer little in childbirth. As an example of how easily they take this incident in their lives, I may quote a case mentioned by Graah. As he was passing by Bernstorffsfiord, on his journey along the east coast, one of the women of his company was taken with labour-pains. They hastened to land upon a naked rock on the north side of the fiord. While the labour continued, the husband stretched himself on the rock and fell asleep; but presently they awakened him with the joyful intelligence that a son had been born to him. As already stated, this is regarded as a piece of good luck, while the birth of a daughter is a matter of indifference. 'Ernenek accordingly (that was the husband's name) expressed his satisfaction by smiling on his spouse and saying "Ajungilatit" (Not so bad for you). With our new passenger, we at once proceeded on our journey.'[35]

The heathen Greenlanders kill deformed children and those which are so sickly as to seem unlikely to live; those, too, whose mother dies in childbirth, so that there is no one to give them suck. This they do, as a rule, by exposing the child or throwing it into the sea.[36] However cruel this may sound to many European mothers, it is nevertheless done from compassion, and it is undeniably reasonable; for under such hard natural conditions as those of Greenland, we cannot wonder that people are unwilling to bring up offspring which can never be of any use, and can only help to diminish the common store of sustenance.[37] It is for the same reason that people who have grown so old as to be quite unable to fend for themselves are held in small esteem and are thought to be better out of the way.

---

[35] W. A. Graah, *Narrative of an Expedition to the East Coast of Greenland*, London, 1837, p. 135.

[36] Compare P. Egede, *Efterretninger om Grönland*, p. 107; and Holm, *Meddelelser om Grönland*, pt. 10, p. 91.

[37] Although, as we have seen, the Eskimos are not greatly delighted at the birth of daughters, they do not, like so many other primitive people, make a habit of killing female children.

On the east coast it sometimes happens that old people, who seem likely to die, are drowned, or else drown themselves. Similar practices also obtained in former days upon the west coast (compare next chapter).

Greenland mothers are very slow to wean their children. They often give suck until the child is three or four, and I have even heard of cases in which children of ten or twelve continued to take the breast. A European at Godthaab told me that he had seen a dashing youth of twelve or so come home in his kaiak with his booty, rush up to his home, and there consume a biscuit, standing between his mother's knees, and drinking, from time to time, from her breast.

All the children of Christian Greenlanders are of course christened and given names. The original Greenland names however, have, owing to the influence of the missionaries, almost entirely died out. In their stead are used all possible Biblical names from both the Old and the New Testament. Nowhere in the world, probably, is one surer to meet with the whole dramatis personæ of the Scriptures, right from Father Adam down to Peter and Paul. Our notable friend Dalager does not seem to have liked this misuse of the Bible, and therefore, he says, 'I once asked a certain missionary why a Greenlander, when he was christened, could not be allowed to retain his former name, which was probably a very natural and good one. "It sounds ill" he replied, "to have a Christian called after a seal or a sea-bird." I smiled and answered that at home there were plenty of Ravens, Hawks, and Crows, who passed for excellent people none the less.' On this point I cannot but agree with Dalager.

The Greenlanders are exceedingly fond of their children and do everything to make them happy, especially if they are boys. These little tyrants will often rule over the whole house, and the words of Solomon: 'Chasten thy son while there is hope, and let not thy soul spare for his crying,' are by no means acted upon. Punishment, especially of course where their own flesh and blood is concerned, they regard on the whole as inhuman. I have never once heard an Eskimo say an unkind word to his child. With such an upbringing, one might expect that the Greenland children would be naughty and intractable. This is not at all the case. Although I have gone about a good deal among the Eskimos on the west coast, I have only once seen a naughty Eskimo child, and that was in a more European than Eskimo home. When the children are old enough to understand, a gentle hint from father or mother is enough to make them desist from anything forbidden. I have never seen Eskimo children quarrelling either indoors or in the open air; not even talking angrily to each other, much less fighting. I have watched them playing by the hour, and have even taken part in their football (a peculiar game of theirs, very like the English football), which, as we know, is rather apt to lead to quarrels; but I have never seen an angry or even an unfriendly look pass between them. Could such a thing happen in Europe? I shall not attempt to determine what may be the reason of this remarkable difference between Eskimo and European children. No doubt it is mainly due to the excessively peaceable and good-humoured temperament of the race, devoid of all nervousness or irritability. It may partly be attributed, also, to the fact that the Eskimo women always live in the same room as their children, and carry them with them in the amauts on their backs even when they go to work.

Thus they can give them much more constant care, and there is a more unbroken intercourse between children and parents in Greenland than in Europe.

We must not judge the Eskimo boys too severely if they now and then amuse themselves with throwing stones at the Colonial Manager's or the Pastor's fowls and ducks, or if they make occasional irruptions into the Manager's garden and root up or destroy the plants. It must be remembered that the conception of property in land, and the notion that one is not at liberty to chase or to appropriate whatever moves or grows upon the face of the earth, are quite foreign to their instinctive ideas. Even if such conceptions are inculcated upon them, they do not grasp them clearly; they are, and will always remain, notions which the European foreigners have tried to introduce in their own interests, and which are founded upon no natural right.

In order to exercise their eyes and their arms, the provident Greenlander gives his sons, even while they are mere children, toy bird-darts and harpoons; and with these, or, failing these, with common stones, one may see the three or four-year-old hunters practising upon small birds and anything else worthy of their passion for the chase which they happen to come across. I have already mentioned that they commence practising in the kaiak at a very early age.

It is, of course, of the greatest importance for the Greenland community that the rising generation should be brought up to be expert hunters. On this their whole future depends.

The girls, too, must be early trained in their life-work; they must learn to sew, and to assist their mother in her domestic labours.

CHAPTER X

MORALS

The Eskimo has, of course, like every other race of men, his virtues and his foibles; possibly with this difference from the civilised European, that the former are more numerous in proportion to the latter. But, on the other hand, neither his virtues nor his foibles are found in such high development.

Even the earliest accounts of Greenland, however, such as Egede's, Cranz's, Dalager's, and others, show clearly enough the falsity of the frequent assertion that the Eskimo stands upon a low moral plane; although in some of these writers, for example in Hans Egede, we can trace an evident tendency to paint the Eskimo, individually and socially, in as dark colours as possible, in order to prove how sadly this people stood in need of the lights of religion, and how necessary it therefore was that the Greenland mission should be supported.

One of the most prominent and attractive traits in the Eskimo's moral character is certainly his integrity. If some Europeans have denied him this virtue, it can only be, I am sure, because these gentlemen have not taken the trouble to place themselves in sympathy with his modes of thought, and to realise what he regards as dishonourable.

It is of special importance for the Eskimo that he should be able to rely with confidence upon his neighbours and his fellow-men; and it is the first condition of this mutual confidence, on which depends all united action in the battle for life, that every man shall be upright in his dealings with his neighbours. The Eskimo therefore regards it as in the highest degree dishonourable to steal from his housemates or from his fellow-villagers, and it is very seldom that anything of the sort occurs. Even Egede tells us that they let their goods and chattels 'lie open to everyone without fear of anyone stealing or taking away the least portion of them.... This misdemeanour is so repulsive to them that if a girl is found stealing, she loses all chance of making a good marriage.'

For the same reason they very seldom lie to each other—especially the men. The following trait, related by Dalager, affords a remarkable proof of this: 'In describing a thing to another person, they are very careful not to paint it in brighter colours than it deserves; especially in the sale of an object which the buyer has not seen, even although the seller may be anxious to get rid of it, he will depreciate it rather than overpraise it.'

When one owes another money, the creditor may, as a rule, be assured that the debtor will pay up as soon as ever he can. The Danish merchants confirm this trait. They have often told me that they lend with confidence to the Greenlanders, because it very seldom happens that they are not repaid in full.

The Eskimo's conception of his duties towards strangers, especially towards people of another race, is not quite so strict. We must remember that a foreigner is to him an indifferent object, whose welfare he has no interest in furthering; and it matters little to him whether he can rely on the foreigner or not, since he has not got to live with him. Thus he does not always find it inconsistent with his interests to appropriate a little of the foreigner's property, if he thinks it can be of use to him.

The first Europeans who came to the country suffered a good deal from this peculiarity. We cannot greatly wonder that the Eskimos stole from them, when we consider how the European expeditions at first conducted themselves, after the land had been discovered anew. They often plundered the natives, maltreated their women, and what was worse, tempted them on board their ships, set sail, and took them as prisoners to Europe. Thus the Eskimos had from the first but little reason to regard us as friends. Nor does it seem by any means irreconcilable with European morality to plunder foreign peoples, if we may judge by the way in which we deal with the native races in Africa and elsewhere. Or let us suppose that it had been the Eskimos who came and planted themselves upon our shores, and behaved to us as we did in Greenland—would it then have been altogether inconsistent with our moral code to rob and filch from them whatever we could?

It must also be taken into account that in comparison with the Eskimos the Europeans possess property in superabundance. According to Eskimo morality, therefore, it appears that we ought to be able to dispense with some of our super-fluity, and if we decline to do so it is because we are miserly and selfish.

As the Europeans have gradually settled down in the country and ceased to be regarded as foreigners, matters have altered a good deal, and theft even from them is now rare. I believe, however, that when an opportunity offers the natives are still inclined to appropriate trifles which they think can never be missed. I have myself seen respectable Greenlanders fill their pockets and gloves with meal from the barrels in the store, quite unabashed by the fact of my observing them. In such a case they no doubt think that it is the Royal Greenland Company from whose superfluity they are helping themselves. The company will neither be richer nor poorer for a few handfuls of meal, which for them are of great moment—and in this comfortable conviction they go on their way rejoicing. I am afraid that such modes of thought are not peculiar to Greenland.

For the rest, it must be remembered as an extenuating circumstance that the Eskimos were from the first, and even down to comparatively recent times, shamelessly defrauded by the European traders, who used false weights and measures, and gave them, in barter, wares of wretched quality. I need only mention, on Saabye's authority, that the traders of last century used excessively large four-bushel measures, which had, in addition, no bottom, but were carefully placed over cavities in the floor. These the natives had to fill with their blubber when they wanted to sell it, so that what passed for four bushels was in reality at least six. They knew and understood quite well that they were being cheated, but they submitted uncomplainingly. Such practices are now, of course, things of the past.

As a proof of the Eskimo's scrupulous respect for the moral law which he recognises, I may remind the reader that he never touches drift-wood which another has placed above high-water mark, though it would often be so easy to appropriate it without fear of detection. And when we Europeans break through this law, and help ourselves without ceremony to their stored-up drift-wood—as we have often done, I am sorry to say, intentionally or otherwise—have not the Eskimos, I wonder, at least as good right to despise us as we have to look down upon them?

Fighting and brutalities of that sort, as before-mentioned, are unknown among them, and murder is very rare. They hold it atrocious to kill a fellow-creature; therefore war is in their eyes incomprehensible and repulsive, a thing for which their language has no word; and soldiers and officers, brought up to the trade of killing, they regard as mere butchers.

It has, indeed, as Egede says, 'occurred now and then that an extremely malicious person, out of rankling hatred, has killed another.' But when he adds that 'this they regard with the greatest coolness, neither punishing the murderer nor taking the thing to heart in any way,' I believe that he is not quite just to them. They certainly abhor the crime, and if they do not actively mix themselves up in the matter, it is because they regard it as a private affair between the murderer and his victim. It is not the business of the community, but simply of the murdered man's nearest relatives, to take revenge for his death, if they are in a position to do so; and thus we find, even among this peaceable folk, traces of a sort of blood-feud, though the practice is but slightly developed, and the duty does not, as a rule, seem to weigh heavily upon the survivors. In cases of extreme atrocity, however, the men of a village have been known to make common cause against a murderer, and kill him.

Here, as elsewhere, women and love are among the most frequent causes of bloodshed.

The attack often takes place at sea, the murderer transfixing his victim from behind with his harpoon, or capsizing his kaiak and cutting a hole in it. It does not accord with the Eskimo's character to attack another face to face, not so much because he is afraid as because he is bashful, and would feel it embarrassing to go to work under the other's eye.

They do not regard it as criminal to kill old witches and wizards, who, they think, can injure and even kill others by their arts. Nor is it inconsistent with their moral code to hasten the death of those who are sick and in great suffering, or of those in delirium, of which they have a great horror.

Of our commandments, the seventh is that which the Greenlanders are most apt to break; for, as the reader may already have gathered from the foregoing chapter, virtue and modesty are not held in high esteem among them. This is especially the case among the Christian Eskimos of the west coast, who have come much in contact with us Europeans. By many of them it is not regarded as any particular disgrace for an unmarried girl to have children. Of this I have seen frequent examples. While we were at Godthaab, two unmarried girls of the neighbourhood who were with child made no sort of attempt to conceal the fact, and even tied up their top-knots with green ribbon[38] long before it was necessary, seeming almost proud of this visible sign that they were not disdained. I have seen green-tops who not only wore the colour in their hair, but trimmed and embroidered their anoraks quite stylishly with ribbons of the same hue, though such a proceeding is neither obligatory nor customary.

The missionaries have, of course, been vehement in their denunciations of the prevalent laxity in this direction, and have tried to inculcate a stricter morality upon the youth of both sexes, from their schooldays onwards; but they do not seem to have succeeded in inducing their flocks to regard the matter from a higher standpoint, for things grow worse rather than better. When a young woman stands in an illicit relation to a man, she attempts no concealment; if the man be a European, indeed, she positively glories in it, and it seems to procure her additional consideration among her female friends. For this state of things the Europeans themselves are chiefly to blame. In the first place, the young men who have come to Greenland have often behaved ill to the native women, and set a bad example; and, in the second place, the Europeans have on the whole managed so to impose upon the natives that the women will now prefer the commonest European sailor to the very best Eskimo hunter. The result is that during the century and a half since we settled in the country, the race has suffered so large an admixture of European blood that it is now extremely difficult to find a single pure-bred Eskimo on the whole west coast.[39] And this although the Europeans form but a small fraction of the population of the country, a few hundred as against ten thousand.

It is obvious that the proneness of the Europeans to this form of immorality has not made it any easier for the missionaries to vindicate the sanctity of the seventh commandment. My experience, and I believe that of most observers, is that the native women of the colonies, where many Europeans reside, are much more immodest than those of the villages where there are no Europeans. For example, I may mention that the women at Sardlok, Kornok, Kangek, and Narsak made an altogether better impression than those at Godthaab and New Herrnhut, where their behaviour was often the reverse of discouraging towards young men who happened to take their fancy.

Sexual morality seems to have been considerably higher among the heathen Eskimos before the Europeans came to the country. Even Hans Egede, who does not, as a rule, depict their moral qualities in too bright colours, says in his 'New Perlustration': 'Young girls and maidens, on the other hand, are modest enough. We have never seen them conducting themselves wantonly with the young men, or making the least approach to such conduct, either in word or deed. During the fifteen years I was in Greenland, I knew of only two or three unmarried girls who

[38] As stated on p. 13, green top-knots are worn by unmarried women who have had children.

[39] One reason of this is also to be found in natural selection, for the half-castes are now generally regarded as handsomer than the pure-bred Eskimos, and are consequently apt to be preferred in marriage.

gave birth to children; for this they regard as a great disgrace.'

Dalager's general testimony to the national character in this respect is that 'the Greenlanders are certainly inclined to the sin of incontinence, but not so much so as other nations.' Of the girls he says that 'in their first years of maturity they bear themselves very chastely, for otherwise they are certain to spoil their chances in marriage.'

Among the heathens of the east coast at the present day, the matter does not seem to be regarded so seriously; for Holm assures us that 'it is not considered any disgrace for an unmarried girl to have children.'

The strict morality which obtained among the unmarried youths and maidens of the west coast in the heathen days, seems to have been very considerably relaxed when once they were married. The men, at any rate, had then the most unrestricted freedom. Egede says that for long 'he could not ascertain that men had to do with other women than their own wives, or wives with other men; but at last we discovered that they were none too particular in this respect.' He describes, among other things, a remarkable game for which 'married men and women come together, as though to an assembly.' The men stepped forth by turns, and, to the accompaniment of a drum, sang songs in honour of women and love; whereupon shameless license became the order of the day for all present. 'But in this game the young and unmarried are forbidden by modesty to take part; married people see in it nothing to be ashamed of.'

Egede also remarks that women regard it as a great honour and happiness to become the concubine of an angekok—that is, 'one of their prophets and learned men.' 'Many husbands even regard this with favour, and will sometimes pay the angekoks to lie with their wives, especially if they themselves have no children by them.'

The Eskimo women, then, are allowed far greater freedom in this respect than women of Germanic stock. The reason probably is that whereas inheritance, and the continuance of the race and name, have been matters of supreme importance to the Teutons, the Eskimos have had little or no property to transmit from father to son, while for them the great consideration is simply that children shall be born.

With reference to the above-mentioned game, however, Dalager declares that it is of very rare occurrence, 'and that it is to be observed that a married woman who has duly become the mother of a family never takes part in it.'

On the other hand, he tells us that widows and divorced wives are not so particular. While it is very seldom that 'a young girl has a child, one sees older women bearing just as many children as if they were living in wedlock. If they are reproved for this, even by their own countrymen, they will often answer that their conduct does not proceed from mere wantonness, but from a natural longing to bear children, which leads them to seduce many a worthy man.'

On the east coast, too, the morality of married people seems to leave a good deal to be desired, according to our ideas. I have mentioned, for instance, that the men often exchange wives; but the exchange is strictly a personal matter, and the husband will usually resent any unfaithfulness on the wife's part to the man to whom he has lent her, he himself, however, claiming full liberty. While living in their winter houses they often play a wife-exchanging or lamp-extinguishing game, like that above-mentioned; but in this the unmarried also take part. Holm tells us that 'a good host always has the lamps put out at night when there are guests in the house.'

So far as I know, this game is no longer practised on the west coast. Married Christian Greenlanders, however, do not seem to have any overweening respect for the seventh commandment, and irregularities of conduct are far from uncommon.

The morals above described seem to us very bad on the whole; but it does not follow that the Eskimos share this feeling. We should beware how we fix ourselves at one point of view, and unsparingly condemn ideas and practices which the experience of many generations has developed among another people, however much they may conflict with our own. There may be underlying reasons which do not at once meet the eye, and which place the whole matter in a very different light.

The conceptions of good and evil in this world are exceedingly divergent. As an example, let me cite the case of the Eskimo girl who, when Niels Egede spoke to her of love of God and her neighbour, said to him: 'I have given proof of love for my neighbour. Once an old woman who was ill, but could not die, offered to pay me if I would lead her to the top of the steep cliff from which our people have always thrown themselves when they are tired of living; but I, having ever loved my neighbours, led her thither without payment, and cast her over the cliff.' Egede told her that this was ill done, and that she had killed a fellow-creature. 'She said no; but that she was filled with pity for her, and cried after she had fallen over.' Are we to call this a good or an evil deed?

Another time, when Egede was explaining how God punishes wicked people, an Eskimo remarked that in that respect he was like God, for he had killed three old women who were witches.

The same divergence of judgment makes itself felt with regard to the seventh commandment. To the Eskimo the other exhortation to increase and multiply seems to be of greater weight. The reason may partly be that his race is by nature unprolific.

Like many other peoples, the Eskimos found it strange that we should not regard polygamy with warm approval. Among them, a man was held in esteem in proportion to the number of wives he possessed, and they therefore thought the Old Testament patriarchs more reasonable than we. This, however, is a view which we find prevailing among our own forefathers, until well on in historical times.

When Paul Egede was remonstrating with the Greenlanders one day upon their polygamous proclivities, one of them fell to eulogising his own wife for her 'good humour in never being angry because he loved strange women.' Egede said that 'women in our country could not endure that their husbands should care for others; they would turn them out of their houses.' 'It is no praise to your women,' replied the Eskimo, 'that they want to have their husbands all to themselves and to be masters over them; we hold that a fault.'

Their way of thinking in these matters is less ideal and more practical than ours, and their point of view entirely different. Their habit of exchanging wives, for example, and their treatment of barren women, seems to us wanton and immoral; but when we remember that the production of offspring is the great end and aim of their conduct, and reflect what an all-important matter this is for them, we may perhaps pass a somewhat milder judgment.

If a Greenlander's wife does not bear children, his marriage fails of its chief purpose, and it is quite natural that he should try to find a remedy. A young man whose wife had no children once offered Niels Egede a fox-skin either to come to his aid himself in the matter, or to order one of his sailors to do so, and was much astonished to find Egede indignant at the proposal. 'There would be no disgrace,' he said, 'for she is married, and she could have one of your married sailors.'

It appears, however, that even the married Greenlanders are not by nature devoid of what we understand as moral feeling, for their everyday behaviour is, as a rule, quite reputable and void of offence; on that point all travellers must agree.

If a heathen—and in many cases even a Christian—Greenlander refrains from having to do with another man's wife, whom he has looked upon with favour, it is generally, no doubt, more because he shrinks from quarrelling with the husband than because he regards adultery as morally wrong; but we may gather from the following saying, current at Angmagsalik, that even on the east coast there is a vague feeling that it is not the right thing. 'The whale, the musk-ox, and the reindeer,' so the saying runs, 'left the country because men had too much to do with other men's wives.' Many men declared, however, that it was 'because the women were jealous of their husbands.' The jealousy of the women was also alleged as a reason for the fact that the channel which formerly went right through the country, from the Sermelik Fiord to the west coast, had been blocked with ice.[40]

Egede relates that, strangely enough as he thought, the women before his arrival had felt no jealousy when their husbands had more wives than one, 'and got on very well with each other'; but as soon as he had preached to them the wickedness of such proceedings, they began to show much annoyance when their husbands wanted to take second wives. 'When I have been reading with them,' he says, 'and instructing them in the Word of God, they have often urged me to bring the seventh commandment sharply home to their husbands.' The men, as may be supposed, did not at all approve of the missionaries' influence over the women in this respect, and one of them, whose two wives had fallen by the ears, said angrily to Niels Egede: 'You have spoiled them with your teaching, and now they're jealous of each other.' It appears to me that the man's anger was not without justification. What should we say if Greenlanders came to our country, forced themselves into our houses, and preached their own morality to our wives?

Before we utterly condemn the morality of the Eskimos, we ought also, per-

[40] Holm: *Meddelelser om Grönland*, pt. 10, p. 100.

haps, to remember the golden maxim that those who live in glass houses should not throw stones. European morality is in many respects of such doubtful value that we have scarcely the right to pose as judges. After all is said and done, it is possible that the most essential difference between our morality and that of the Eskimos is that with us the worst things take place behind the scenes, in partial or complete secrecy, and therefore produce all the more demoralising effect, while among the Eskimos everything happens on the open stage. The instincts of human nature cannot be altogether suppressed. It is with them as with explosives: where they lie unprotected on the surface, they may be easily 'set off,' but they do little mischief; whereas when they lie deeper and more concealed, they are perhaps less easily kindled, but when once they take fire the explosion is far more violent and destructive, and the greater the weight that is piled upon them, the greater havoc do they work.

According to the Eskimo code, marriage between first cousins, or between any near relations, is prohibited. Even foster-children, who happen to have been brought up in the same household, cannot marry. A man should, if possible, seek his wife in another village.

This rule answers to the so-called law of exogamy, or prohibition of marriage with blood relations, with people of the same family name, or even belonging to the same clan (among the Chinese), gotra (among the Hindus), or gens (among the Romans?), which is also found in slightly different forms in the Greek, and formerly in the Catholic, Church, among the Slavonic and Indian races, and in many other quarters. Plutarch says of the Romans that in earlier times they no more thought of marrying women of the same stock than they would in his day think of marrying aunts or cousins. Our own forefathers, in long past ages, probably observed the law of exogamy, which, however, stands in sharp opposition to the feeling now dominant in Norway, that natives of the same place should be chosen in marriage, and if possible near relatives, even first cousins. It seems to be the general rule that we find the widest circles of prohibition against marriage among savage peoples, while among modern and civilised nations a greater freedom prevails. Exogamy would thus appear to be a relic of barbarism from which we Norwegians have very thoroughly freed ourselves. It is very difficult to explain the origin of this law. Many writers, as we know, seek to trace it to the primitive conception of woman as a chattel, and commonly as a captive of the spear, whence it followed that a wife ought not to be taken from among relations or friends, but should be carried off from another tribe. Although the scientific authorities are against me, it appears to me by no means impossible that we may also find at the root of the custom the belief that marriage between near relations produces a weakly progeny. This belief, at any rate, prevails among almost all nations in the form of a dread of incest. It is true that modern research has sought to show that marriage between kinsfolk is not injurious; but whether well-founded or not, the contrary belief has undoubtedly been entertained, and from it the law of exogamy would naturally follow. The fact that among the Greenlanders it goes the length of forbidding marriage between people of the same village is easily explicable when we think of the above-mentioned customs, which render it impossible to be sure who may or may not be half-brothers and sisters.

In several respects the morality of the heathen Eskimos stands considerably higher than that which one generally finds in Christian communities. As I have already pointed this out (in Chapter VIII.), I will here only remind the reader of their self-sacrificing love of their neighbour and their mutual helpfulness, to which, indeed, we find no parallel in European society. These virtues, however, are not unfrequently to be found among primitive peoples, and are probably in the main due to the simpler structure of society. A more developed and consequently more complicated social order leads to the decline of many of the natural virtues of humanity.

But the Eskimo's love of his neighbour goes the length of restraining him from slandering him, and even from any sort of evil-speaking, especially in the case of a neighbour in the literal sense of the word. Scandal and malice are inconsistent with his peaceable and kindly disposition. As before remarked, the women do not seem to be quite so exemplary in this respect; but we know that such weaknesses are commonly attributed to the softer sex all the world over.

Reverence for the aged is not a prominent feature of the Eskimo character. They are honoured, indeed, so long as they are able to work, and if they have in their younger days been good hunters, and have sons, they may retain great influence and be regarded as the head of the household. A woman who has able-bodied sons may also be treated with reverence, even should she attain a great age. A widow especially has often great power, governing the house as long as she lives, and having the upper hand of her daughters-in-law. But, as a rule, when people grow so old that they cannot take care of themselves, they are apt to be treated with scant consideration, especially women. Sometimes the younger generation will even go the length of making fun of them, and to this the poor old people submit with great patience, regarding it simply as the way of the world.

That the reader may form some conception of a primitive Eskimo's habits of thought on moral questions, I quote the following letter from a converted Greenlander to Paul Egede.[41] I reproduce it here, because it in many respects bears out the views above expressed, and Egede's book 'Accounts of Greenland,'[42] in which this translation is printed (pp. 230-236) is now not easily obtainable. The writer was a heathen who had been baptised by Paul Egede's father, Hans Egede. The letter, which was of course written in Eskimo, gives evidence not only of a peculiar moral point of view, but also of a keen understanding, and of feelings which, as Paul Egede says, one would scarcely expect 'in so stupid a people as we have hitherto taken them to be.' It is, as will be seen, an answer to an epistle of Egede's, and runs as follows:—

Amiable Pauia![43]

You know how precious and agreeable your letter is to me;

[41] Paul Egede was for many years a missionary in Greenland, but had at this time (1756) returned to Copenhagen.

[42] *Efterretninger om Grönland.*

[43] Pauia or Pavia is the Eskimo corruption of Paul.

but how appalled I was when I read of the destruction of such multitudes of people in the great earthquake,[44] inconceivable to us, which you say devoured in one moment more people than there are in all our country. I cannot tell you how this moved me, or how frightened we were, so that many fled from the place where they lived to another, which was quite as unsafe, though it was on a rock; for we see even here that rocks have been split open from the top to the very depths, though when it happened none of us know. Granite rocks, such as our land consists of, and sand-hills like your land, are equally easy for God to overthrow, in whose power the whole world stands, and we poor little animals are easily buried in the ruins. You give me to understand that with you there have been neither snow nor great cold this winter, and conclude that it must have been all the severer with us; but we, too, have had an unusually mild winter. I hear that your learned men are of opinion that this mild weather has been caused by the warm vapours emanating from the earth at the time of the earth-quake, which have warmed the air and melted the snow-material. But if I had not heard that this was the opinion of the learned, I should have thought that the warmth of the earth would avail little to heat the height and breadth of the air—as little as a man's breath avails to warm a large house in which he simply breathes for a moment and then goes out again. The south winds, which are always warm, and have blown all the year through with us, are the cause of the moderate cold we have had; but why the south wind blew I cannot tell, nor the learned either, perhaps. Were these wretched people killed by the heat, or did the earth swallow them up, or were they shaken to death? Skipper B. thought that their own houses must have fallen upon them and killed them. Your people do not seem to care very much about it; for they are not only cheerful and merry, but they relate that the two nations[45] who come here whale-fishing, not your countrymen, but of the same faith as you, are fighting with and shooting each other both by land and sea, hunting each other as we hunt seals and reindeer, and stealing and taking away ships and goods from each other, from people they have never seen or known, simply because their lord and master will have it so. When I asked the skipper, through an interpreter, what could be the cause of such inhumanity, he answered that it was all about a piece of land right opposite ours,[46] so far away that it could only be reached after three months' sailing. Then I thought that there must be great scarcity of land where these people dwell; but he said no, that it was only because of the great lords' greediness for more riches

[44] Evidently the earthquake at Lisbon.—*Trans.*
[45] Probably the Dutch and English.—[Surely rather the French and English.—*Trans.*]
[46] Doubtless America.

and more people to rule over. I was so astounded by this greediness, and so terrified lest it should fall upon us too, that I was almost out of my mind; but I presently took heart again, you will scarcely guess why. I thought of our snow-clad country and its poor inhabitants, and said to myself: 'Thank God! we are poor and possess nothing which these greedy Kablunaks [so they call all foreigners] can desire. What we have upon the earth they do not care to possess, what we require for food and clothing swims in the great sea; of that they may take as much as they can, there will always be enough for us.' If only we have as much food as we can eat, and skins enough to keep us from the cold, we are quite contented; and you know very well that we let to-morrow take care of itself. Therefore we will not fight with anyone, even if we were strong enough; although we can as justly say that the sea belongs to us as the believers in the East can say of the unbelievers in the West that they and their possessions belong to them. We can say it is our sea which surrounds our land, and that the whales, cachalots, grampuses, porpoises, unicorns [that is, narwhals], white whales, seals, halibuts, salmon, cod, and sea-scorpions which swim in it belong to us too; but we willingly allow others to take of this great store as much as they please. We are happy in that we have not so great a natural covetousness as they. I have often wondered at the Christians, and have not known what to think about them—they leave their own beautiful land, and suffer much hardship in this country, which is to them so rough and disagreeable, simply for the sake of making us good people; but have you seen so much evil in our nation, have you ever heard such strange and utterly senseless talk among us? Their teachers instruct us how we are to escape the devil, whom we never knew; and yet the roystering sailors pray with the greatest earnestness that the devil may take them, or may split them. I daresay you remember how I, in my youth, learned such phrases from them to please them, without knowing what they meant, until you forbade me to use them. Since I have come to understand them myself, I have heard more than I wanted of them. This year in particular I have heard so much of the Christians, that if I had not, in the course of long familiarity with them, known many good and worthy men among them, and if Hans Pungiok and Arnarsak, who have been to your country, had not told me that there were many pious and virtuous people there, I could have wished that we had never set eyes upon them lest they should corrupt our people. I daresay you have often heard how my countrymen think of you and yours that you have learned good behaviour among us; and when they see a pious person among you, they will often say, 'He is like a human being,' or 'a Greenlander.' You no doubt remember that funny fellow Okako's idea of sending angekoks [that is, medicine-men] to your country to teach the people to be good, as your king has sent preachers hither to teach us that there is a God, which we did not know before. But I know that your people do not lack instruction, and therefore that proposal is of no use. It is strange enough, my dear Pauia!—your people know that there is a God, the creator and upholder of all things, that after this life they will either be happy or miserable, according as they shall have conducted themselves here, and yet they live as if they were under orders to be wicked, and it was to their honour and advantage to sin. My countrymen, on the other hand, know nothing either of a God or a devil, believe neither in punishment nor in reward after this life; and yet they live decently, treat each other kindly, and share with each other peaceably when they have food to share. There are, of course, bad people among us too, which proves that we must be of one stock; and perhaps we must thank our barren land for the fact that most of us are above reproach. (You do not think, I hope, that I am talking hypocritically about my countrymen, for you know by experience that what I say is true.) When I have heard accounts of your pleasant country I have often envied its inhabitants; for they have great abundance of the delicious fruits of the earth, and of animals, birds, and fishes of innumerable sorts, fine large comfortable houses, fine clothes, a long summer, no snow or cold, no midges, but everything pleasant and desirable; and this happiness, I thought, belonged to you alone because you were believers, and, as it were, God's own children, while we, as unbelievers, were placed in this country as a punishment. But, oh, we happy Greenlanders! Oh, dear native land! How well it is that you are covered with ice and snow; how well it is that if in your rocks there are gold and silver, for which the Christians are so greedy, it is covered with so much snow that they cannot get at it! Your unfruitfulness makes us happy and saves us from molestation! Pauia! we are indeed contented with our lot. Fish and flesh are our sole food; dainties seldom come in our way, but are all the pleasanter when they do. Our drink is ice-cold water; it quenches thirst and does not steal away the understanding or the natural strength like that maddening drink of which your people are so fond. Our clothing is of unsightly thick-haired skins, but it is well suited to this country, both for the animals, while the skins are still theirs, and for us when we take them from them. Here then, thank God, there is nothing to tempt anyone to come and kill us for its sake. We live without fear. It is true that here in the North we have the fierce white bears; but to deal with them we have our dogs, which fight for us, so that we do not run the slightest risk. Murder is very seldom heard of among us. It does not happen unless someone is suspected or accused of being a magician and of having killed someone by his witchcraft, in which case he is killed without remorse by those whose duty it is, who think they have just as good right as the executioner in your country to take the lives of malefactors; but they make no boast of it, and do not give thanks to God for it like the great lords in your country, when they have killed all the people of another land, as D. has told me. It surely cannot be to the good God of whom you teach us, who has forbidden us to shed blood, that they give thanks and praises; it must be to another who loves slaughter and destruction. I wonder if it is not to the Tornarsuk [the devil]? Yet that cannot be either; for it would be flying in the face of the good God to give any honour to Satan. I hope you will explain this to me at your convenience. I promise not to tell my countrymen about it. It might lead them to think like Kaua, who dared not become a Christian for fear he should come to be like the wicked sailors. I will not tell you anything about the conversion of my countrymen, for I know that our teacher has given you all information. The thing you desired me to look into I will, as far as I am able, attend to. I have not been able to make the experiment with the compass, since the cold this year has been only moderate. The cause of the two conflicting currents is no doubt what you say. Since you value so much the two fishes almost turned to stone, I shall try to procure more for you; they are found in clay beds, as you suppose. Now I seem to have been speaking to you and you to me—now I must close my letter. The skipper is ready and the wind is fair. The mighty Protector of all of us guide them over the great and perilous sea, and preserve them, especially from the wicked men-hunters, of whom I see they are most in dread, so that they may come scatheless to their fatherland and find you, my beloved, with gladness.

Paul Greenlander.

Greenland, 1756.

This letter, as well as what has been stated in the earlier part of this chapter, surely justifies us in saying that the primitive morality of the Eskimo stands in many respects close to that of ideal Christianity, and is even in one way superior to it; for, as the letter-writer says, the Greenlanders 'know nothing either of a God or a devil, believe neither in punishment nor in reward after this life, and yet they live virtuously' none the less.

Many people will, no doubt, think it astonishing that we should find so highly developed a morality among a race so uncultivated, and so unclean in their outward habits. Others will perhaps find it more surprising that this morality should have been developed among a people who have no religion, or at any rate a very imperfect one, as we shall presently see. Such facts are inconsistent with the theory which is still held in many quarters, that morality and religion are inseparable. A study of the Eskimo community shows pretty clearly, I think, that morality to a great extent springs from and rests upon natural law.

CHAPTER XI

JUDICIAL PROCEEDINGS—DRUM-DANCES AND ENTERTAINMENTS

I have again and again sought to impress upon the reader that the Eskimos are a peaceable and kindly race. There is no more striking proof of this, I think, than their primitive judicial process.

It is a mistake to suppose that the heathen Eskimos had no means of submitting any wrong they had suffered to the judgment of their fellows. Their judicial process, however, was of a quite peculiar nature, and consisted of a sort of duel. It was not fought with lethal weapons, as in the so-called civilised countries; in this, as in other things, the Greenlander went more mildly to work, challenging the man who had done him wrong to a contest of song or a drum-dance. This generally took place at the great summer meetings, where many people were assembled with their tents. The litigants stood face to face with each other in the midst of a circle of on-lookers, both men and women, and, beating a tambourine or drum, each in turn sang satirical songs about the other. In these songs, which as a rule were composed beforehand, but were sometimes improvised, they related all the misdeeds of their opponent and tried in every possible way to make him ridiculous. The one who got the audience to laugh most at his jibes or invectives was the conqueror. Even such serious crimes as murder were often expiated in this way. It may appear to us a somewhat mild form of punishment, but for this people, with their marked sense of honour, it was sufficient; for the worst thing that can happen to a Greenlander is to be made ridiculous in the eyes of his fellows, and to be scoffed at by them. It has even happened that a man has been forced to go into exile by reason of a defeat in a drum-dance.

This drum-dance is still to be found upon the east coast. It seems clear that it must be an exceedingly desirable institution, and for my part I only wish that it could be introduced into Europe; for a quicker and easier fashion of settling quarrels and punishing evil-doers it is difficult to imagine.

The missionaries on the west coast of Greenland, unfortunately, do not seem to have been of the same opinion. Being a heathen custom, it was therefore, in their opinion, immoral and noxious as well; and on the introduction of Christianity they opposed it and rooted it out. Dalager even tells us that 'there is scarcely any vice practised among the Greenlanders against which our missionaries preach more vehemently than they do against this dance, affirming that it is the occasion of all sorts of misbehaviour, especially among the young.' This policy he did not at all approve. He admits, indeed, that the dances may be the occasion of a few irregularities, but adds that if a girl has made up her mind to part with her virtue, she is not likely to select so unquiet a time and place; and one cannot but agree with him when he exclaims, 'And in truth, if people danced to such good purpose among us, we should presently see every second moralist and advocate transformed into a dancing-master.'

The result of this inconsiderate action on the part of the missionaries is that, in reality, no law and no forms of justice now exist in Greenland. The Europeans cannot, of course, or at any rate should not, mix themselves up in the Greenlanders' private affairs. But when, on some rare occasion, a crime of real importance occurs, the Danish authorities feel that they must intervene. The consequences of such intervention are sometimes rather surprising. At a settlement in North Greenland some years ago (so I have been told), a man who had killed his mother was punished by banishment to a desert island. In order that he should be able to support himself in solitude, they had to give him a new kaiak, and a small store of food to begin with. Some time afterwards, the food having run out, he returned to the settlement and declared that he could not live on the island, because there was not enough game in the waters around it. He therefore settled down again in his old house, and the only change in his life brought about by his matricide was that he got a new kaiak.

The managers of the colonies sometimes have recourse to a more effective method of punishment in the case of women: it consists in excluding them for a certain time from dealing at the stores.

Besides being a judicial process, the drum-dance was also a great entertainment, and was often danced merely for the sake of pastime. In this case the dancers sang songs of various kinds, beating a drum the while, and going through a varied series of more or less burlesque writhings and contortions of the body. This is another consideration which ought to have made the missionaries think twice before abolishing the drum-dances, for amusement is a necessity of life, serving to refresh the mind, and is of quite peculiar importance for a people which, like the Greenlanders, inhabits an inhospitable region and has few diversions. To make up for the loss of the drum-dances, they have now borrowed from the European whale-fishers and sailors many European dances, especially reels, which they have to some extent modified according to their own taste. At the colonies, the carpenter's shop, the blubber-loft, or some other large apartment, is generally used as a ball-room, and here dances take place as often as the managers or other authorities will give permission—generally once a week. In the other villages the dancing takes place in the Greenlanders' own houses.

A Greenland ball offers a picturesque spectacle—the room half lighted by the train-oil lamps, and the crowd of people, young and old, all in their many-coloured garments, some of them taking part in the dance, some standing as on-lookers in crowded groups along the walls and upon the sleeping-benches and seats. There is plenty of beauty and of graceful form, commingled with the most extravagant hideousness. Over the whole scene there is a sense of sparkling merriment, and in the dance a great deal of grace and accomplishment. The feet will often move so nimbly in the reel that the eye can with difficulty follow them. In former days the music was generally supplied by a violin, but now the accordion, too, is much in use.

The unhappy Eskimos who belong to the German or Herrnhut communities, of which there are several in the country, are forbidden to dance, and even to look at others dancing. If they do, they are excommunicated by the missionaries, or put down in their black books.

A GREENLAND DANCE

Among other amusements, church-going takes a prominent place. They find the psalm-singing extremely diverting, and the women in particular are very much addicted to it.

The women, however, find shopping at least as entertaining. As the time for opening the stores approaches, they are to be seen, even in the winter snowstorms, standing in groups along the walls and waiting for the moment when the doors of Paradise shall be flung wide and they can rush in. Most of them do not want to buy anything, but they while away the hours during which the store is open, partly in examining all the European articles of luxury, especially stuffs and shawls, partly in flirting with the storekeepers, and partly in exchanging all sorts of more or less refined witticisms and 'larking' with each other.

The rush is particularly great every summer, after the arrival of the ships with cargoes of new wares from Europe. Then the stores are literally in a state of siege the whole day long. Like their European sisters, the Eskimo women are fond of novelties of all sorts, so that as soon as they arrive the stores do a roaring trade in them. The main point, so far as I could understand, is that the wares shall be new; the use they are to be put to is a minor consideration.

CHAPTER XII

MENTAL GIFTS—ART—MUSIC—POETRY—ESKI-MO NARRATIVES

The Greenlanders are endowed with good mental faculties and great inventiveness. Their implements and weapons, as we have seen, afford a striking proof of this. The missionaries, too, especially at first, found only too ample opportunity to judge of the keenness of their understanding, when they were so foolish as to let themselves be drawn into discussions with the heathen angekoks. When the missionaries were cornered, however, they had often arguments in reserve which were much more forcible than those of the natives. They wielded, as my friend, the master carpenter at Godthaab used to say, 'a proper fist,' and to its persuasions the peaceable Greenlanders could not but yield.

To prove that their natural parts are good, I may mention that they learn to read and write with comparative ease. Most of the Christian Eskimos can now read and write, many of them very well; indeed, their faculty for writing is often quite marvellous. Even the heathen Eskimos learn to play dominoes, draughts, and even chess, with ease. I have often played draughts with the natives of the Godthaab district, and was astonished at the ability and foresight which they displayed.

All our ordinary branches of education they master with more or less readiness. Arithmetic is what they find most difficult, and there are comparatively few who get so far as to deal competently with fractions; the majority have quite enough to do with addition and subtraction of integers, to say nothing of multiplication and division. The imperfection of their gifts in this direction is no doubt due to age-old causes. The Eskimo language, like most primitive idioms, has a very undeveloped system of numerals, five being the highest number for which they have a special word. They count upon their fingers: One, *atausek*; two, *mardluk*; three, *pingasut*; four, *sisamet*; five, *tatdlimat*, the last having probably been the original word for the hand. When an Eskimo wants to count beyond five, he expresses six by saying 'the first finger of the other hand' (*arfinek* or *igluane atausek*); for seven he says 'the second finger of the other hand' (*arfinek mardluk*), and so forth. When he reaches ten he has no more hands to count with, and must have recourse to his feet. Twelve, accordingly, is represented by 'two toes upon the one foot' (*arkanek mardluk*), and so forth; seventeen by 'two toes on the second foot' (*arfersanek mardluk*), and so forth. Thus he manages to mount to twenty, which he calls a whole man (*inuk nâvdlugo*). Here the mathematical conceptions of many Eskimos come to an end; but men of commanding intellect can count still further, and for one-and-twenty say 'one on the second man' (*inûp áipagssâne atausek*). Thirty-eight is expressed by 'three toes on the second man's second foot' (*inûp áipagssâne arfinek pingasut*), forty by 'the whole of the second man' (*inûp áipagssâ nâvdlugo*), and so forth. In this way they can count to a hundred, or 'the whole of the fifth man'; but beyond that his language will not carry even the most gifted Eskimo.

This is, as will be easily understood, a somewhat unwieldy method of expression when one has to deal with numbers over twenty. In former days there was seldom any need to go further than this; but the introduction of money and trade has, unfortunately, rendered this more frequently necessary. It is therefore not surprising that, in spite of their remarkable power of resistance to foreign words, the Greenlanders have begun more and more to adopt the Danish numerals, even for the smaller numbers. By their aid they have now got so far that they can count to over a hundred, which they call *untritigdlit*[47]; but I strongly suspect that they have still a difficulty in forming any distinct conception of so high a number. A thousand they call *tusintigdlit*.[48]

This primitive Eskimo method of numeration answers to what we find among most primitive peoples, the fingers and toes having been from all time the most natural appliances for counting with; even our forefathers no doubt reckoned in the same way. Imperfect though it be, however, this method is a great advance upon that of the Australian tribes, who cannot count beyond three, or in some cases not beyond two, and whose numerals consist of: 'One, two, plenty.' That the forefathers of the Eskimos, as of all other peoples, at one time stood on this level appears from their original grammar, in which we find a singular, dual, and plural, as in Gothic, Greek, Sanscrit, the Semitic languages, and many others.

All travellers agree in acknowledging the Eskimo's remarkable sense of locality and talent for topography. When Captain Ommaney, in 1850, asked an Eskimo from Cape York to draw the coast, he took a pencil, a thing he had never seen before, and sketched the coast-line along Smith's Sound from his birthplace northwards with astonishing accuracy, indicating all the islands, and the more important rocks, glaciers, and mountains, and mentioning the names of all of them. The heathen natives brought to Captain Holm a map of the east coast north of Angmagsalik, which they had cut out in wood.

The Greenlanders have, in my opinion, an indubitable artistic faculty, and if their culture in this direction is but little developed, I believe the reason lies in their hard fight for existence, which has left them no time for artistic pursuits. Their art[49] consists chiefly in the decoration of weapons, tools, and garments with patterns and figures, cut out of bone or wood, or embroidered in leather. The designs often represent animals, human beings, woman-boats, and kaiaks; but they are conventional, and intended rather for decorative or symbolic effect than as

[47] Danish, *hundrede*.

[48] Danish, *tusinde*.

[49] The most important contribution to our knowledge of Eskimo art in its primitive condition is to be found in Captain Holm's instructive account of the Eskimos at Angmagsalik, *Meddelelser om Grönland*, pt. 10, p. 148, &c., with illustrations.

true reproductions of Nature; indeed, they have as a rule assumed quite traditional forms. Some, too, are of religious significance, and represent, for example, the *tôrnârssuk*—one of their spirits or supernatural beings. When they really try to copy Nature, they sometimes display a rare sense of form and power of reproducing it, as may be seen from the remarkable pictures given by Captain Holm of dolls and toys from the east coast, which are therefore quite uninfluenced by European art-products.

Weapons and tools were doubtless among the first things upon which the human artistic faculty thought of exercising itself; but the human body itself was perhaps a still earlier subject for artistic treatment. Relics of this early form of art are found among the Eskimos, the women seeking to heighten their attractions by means of geometrical lines and figures which they produce upon face, breast, arms, or legs, by means of drawing sinews, blackened with lamp-soot, through the skin.

Hieroglyphics, which many believe to have been, in part at least, the origin of art, seem oddly enough to have been unknown among the Greenlanders, unless indeed the symbolic designs in their ornamentation can be supposed to have some such significance. The only attempt at real picture-writing which I have been able to discover among them does not evince a very high order of talent. It was a missive to Paul Egede from an angekok, which consisted simply of a stick, upon which was drawn, with soot and train-oil, a figure like this: Λ. The angekok called after the letter-carrier, as he took his departure, 'If Pauia Angekok does not understand what I mean (though he probably will), then say to him: "This means a pair of trousers which I want him to buy for me at the stores." But he will understand it well enough.'

Eskimos who have seen specimens of European art and methods of representation, will sometimes produce remarkable things without any sort of instruction. A Greenlander named Aaron once fell sick and had to keep to his bed. Dr. Rink sent him some materials for wood-engraving and some old woodcuts. Lying in bed, he at once began to illustrate the Eskimo legends, and he not only drew his pictures, but also cut them on the wood.

As an example of their talent for sculpture I here reproduce two heads, carved in wood, which a native of a village in the Godthaab district brought to me. They seem to me to betray a marked sense of humour; and one can scarcely doubt that it is the features of his own race which the artist has immortalised.

Of musical talent the Greenlanders have a good share. They pick up our music with remarkable ease, and reproduce it, sometimes vocally, for they are very fond of singing, sometimes on the violin, guitar, organ, accordion, or other instruments, which they quickly teach themselves to play upon. This is the more remarkable as their primitive music, which was performed at the drum-dances, is monotonous and undeveloped, like that of most primitive peoples. It employs only a few notes, as a rule not more than five; but it is nevertheless peculiar and not without interest. It is believed to be in the main an imitation of the rushing of the rivers. The East Greenlanders told Holm that when they sleep beside a river they hear the singing of the dead, and this they seek to imitate.

ESKIMO VENUS AND APOLLO

The primitive characteristics of their music have of course been more or less destroyed by their intercourse with Europeans. They have now adopted many European airs, and it produces a quaint and surprising effect, among the mountains and the glaciers, suddenly to hear a snatch of a Copenhagen street song, as for example, 'Gina, lovely maiden mine, ... won't you come along?'

The Greenlanders have a great wealth of fairy tales and legends, many of them very characteristic. Nothing affords a better insight into the whole spiritual life of the people, their disposition, feelings, and moods, than the matter of these legends and the manner in which they are told. We find in them a considerable talent for narrative and gift of imagination, along with a grotesque humour, which of course often takes the form of coarseness.

Besides this legendary lore (see next chapter) and narratives of exploits and adventures, the Greenlanders had a poetry of their own. The songs were either lampoons, such as they used to sing at the before-mentioned drum-dances, or else descriptions of different objects and events.

When, on the introduction of Christianity, the drum-dance was abolished, the art of versification also fell into disuse or assumed new shapes. Still, however, the Greenlanders make up songs. They are often of a jocose character, the poet setting forth to ridicule, in a more or less innocent manner, the peculiarities of others. I understand that several songs of this nature were composed with reference to members of my expedition. Indeed I have often heard them sung about the settlement of an evening, though I never succeeded in obtaining the text of any of them.

Thanks to the initiative of Dr. Rink, an Eskimo newspaper, *Atuagagdliutit*, has ever since 1861 been published in Godthaab. It is printed by a native, Lars Möller, who has been to Copenhagen to learn the trade, and who even draws and lithographs pictures for it. It is published twelve times a year, and is distributed gratis to the community, the expenses being borne out of the public funds. Its contents consist partly of translations from the Danish, partly of independent contributions from the natives describing their hunting, their travels, and so forth. Thus a whole new literature has been called into existence.

A specimen of their method of narration was given in 'The First Crossing of Greenland,' Vol. II. pp. 217-236. It consisted of the account given by an Eskimo named Silas, in the *Atuagagdliutit*, of his expedition from Unanak on Godthaab-fiord to the Ameralik fiord to render assistance to the four members of our expedition who had remained behind there in October 1888, after Sverdrup and I had proceeded to Godthaab. The following narrative, from the *Atuagagdliutit*, is also a good sample of their style. It exemplifies, moreover, the strong hold which their superstitions still possess upon the Eskimo mind, and is thus of interest with reference to the matter of my next chapter. I have to thank Mrs. Signe Rink for her kindness in translating it for me.

At last I send you something which I have long thought of contributing to your 'Varieties' column. There is not much in what I have to tell, but what there is I have seen with my own eyes. I refer to the comical customs in connection with the killing of a bear in certain southern districts, which are quite unknown elsewhere. These things took place in the year 1882-83 down at Augpilagtut, a little way from Pamiagdluk.[50] There are two Eskimo houses at Augpilagtut. In one of them lived three seal-hunters with their families, to wit, Benjamin, surnamed Akâtit, Isaac, or Umangûjok, and lastly Moritz; and in the other dwelt Mathæus, who was generally called Ulivkakaungamik, or 'the full-stuffed,' from a catch-word he himself was in the habit of using. He was over seventy, but still went hunting very often, and had even killed many bears all by himself.

It happened one Sunday, when all the other hunters had gone to sea, that we who remained behind held a prayer-meeting in Mathæus's house. When it was over, Benjamin's son was the first who went out, and he came rushing back again crying, 'There's a bear right outside here, eating the blubber.'

I was half frightened, half rejoiced by this news; but old Mathæus positively trembled with delight, and burst forth, 'Thanks to him who brings such good tidings; I must go out at once and kill the bear.' I looked at him, thinking that he was going to pick out for himself a good weapon, a long knife or spear. But nothing of the kind! The weapon he had taken scarcely stuck out from his clenched fist. What use can that be, I thought, against the bear's hide and thick layer of fat. However, the women of the house would not let him attack the bear, and all seized upon him to hold him back, I helping them. The women all untied their top-knots and let their hair spread loose, that the bear might think they were men, and therefore keep his distance. For our heathen forefathers thought that bears had human understanding.

[50] Near Cape Farewell.

As we were afraid lest this bear should take it into his head to come into the house through the gut-skin window, I, too, had to think about getting hold of some weapon or other, and therefore asked for their axe; but I of course found that it had been lent to the people of the other house. At the same time I caught sight of a woman's knife lying upon the *ipak*[51] beside the lamp, and that I seized, along with a piece of wood from an old kaiak-keel, which I wanted to tie to the knife and use as a spear-shaft. But no sooner had I taken these things than someone behind me cried, 'Give them to me; I am ever so much stronger than you!' It was no other than Mathæus's daughter, a widow. She took them both away from me.

The house-clock[52] now began to strike eleven, and that brute of a bear forthwith began to look hungrier. I rushed at once to stop the striking, but in my consternation I made a mistake and increased the racket, until at last I managed to get the weight loosened and the striking stopped. The women were still holding tight to Mathæus to keep him back. Then, all at once, the mother of the boy who had seen the bear began to slip her trousers down to her knees, and so go shuffling round the room, while she plaited some straws. This, they said, was to weaken the bear, so as to make it easier to get the better of him. In the meantime, old Mathæus shook the women off and set forth. I rushed after him, and came up with him before he had quite got out of the entrance-passage. He told me to go quietly, and said, 'Hush, hush, now he's going down towards the sea.'

Mathæus's rifle was lying in his kaiak on the beach, and as soon as the bear had passed the kaiak, the old man crept cautiously on all fours in the same direction. I stood at the entrance to the passage and saw the bear suddenly turn and rush roaring towards him. This frightened me so that I fled over to the other house where, in my hurry, I came tumbling in at the door. While I still lay grovelling upon the floor, I could see through the window[53] how the bear and Mathæus stared each other straight in the face, each on his own side of the kaiak, Mathæus making grimaces, and the bear roaring with his mouth wide open, ready to bite him; but Mathæus planted his foot firmly against the kaiak and aimed, without once taking his eyes off the bear for a single moment; and then he fired. I now hurried out, just in time to see him thrust his sealing-lance into its carcase. Then he called loudly to those in the house that now they had better come and get their *ningek* (slice of fat). In their hurry to outstrip each other, the women almost stuck fast in the narrow house-passage, part of which they tore down. When they reached the bear, they all thrust their hands into the wound and lapped some of the blood, while each of them named the part of the animal which she wanted to have. At last my turn came to drink the blood, and I did so, saying that I wanted one ham as my portion; but thereupon they answered that all the limbs were already bespoke, and that I, moreover, had neglected to touch the bear when I came up to it. It was extremely

---

[51] The *ipak* is an extension of the sleeping-bench (generally square) on which they place the lamp with its wooden stand.

[52] Cheap Nuremberg or Swiss clocks are among the articles of luxury which commerce has introduced into Greenland; they are to be found in the remotest corners of the country.

[53] Which is very low in the genuine Eskimo huts.

vexatious that I had forgotten this detail. The mother of the boy who had first seen the bear now ran for a bowl of water and made us all take a mouthful of it, though none of us was thirsty. This she did in order that her son might always have good luck in spying bears. The drinking of the blood was meant to prove to the whole race of bears how they thirsted after them. Before they set to work to cut up the bear, they kept drumming at his skin and crying: 'You are fat, fat, beautifully fat.' This they do out of politeness, in the hope that the bear may really be fat; but when we skinned this one it was found to be quite unusually lean.

When they carried the head into the house, I went along with them, knowing that they would go through certain ceremonies with it. First it was placed on the edge of the lamp-table with the face towards the south-east; then they stopped its mouth and nostrils with sediment from the lamps and other sorts of grease; and lastly, they bedecked the crown of the head with all sorts of little things, such as shoesoles, sawdust, glass beads, knives, &c. The south-east direction is due to the fact that it is from this quarter of the compass that the bears generally come, being carried by 'the great ice' round the southern extremity of the land. The lamp-moss in the nostrils is meant to prevent the bear they next attack from scenting the approach of men; and the greasing of the mouth is designed to give it pleasure, as the bear is supposed to be a lover of all sorts of fried grease. The head is covered with knick-knacks because they think that the bear is sent to them by their forefathers for the purpose of bringing these things with it to the other world; and as they reckon that the bear's soul cannot reach its home in less than five days, they always refrain for that time from eating its head, lest its soul should die on the way, and the little gifts to their relatives should thus be lost. They are even careful to stop up all the holes in the neck where the head has been cut off, in order to prevent the soul from bleeding to death on its journey. For my part, I call all this idolatry. The heathens, indeed, believed in the old days that everything, whether living or dead, had its soul; but there is nothing that one ought to mix up with man's immortal soul. The fact that, even in our days, so long after the introduction of Christianity, the people here in the far south still cling to some of the habits of their forefathers is due to their frequent (almost yearly) intercourse with the heathens of the east coast.

I left Augpilagtut in 1885. I am not quite sure whether even out at Pamiagdluk there may not be a few families who still lean to these bear superstitions; but all certainly do not—not Isaac's family, for one. At other places, for example here at the Colony, they have scarcely even heard of the customs I have described.

I had not been told on what day they intended to cook the bear's head, and was therefore surprised by a sudden invitation to come and share in it. I cut the snout off without ceremony; but they soon let me know that I had made a mistake, at once tearing it out of my hands. I confess I was a good deal offended, and told them straight out that, however foolish they might think me, I did not believe a bit in all this. They assured me quite earnestly that in that case I would never kill a bear, whereupon I answered that this prophecy was very likely to be fulfilled, since I was so short-sighted that the bear would probably be licking me before I was aware of its presence.

They have also these further customs: If they see the track of a bear in the snow, they eat a little of it in order to assure themselves of killing the bear if it should happen to come back the same way. Little boys are given the kidneys of bears to eat, in order that they may be strong and courageous in bear-hunting. Furthermore, they are careful during the aforesaid five days not to make any jingling noise, for the bear is supposed to dislike any sort of clinking or clanking.

Mathæus told me that the bear I had seen him kill was his eleventh, and that he had not been in the least afraid of it because in this case he knew he had his rifle to trust to; but that once before when he had seen a bear come crawling up the beach in the same way, he had rushed right in upon it with only his lance. He said he could not remember how long ago that was.

CHAPTER XIII

RELIGIOUS IDEAS

Religion and religious ideas are among the most remarkable products of the human spirit. With all their reason-defying assertions and astounding incongruities, they seem at first sight inexplicable. Time out of mind, therefore, men have found it difficult to conceive them as having arisen otherwise than through a supernatural or divine revelation, which, it would follow, must originally have been imparted to all men alike. But gradually, as people became acquainted with the more or less rudimentary religions of the various races, which often differ greatly on the most essential matters, they began to doubt the accuracy of this assumption, and came more and more to consider whether religious ideas must not be reckoned as a natural product of the human mind itself, under the influence of its surroundings.

The first theory was that they arose from a religious craving common to all human beings, which was itself, therefore, in a certain sense supernatural. It is a mysterious incomprehensible presentiment, says Schleiermacher, which drives mankind across the boundaries of the finite world, and leads everyone to religion; only by the crippling of this natural proclivity can irreligiousness arise. 'Religion begins in the first encounter of the life of the All with that of the individual; it is the sacred and infallible inter-marriage—the creative, productive embrace—of the universe with incarnate reason.'

Gradually the explanations became less vague and high-sounding. Peschel and others held that religious ideas arose from the need of conceiving the cause or beginning of all things, or, in other words, that it was the sources of movement, life, and thought, which mankind sought after, with its inborn longing to realise the absolute. Others hold, with Max Müller, that a longing for the infinite, a striving to understand the incomprehensible, to name the unnameable, is the deep spiritual bass-note which makes itself heard in all religions. Others again, like O. Pfleiderer, see in mankind's inborn and incomprehensible thirst for beauty, its fantasy, and its æsthetic sense, the first germs of religious consciousness. Some theorists, finally, have sought to explain religious ideas as an outcome of the moral sense of mankind, of its thirst for righteousness.

In the light of a moderately penetrating study of the religious ideas of the Eskimos, as of every other primitive people, all these philosophic theories vanish away. In our empirical age, people have come more and more to recognise that religious ideas must be ascribed to the same natural laws which condition all other phenomena, and to hold, as David Hume first maintained, that they can be traced for the most part to two tendencies in our nature—or perhaps we should rather call them instincts—which are common to all animals; to wit, *the fear of death and the desire of life*. From the former instinct arises fear of the dead and of external nature with its titanic forces, and the craving for protection against them. From the latter arises the desire for happiness, for power, and for other advantages. Thus, too, we understand the fact that the early religions are not disinterested, but egotistical, that the worshipper is not so much rapt in contemplation of the enigmas of nature and of the infinite, as eager to secure some advantage to himself. When, for example, amulets and fetishes are supposed to possess supernatural power, they are not only treasured, but worshipped.

It is difficult, not to say impossible, to search back to the first vague forms in which religious ideas dawned in the morning of humanity, when thought began to emerge from the primal mists of animal consciousness. It was with religious ideas in that time as with the first organic beings which arose upon our earth—they had not yet assumed such determinate forms, their component parts were not yet so definitely fixed, as to leave traces behind them; what we find are the more advanced stages of development. The first ideas must have been exceedingly obscure impressions, dependent upon many outward chances, and we can no more reason ourselves back to them, than we can conceive the appearance of the first organisms. Nor can we determine at what stage of the development of humanity these first vague germs of religious ideas appeared—whether, for example, they were present in our simian forefathers. It does not even seem to me certain that the lower animals are devoid of all superstitious feeling. We cannot, therefore, expect to discover in any now existing race a total lack of even the most rudimentary superstitious conceptions. We must rather wonder that in a people otherwise so highly developed as the Eskimos, they should still remain on such a remarkably low level.

In the light of our knowledge of the primitive religions, it seems to me best not to regard the aforesaid instincts as the direct cause of superstitious conceptions, but rather to distinguish between at least three germs or impulses, which have provided the material out of which these instincts—in reality resolvable into one, the instinct of self-preservation—have fashioned all religious systems. The three germs are: our tendency to personify nature, our belief in its and our own duality and in the immortality of the soul, and the belief in the supernatural power and influence of certain inanimate objects (amulets). In order to recognise the great importance of these germs, especially at a primitive stage of development, we must try to throw our minds back to the standpoint of the child, which most nearly answers to that of primitive man. To personify nature is for the child no mere passing fancy; he consistently regards all surrounding objects, animate and inanimate, as persons, and will, for example, carry on long conversations with his toys. A child of my acquaintance, standing one day in the kitchen watching some long sausages boiling in a pot, exclaimed to the cook: 'I say, are these sausages killed yet?' All of us, probably, can remember from our childhood how we personified trees, certain mountains, and the like. It is the same proclivity, as Tylor says, which reappears in our often irrational desire or thirst for vengeance upon inanimate things which in one way or another have caused us pain or injury. For example, when we were crossing Greenland, Sverdrup and I had a sledge which was heavy to draw; it would have caused us quite real satisfaction to have destroyed it, or otherwise revenged ourselves upon it, when we at last left it behind. Another inseparable characteristic of the child-mind is its determination to see in every movement or occurrence in its little world the activity of a personal will.

In the first childish philosophy of the human race, the same method of regarding all natural objects as persons must have been quite inevitable. Trees, stones, rivers, the winds, clouds, stars, the sun and moon became living persons or animals. The Eskimos, for example, believe that the heavenly bodies were once ordinary men and women before they were transferred to the sky.

But after or along with this proclivity there must also have arisen quite naturally the tendency to conceive a twofoldness, a duality, in nature and in man, the feeling of a visible and tangible, and of an invisible and super-sensible, existence. Let us, for instance, with Tylor, conceive an ignorant primitive man hearing the echo of his own voice; how can he help believing that it is produced by a man? He knows nothing of the theory of sound-waves. But when he hears it time after time, and can find no man who produces the sound, it is inevitable that he should attribute it to invisible beings.

Or take, for example, the dew, which he sees appearing and disappearing, he cannot tell whence or whither; the stars which are lighted in the evening, and put out again at morning; the clouds which gather all of a sudden, and of a sudden are dispersed; the rain, the wind, the currents in the water—must not all these arouse in him the thought or conception of visible and invisible existences? When the primitive Eskimo first met with the glacier which he saw gliding out into the sea, and giving birth, from time to time, to mighty icebergs, could he see in this anything else than the activity of a live being? He attributed life to the thing itself, and regarded these monstrous births as voluntary and awe-inspiring actions.

Or, to take another example, when a primitive man saw his own shadow or his own image in the water, now here, now gone again, eluding alike his touch and his grasp, how could this fail to arouse in him the conception of tangible and intangible existences, things that could now be here and at the next moment could vanish away?

There were plenty of grounds, in short, for the evocation of the idea of duality in nature, of a visible and an invisible phase of existence. But this belief in the duality of nature must have been greatly strengthened by the primitive man's conceptions of himself. When he slept, and dreamed that he was out hunting, was dancing, was visiting others, in short, was wandering far and wide, and then awoke and discovered that his body had not moved from his cave or hut, and heard his wife or his companions corroborate this, he naturally could not but believe that he consisted of two parts, of one part which could leave him at night and go through all these experiences, and one which lay still at home. To distinguish between dreams and reality was far more than could be expected of him. The speech of many primitive races cannot to this day, as Spencer points out, express this distinction, having no means of saying 'I dreamed that I saw' instead of 'I saw.' When he had further noticed that his shadow followed him by day but not by night, it was quite natural that he should give to the part that was separable from him the name of 'shadow' or 'shade,' which, therefore, came to mean the same thing which others denominate soul or spirit. We shall presently see that the Eskimo has acquired in this way his belief in, and his name for, the soul. The conviction of his own kinship with all the objects around him is further strengthened by the observation that they have shadows as well as himself.

But when primitive man was brought face to face with death it must have made a powerful impression upon him, and the belief in his own duality must have been confirmed in a still higher degree. Here, he saw, was the same body, the same mouth, and the same limbs; the only difference was that in life they spoke and moved, whereas now all was still. Their speech and motion must be due to some life-giving principle, and this must of course be the soul, which, as he knew from dreams, had the power of quitting the body. We must also hold it only natural that the soul, which at death departed from the body, came to be associated with the breath of the mouth, which was now gone; and therefore (as for example among some of the Eskimos) man was endowed with two souls, the *shadow* and the *breath*. This belief in the duality of the soul, which is sometimes also traceable to the shadow and the reflection in the mirror, is very widely spread, and to it we may probably trace our own distinction between soul and spirit, *psyche* and *pneuma*.

It might at first sight seem natural for primitive man to conclude that the soul no less than the body dies at death. There are, in fact, some who think so; but most of them, on meeting the dead again in their dreams, were driven to the conclusion that their souls still lived. Furthermore, it was not at all difficult to conceive that, as the soul was temporarily absent from the body in sleep, delirium, and so forth, it was permanently absent in death. Thus the belief in the continued life of the soul has quite naturally and inevitably arisen; and as the idea of annihilation is very unattractive to every living creature, this conception of immortality has appealed forcibly to the human mind.

But as most men are afraid of death and of the dead, they do not like to meet them again as ghosts; and, terror stimulating the imagination, a supernatural power is attributed to them, mainly hurtful, but sometimes helpful as well. People therefore come to think it wisest to propitiate and make friends with them. Thus has arisen that worship of the dead which plays so great a part in the religion of most races, and which lies, if not at the foundation, at any rate, very near to it, in almost all religions—as, for instance, among the Eskimos.

It cannot be thought unnatural that the spirits of the dead, and especially those of the more eminent among them, such as chiefs and princes, were gradually converted into gods.

The word for God among the Hebrews (*il* or *el*), among the Egyptians (*nutar*), and among many other peoples, meant only a powerful being, and could be applied as well to heroes as to gods. As there were upon the earth peculiarly powerful men, so there must be in the spirit-world peculiarly powerful spirits; and these naturally became the divinities *par excellence* whom it was specially important to worship. Thus we arrive at last at the belief in one God, at the moment when absolute monarchy is established in the spirit world.

But alongside of this ancestor-worship, we recognise as a powerful factor in the development of superstitious ideas the marked tendency of the human race to attribute supernatural power to certain inanimate objects, which, in the primitive stage, are used to avert or influence the power of the dead or to attain other advantages; and from this has developed the whole widespread belief in amulets, and possibly also, in a measure, fetish-worship. We shall consider later how the belief in the power of the amulet may have arisen.

An important force tending towards the continuance and development of superstitious conceptions, when they have once arisen, is of course to be found in the authority of the medicine-men (spirit-exorcisers), or of the priests, over their fellow-men. Some minds, and these the ablest, naturally came to have a better understanding than the others of supernatural things, and to stand in a closer relation to the dead. It was clear that they could thus help their neighbours, when, for example, there was question of applying the powers of the dead to the benefit of an individual or of a body of men; and the priest thus attained power and influence in the community, and often advantages of a more material nature as well. It has thus always been to the interest of the medicine-men and priests to sustain and nurture superstitious or religious ideas. They must themselves appear to believe in them; they may even discover new precepts of divinity to their own advantage, and thereby increase both their power and their revenues.

Among people like the Eskimos, yet another influence comes into play, which colours their superstition; the influence, to wit, of the natural surroundings among which they are placed, and of the hard and hazardous life they lead. It is a recognised fact that a race which lives by hunting and fishing has a special tendency to become superstitious; of this we have a striking example in our own country. Compare the men of the west and north coasts with those of the eastern districts. The former have to look mainly to the sea for their livelihood, they are dependent on wind and weather, on the coming of shoals of fish, &c.—in short, on a whole series of influences unfathomable by man, which they describe in one word as chance, and which may be not only unfavourable but even fatal to them. Inevitably, therefore, they become superstitious; nor is there any part of the country where pietism and obscurantism find such fertile soil as on the west coast. When we turn to the peasant of the eastern districts we find a remarkable difference. He dwells at ease upon his farm; somewhat dependent, it is true, on wind and weather, but in a comparatively secure position; and therefore he is less superstitious. How much more strongly must the stimulus towards superstition act upon the Eskimo, whose whole life depends upon hunting and fishing! And it is still further intensified by the perpetual danger in which he lives, and by his Arctic surroundings. Nature so wild and majestic as that of Greenland—with its glaciers, icebergs, mirages, tempests, and the long winter nights with the shimmering Northern

Lights—obtains an irresistible power over the mind, evokes reverence and terror, and feeds the imagination. We look upon all these marvels in the dry light of reason; but primitive man, like a child, ekes out defective comprehension with wild fantasy, and his belief in the supernatural is strengthened and developed.

Morality, which many believe to be intimately connected with religious conceptions, has in its origin little or nothing to do with them. As already indicated in Chapter X. it springs from the social instinct, and is, among primitive races, quite distinct from superstitious ideas. Thus they have no rewards beyond the grave for a life of moral excellence.

The Eskimos are in some measure an example of this. It is true that we find hints in the Greenland legends of punishment in this life for evil-doing, and especially for witchcraft, at the hands of supernatural powers. The dead may possibly to a certain extent requite survivors for benefits conferred upon them during their life; the souls (or inue?) of animals can revenge a too cruel slaughter of their offspring; the soul or spirit of a murdered man demands that his murder shall be avenged; wrong done to the weak is punished in divers fashions, and so forth. But all these notions are so vague that they cannot be conceived as primary or fundamental, but rather as a sort of occasional overgrowth, due to the natural mingling of social relations and laws with the primitive legends. They may therefore be regarded as the first hesitating steps of the religious ideas towards morality. It is not until a considerably later stage that religion has consciously and in earnest entered into an alliance with morality which helps to strengthen both. Religion has thereby acquired a strong back-bone, and moral precepts produce a deeper impression when they come from an exalted and divine source, and are moreover reinforced by promises of rewards and punishments beyond the grave.

A remarkable feature in all religions is that in spite of their great differences in many essentials, there are also such great and important similarities spread over the whole earth. This may be explained in two ways: either on the theory that all religion is the result of the same causes, acting independently in different places, or on the theory that religious conceptions have arisen in one place and have thence spread all the world over. For my part I believe that we may have recourse to both theories in order to explain this similarity of religions. The human brain and nerve-system are astonishingly similar among all races; the differences consist chiefly in the development which must be associated with the progress of the higher races. It follows that we must assume the same laws of thought to hold good throughout, especially in earlier and less complex stages of development; and as experiences must in a certain measure have been everywhere identical, people must not only have arrived at the same right conclusions, but must have also, when the right explanation did not lie on the surface, have everywhere fallen into the same fundamental errors; and upon these errors religions are built. But in addition to this, certain definite religious conceptions have presumably shaped themselves in particular places, and have, in the form of mouth-to-mouth traditions and legends, permeated all races of the earth. We shall subsequently find speaking evidence for the belief that they may have reached even such remote races as the Eskimos.

The faith of the Greenland Eskimo is of great interest towards the elucidation of the questions above touched upon. It is so primitive that I doubt whether it deserves the name of a religion. There are many legends and much superstition, but it all lacks clear and definite form; conceptions of the supernatural vary from individual to individual, and they produce, as a whole, the impression of a religion in process of formation, a mass of incoherent and fantastic notions which have not yet crystallised into a definite view of the world. We must assume that all religions have at one time or another passed through just such a stage as this.

The Greenlanders, like all primitive races, originally conceived nature as animate throughout, every object—stone, mountain, weapon, and so forth—having its soul. We still find traces of this belief. The souls of tools, weapons, and clothes, follow the dead on his wandering to the land of the shades; therefore they are laid in the grave, that there they may rot and their souls may be set free. Gradually, however, this belief has, in the confused and illogical way peculiar to primitive races, mixed itself up with a totally different one: the belief, to wit, that the souls of the dead can take up their abode in different animals, objects, mountains, and the like, which they subjugate to themselves, and from which they can issue from time to time, even showing themselves to the living. There has thus arisen the belief that in every natural object there dwells a particular being, called its *inua* (that is, its owner)—a word which, characteristically enough, originally signified human being or Eskimo.

According to the Eskimos, every stone, mountain, glacier, river, lake, has its inua; the very air has one. It is still more remarkable to find that even abstract conceptions have their inue; they speak for example of the inue of particular instincts or passions. This may seem surprising in a primitive people, but it is not very difficult to explain. When, for example, a primitive man suffering from violent hunger, feels an inward gnawing, it is quite natural that he should conceive this to be caused by a being, whom he therefore describes as the inua of hunger or appetite. As a rule, these inue are invisible, but when they are seen, according to Rink, they take the form of a brightness or fire, and the sight of them is very dangerous.

Man himself, according to the Greenlanders, consists of at least two parts: the *body* and the *soul*—and these they hold to be quite distinct from each other. The soul can only be seen by aid of a particular sense which is found in men under certain conditions, or in those who possess a special gift: to wit, the angekoks. It appears in the same shape as the body, but is of a more airy composition. The angekoks explained to Hans Egede that souls were 'quite soft to the touch, indeed scarcely tangible at all, just as if they had neither muscle nor bone.'[54] The people of the east coast hold that the soul is quite small, no larger than a hand or a finger. The Greenlanders' word for the soul is *tarnik*; this resembles the word *tarrak*, which signifies shadow, and I think there can be no doubt that they have originally been the same word, since the Eskimo, as before indicated, used to regard the soul and the shadow as one and the same thing.[55] This tallies exactly with what we

[54] As to the constitution of the soul see also Paul Egede, *Efterretninger om Grönland*, p. 149, and Cranz, *Historie von Grönland*, p. 258.

[55] Paul Egede says expressly (*Efterretninger om Grönland*, p. 126) that the natives make

find among other peoples. The Fijian, for example, calls his shadow his dark soul, which leaves him during the night; his image in the mirror is his light soul. *Tarrak* in the Greenland language means both shadow and reflection, so that the original word for soul meant all these three things. According to Cranz,[56] some of the Greenlanders believed that man had two souls: his shadow and his breath (compare above, pp. 216, &c.). The general belief in Egede's and Cranz's time seems to have been that the soul was most intimately connected with the breath. For instance, the angekok used to blow upon a sick man in order to cure him or give him a new soul.

It is worth noting that Hanserak, a native catechist from West Greenland who accompanied Captain Holm on his journey along the east coast (in 1884-85), stated in his diary (written in Eskimo), with reference to the Angmagsaliks' belief in the soul, that 'a man has many souls. The largest dwell in the larynx and in the left side, and are tiny men about the size of a sparrow. The other souls dwell in other parts of the body and are the size of a finger joint. If one of them is taken away, its particular member sickens.'[57] Whether this belief has ever been widespread among the Eskimos does not appear from other sources of information.

The soul is quite independent, and can thus leave the body for any time, short or long. It does so every night, when, in vivid dreams, it goes hunting or joins in merrymakings and so forth. The soul can also remain at home when the man is on a journey, a notion which Cranz believes to arise from home-sickness. It can also be lost, or stolen by means of witchcraft. Then the man falls ill and must get his angekok to set off and fetch his soul back again. If, in the meantime, any disaster has happened to it, for example if it has been eaten up by another angekok's tornarssuk, the man must die. An angekok, however, had also power to provide a new soul or exchange a sick soul for a sound, which, according to Cranz, he could obtain from, say, a hare, a reindeer, a bird, or a young child.

The strangest thing of all is that the soul could not only be lost in its entirety, but that pieces of it could also go astray; and then the angekok had to be called in to patch it up.

Among the Greenlanders of the east coast, according to Holm, a third element in addition to these two enters into the composition of man: to wit 'the name' (*atekata*). 'The name is as large as the man himself, and enters into the child after its birth, on its mouth being damped with water, while at the same time the "names" of the dead are spoken.' Among all the Greenlanders, even the Christians, the first child born after the death of a member of the family is almost always called after him, the object being to procure peace for him in his grave. The East Greenlander believes that the 'name' remains with the body or migrates through different animals,[58] until a child is called by it. It is therefore a duty to take care that this is

no distinction between *tarrak* and *tarnek* (*tarnik*), and he himself uses the two words indifferently. See also the same work, p. 92.

[56] *Historie von Grönland*, p. 257.

[57] See Holm, *Meddelelser om Grönland*, pt. 10, p. 112.

[58] A similar idea is also current on the west coast (compare *Meddelelser om Grönland*, pt. 10, p. 342), but seems there to have reference to the ordinary soul of the deceased. The

done; if not, evil consequences may follow for the child to whom the name ought to have been given.

This belief is remarkably similar to one which (as Professor Moltke Moe[59] informs me) is current in Norway: to wit, that the dead 'seek after names.' A pregnant woman dreams of one or other departed relative who comes to her ('seeking after a name'), and after him she must call her child; if not, she is guilty of an act of neglect, which may injuriously affect the child's future.[60] The same superstition is also found among the Lapps. Among the Koloshes in North-West America, the mother sees in a dream the departed relative whose soul gives the child its likeness. Among the Indians also the naming of children is made to depend on a dream.[61]

In Greenland, as everywhere else, the name is of great importance; it is believed that there is a spiritual affinity between two people of the same name,[62] and that the characteristics of a dead person are transmitted to one who is called after him, who, moreover, is specially bound to defy the influences which have caused his predecessor's death. Thus the name-child of a man who has died at sea must make it his special business to defy the sea in his kaiak—a notion which is also found among other races, for example, the Indians.

The Greenlanders are very much afraid of mentioning the names of the dead. On the east coast, according to Holm, this fear goes so far that when two people have borne the same name the survivor must change his; and if the deceased has been named after an animal, an object, or an abstract idea, the word designating it must be altered. The language is thus subjected to important temporary changes, for these re-christenings are accepted by a whole tribe.[63] The same custom is very widely diffused among the Indians of North America and of Patagonia, among the Samoyedes in Asia, and the Gipsies in Europe. It is also found in Eastern Africa, in Madagascar, Australia, Tasmania, New Guinea, and the Society Islands. When Queen Pomare of Tahiti died, the word *po* (night) was dropped from the language,

---

distinction between the soul and the name cannot, therefore, be sharply drawn among the different tribes.

[59] Throughout the footnotes to this chapter, Dr. Nansen is profuse in his acknowledgments of the assistance rendered him by Professor Moltke Moe. I have ventured to concentrate these recurrent acknowledgments into this one note, and shall refer to Professor Moe only where he figures as the authority for a statement of fact.—*Trans.*

[60] See also Liebrecht, *Zur Volkskunde*, p. 311.

[61] Klemm, *Culturgeschichte*, iii. p. 77; Tylor, *Primitive Culture* (1873), ii. p. 4; *Antiquarisk Tidsskrift*, 1861-63, p. 118.

[62] It appears to me that exogamy between two of the same surname, which is found among many races (see p. 175), can easily be explained on this principle, since the same name creates a close spiritual affinity, which may, like blood-affinity, act as a bar to marriage.

[63] See Holm, *op. cit.* p. 111, where examples of such re-christenings are given. Holm thinks that 'the old names reappear when the deceased is quite forgotten.' It seems to me more natural to suppose that this occurs as soon as a child has been called after the dead man.

and *mi* took its place.[64]

The fear of mentioning the names of the dead is also found in Europe—in Germany, the Shetland Islands,[65] and elsewhere—and, no doubt, among us in Norway as well. In Greenland, as among some native races in America and in the Sunda Islands,[66] sick people who bear the same name as one who is dead change it in order to cheat death.

The East Greenlanders are also afraid to speak their own names. Holm says that when they were asked what they were called they always got others to answer for them. When a mother was asked 'what was the name of her child, she answered that she could not tell. The father likewise refused to say; he intimated that he had forgotten it, but that we could learn it from his wife's brother.'[67]

Among the Indians, the name plays a great part; they even try to keep it secret, and therefore a man is often called by a nickname.[68] Among many races, custom forbids the mention of the names of relations, as, for instance, a husband's, a mother-in-law's, a son-in-law's, the names of parents, or the name of the king. This potency of the name goes to considerable lengths amongst certain races. When the King of Dahomey, Bossa Ahadi, ascended the throne, he had everyone beheaded who bore the name of Bossa.

The fear of mentioning names is common to humanity; we find it in many of our legends,[69] and it prevails among us even to this day, especially upon the west coast.[70] It may probably be traced to the fact that the name and the thing are apt to melt into one. People come to think that when once the name is known the thing[71] is known as well, so that the mention of its name comes to exercise an influence upon the thing itself. A man may thus lose his strength by revealing his name. Therefore, too, we may suppose that dead people do not like to be called by their names, and that to name them may be a means of summoning them from their graves or of disturbing them in their rest. The Greenlanders dare not even speak the name of a glacier (*puisortok*) as they row past it, for fear lest it should be offended and throw off an iceberg.[72] A similar notion is very prevalent among the

---

[64] Nyrop, *Mindre Afhandlinger udgivne af det philologisk-historiske Samfund*, Copenhagen, 1887, pp. 147-150.

[65] Nyrop, *op. cit.* pp. 136 & 137.

[66] Liebrecht, *Academy*, iii. (1872), p. 322.

[67] *Meddelelser om Grönland*, pt. 10, p. 113.

[68] See Schoolcraft, in *Antiquarisk Tidsskrift*, 1861-63, p. 119, &c., also Andrée, *Ethnographische Parallelen und Vergleiche*, p. 180; Tylor, *Early History of Mankind*, p. 142.

[69] The reluctance prevailed among our forefathers. 'Sigurd concealed his name because people believed in the old days that a dying man's curse had great power, when he called his enemy by name.'—*Sæmundar Edda*, ed. by Sophus Bugge, p. 219.

[70] Information received from Prof. Moltke Moe.

[71] The way in which name and thing melt into one appears clearly, to mention one instance, in the Swabian custom of 'throwing the names of three shrewish women' into the wine, in order to turn it into good vinegar.

[72] Compare Nansen: *The First Crossing of Greenland*, i., p. 328; abridged edit., p. 160.

Indians and others, who dare not speak the names of places or of rivers.[73]

With reference to the soul's life after death, the Greenlanders seem to have had diverse opinions. Some, whom the missionaries call stupid and brutish people, thought that all was over at death, and that there was no life beyond the grave. Most of the Greenlanders, however, seem to have thought that even if the soul was not quite immortal, it was yet in the habit of continuing to live after leaving the body, or at any rate of coming to life again even if it had died along with the body. In that case it went either to a place under the earth and the sea or to the upper world in the sky, or rather between the sky and the earth.[74] The former place is regarded as the better of the two; it is a very good land, where, according to Hans Egede, there is 'lovely sunshine, excellent water, animals and birds in abundance.' To many it may seem strange that, unlike us, they should place their happiest region under the earth or the sea; but this, it seems to me, may easily have arisen from their having seen the heaven and the mountains reflected in the water, and believed that it was another world they saw. No doubt they have in process of time discovered that it is only a reflection, but the original belief in an under-world has maintained itself none the less. It is particularly characteristic that this under-world is placed under the water, and that there is much sunshine in it; for it must have been chiefly in the sunshine that they saw the reflection.

The other region, in the over-world, is colder; it is like the earth with its hills and valleys, and over it is arched the blue heaven. There the souls of the dead dwell in tents round a lake, and when the lake overflows it rains on earth. There are many crowberries there, and many ravens, who always settle on the heads of old women[75] and cling on to their hair; it is difficult to drive them off, and they seem to fill the place of lice here on earth. The souls of the dead can be seen up there by night, in the form of northern lights, playing football with a walrus head. On the east coast, however, it is believed that the northern lights are merely the souls of stillborn or prematurely born children, or of those who are killed after their birth. These children's souls 'take each other's hands and dance around in mazy circles. They play at ball, too, and when they see orphan children, they rush upon them and throw them to the ground. They accompany their sports with a hissing, whistling sound.'[76] Therefore, the northern lights are called *alugsukat*, which appears to mean untimely births, or children born in concealment. This notion of the Greenlanders seems to be closely related to the Indians' belief[77] that the northern lights are the dead in dancing array.

---

[73] As to the significance of the name and its mention among the different races, compare Kristoffer Nyrop's comprehensive essay, 'The Power of the Name,' in *Mindre Afhandlinger udgivne af det philologisk-historiske Samfund*, Copenhagen, 1887, pp. 119-209. See also B. Gröndahl in *Annaler for nordisk Oldkyndighed*, 1863, p. 127, &c.; Moltke Moe, in *Letterstedtske Tidsskrift*, 1879, p. 286, &c.; S. Grundtvig, *Danmarks gamle Folkeviser*, ii. p. 339, &c.; H. Spencer, *Principles of Sociology*, vi. p. 701.

[74] Compare Rink, *Aarböger for nordisk Oldkyndighed og Historie*, 1868, iii. p. 202.

[75] Compare Paul Egede, *Efterretninger om Grönland*, p. 149.

[76] Holm, *Meddelelser om Grönland*, part 10, p. 113.

[77] Communicated to me by Moltke Moe.

The Eskimos have no hell. Both the above-named regions are more or less good, and whether the soul goes to the one or to the other does not seem to depend particularly upon the man's good or evil acts.

Egede, however, asserts that to the lovely land under the earth there go only 'women who die in childbirth, men who are drowned at sea, and whale-fishers, as a reward for the evil they have suffered here on earth; all others go to the sky.'[78] It seems doubtful whether this was ever a general belief. An exactly analogous idea is to be found among ourselves. An old woman in Telemark said to Moltke Moe, speaking of her son: 'Ah, yes, he is certain enough to have gone straight to heaven; for you know it's said in God's Word that those who are drowned at sea or die in childbirth go straight away to the Kingdom of God.'[79]

From other accounts, in any case, it seems that these are not the only souls which go to the under-world. The destination of the soul may partly depend on the treatment of the body. Paul Egede says (*Efterretninger om Grönland*, p. 174) that 'it was their custom to take people who were sick unto death gently out of bed, and, laying them on the floor, to swathe them in their grave-clothes. This lowering them down from the bed probably symbolises their wish that after death they may descend beneath the earth. But if a man dies before he is taken from the bed, his soul goes upward.' On his inquiring why a dog's head was laid beside the grave, he was answered 'that it was a custom among some of their fellows to lay a dog's head beside a child when it was buried, in order that it might scent about and guide the child to the land of spirits when it came to life again, children being foolish and witless, and unable to find their own way.'[80] It seems as though Captain Holm[81] doubted the correctness of this trait (which, however, he quotes from Hans Egede), on the ground that he could discover no such poetical custom among the East Greenlanders. But in this he does not seem to be quite justified; for, on the one hand, we are scarcely entitled to doubt so definite a statement by a man like Paul Egede, who knew the Greenlanders and their language so well, while, on the other hand, we must always remember how fluctuating and changeable are religious conceptions. Analogous customs, moreover, are found among the Indians. The Aztecs killed a dog at funerals, and burned or buried it along with the body, with a cotton thread tied around its throat. Its function was to lead the deceased over the deep waters of Chiuhnahuapan on the way to the land of the dead.[82]

The journey to the beautiful region is, however, no easy matter. Egede says that there is on the way a high sharp rock, 'down which the dead must slide on their backs, wherefore the rock is bloody.' Cranz asserts that it takes the souls five

[78] See on the same subject Paul Egede, *Efterretninger om Grönland*, p. 117. According to some accounts, witches and 'wicked people' go to the over-world.

[79] Communicated by Moltke Moe. Compare also J. Flood, *Grönland*, Kristiania, 1873, p. 10, note. Similar notions are said to be current in Bavaria and in the Marquesas islands. Compare Liebrecht, in the *Academy*, iii. (1872), p. 321.

[80] P. Egede, *Efterretninger om Grönland*, p. 109. See also H. Egede, *Det gamle Grönlands nye Perlustration*, p. 84. Cranz, *Historie von Grönland*, p. 301.

[81] *Meddelelser om Grönland*, part 10, p. 106, note.

[82] Tylor, *Primitive Culture* (1873), i. p. 472.

or even more days to slide down this rock or mountain; and those luckless ones are especially to be pitied who have to make the journey in winter or in stormy weather, for then they can easily come to harm. This they call the second death, after which nothing is left of them.[83] They fear this very much, and, in order to avert it, the survivors, during the critical days, are bound to observe certain precautions. Similar legends as to the many difficulties besetting the long journey of souls to the land of the dead are to be found amongst most races.[84] It seems probable that these difficulties have arisen in order to serve as tests through which the good can pass more easily than the wicked. But since, among the Eskimos, the difficulties afford no touchstone of moral qualities, we must conclude that the legend describing them must be borrowed from others, and most probably from the Indians. The sharp rock in particular reminds us of the Indians' 'mountain ridge, which was as sharp as the sharpest knife,' along which the souls had to pass on the way to their dwelling-place, *Wanaretebe*.[85]

The Greenlanders seem generally to have attributed a soul to animals, which, like the human soul, could survive the body and journey to the regions beyond. This appears clearly enough from the bear story related in Chapter XII (see p. 206). It also appears from the custom mentioned on p. 237 of laying dogs' heads in the graves of children; for it is of course the dog's soul, dwelling in its head, which is to accompany the child. For the rest, this is a general belief among primitive peoples. The Kamtchatkans, for instance, believe that the souls of all animals, even of the smallest fly, come to life again in the under-world.

The Greenlanders know of many supernatural beings of a higher order. Among those who stand nearest to man, and are most useful to him through the medium of the angekoks, we must first name the so-called *tôrnat* (the plural of *tôrnak*). These are the angekoks' ministering spirits, who impart to them their supernatural power. They are often said to be souls of the dead, especially of grandfathers or other ancestors; but they may also be the souls of various animals, or other supernatural beings, either of human origin, like the *kivigtut*, to be hereafter mentioned, or independent spiritual essences dwelling in the sea or far inland. They may also be the souls of absent Europeans. An angekok would as a rule have several, some acting as councillors, others as helpers in danger, and others, again, as avengers and destroyers. These last were despatched by the angekok to show themselves in the form of ghosts, and thus to frighten to death those against whom the vengeance was directed.

In connection with, or superior to, the tornat, we find the *tôrnârssuk*, which is generally held to be their master, or a particularly powerful tornak. The tornarssuk was regarded as, on the whole, a benevolent power; through his tornak the angekok could get into communication with him and obtain wise counsels. But evil deeds seem often to have been attributed to him. With him, as with all the other supernatural beings, it probably depended on the angekoks whether he should

[83] This conception of a second death, or the death of the soul, is found among many races: Hindus, Tartars, Greeks, Kelts, Frenchmen, Scandinavians, Germans, &c.

[84] Tylor, *Primitive Culture*, ii. p. 44.

[85] Knortz, *Aus dem Wigwam*, Leipzig, 1880, p. 133; compare p. 142.

be beneficent or the reverse. His home lay in the under-world, in the land of the souls. As to his appearance, ideas were very vague; some holding that he had no form at all; others that he was like a bear; others, again, that he was huge and had only one arm; and some, finally, that he was no larger than a finger. As to his nature, according to Hans Egede, there was no less difference of opinion; for while some held that he was immortal, others believed that it needed very little to kill him. Thus Egede relates that during an angekok's magic operations, or while he is communing with the tornarssuk, 'no one must scratch his head, or fall asleep; for by such means they say the wizard may be killed, and even the devil [that is, the tornarssuk] himself.' Dr. Rink holds that all this is founded upon misunderstandings on the part of Egede and the other missionaries, and that, on the whole, very little was known either as to the tornarssuk's appearance or as to his nature. The heathens on the east coast, however, seem, as we shall see, to know all about him.

In this tornarssuk many have been fain to see a beneficent supreme being whom the Eskimos worship; answering, accordingly, to our God. Nevertheless he was, on the introduction of Christianity, transformed into the devil, with whom he is now synonymous. I cannot help believing that Egede and the first missionaries have had some hand in working-up this conception of him as God. They no doubt started, as many missionaries do even to this day, from the hypothesis that every people must have a conception of God or of a beneficent supreme being, and, assuming this, they probably cross-questioned the poor heathen so long about their tornarssuk, that they at last came to answer just what their questioners desired. Moreover, they doubtless talked so much of their good and almighty God that the heathen priests, in order not to be beaten, began to maintain that they, too, had such a God to help them. That the tornarssuk was not so great a spirit as is commonly stated seems evident from Captain Holm's account of the heathen East Greenlanders' belief. Their tornarssuk is a much less imposing creature, who dwells in the sea, and whom many people, both angekoks and others, can see and have seen. They therefore describe him with great exactitude, and have even numerous representations of him. He is long, like a large seal, but fatter than a seal, and has, among other things, long tentacles. Holm, judging from their descriptions, has come to the heretical opinion that he must be an ordinary cuttle-fish. He devours the souls of those whom he can capture, and is often quite red with blood. One must admit that if this creature is descended from our innate conception of God, he has deplorably degenerated. Moreover, he is not, on the east coast, one and indivisible; but every angekok, according to Holm, has his tornarssuk. He has also a coadjutor, *aperketek*, a black animal as much as two ells in length, and with great 'knife-tongs in his head.' Holm says expressly that he could discover no trace of a conception of the tornarssuk as the master of the tornak; and we are thus forced to subtract a little from the power and importance attributed to this spirit by former authors.[86]

It seems to me clear that this belief in the tornarssuk, no less than in the tornat,

____

[86] It is interesting to note that the Alaska Eskimos seem to believe in a being similar to this tornarssuk of the east coast of Greenland, with long tentacles, &c. See Holm: *Meddelelser om Grönland*, part 10, p. 115, note 1.

must be traced to a belief in the spirits or ghosts of ancestors. We may possibly find evidence of this in the words themselves. It seems probable that *tôrnak* may have been the same word as *tarnik* or *tarne* (that is, soul), which again resembles *tarrak* (shadow—compare p. 226). We find some support for this theory in the fact that *tôrnak* appears on the east coast in the form of *tartok* or *tartak*, which is the same word as *tarrak*.[87] Thus it appears to me probable that all these words were originally one and the same, signifying shadow, reflection, or soul, and also designating the souls of the dead. *Tôrnârssuk*, again, is certainly a derivative of *tôrnak*, having probably been in its origin the same as *tôrnârssuak*, that is to say, 'the big, or the bad and horrible, tornak.' This implies that he was originally a particularly powerful tornak, which, among some tribes, has gradually obtained a sort of dominion over the other tornat or souls of the dead.

That these souls should have become the subject of peculiar superstitions is readily comprehensible when we observe the fear with which they still regard the dead, and still more, of course, their spectres. These *gengangere* are often visible and may be very dangerous, though sometimes, too, they are tolerably well-disposed. The most amiable way in which they can manifest themselves is in a whistling sound, or a singing in people's ears. In the latter case they are begging for food, and to such a request a Greenlander will reply: 'Help yourself'—meaning 'from my stores.'[88] That the ghost is not always hostile appears from what Niels Egede[89] relates of a boy at Godthaab who, playing one day with several others in the neighbourhood of his mother's grave, suddenly saw a shape rising up from it. He and the others took to their heels, but the ghost ran after them, caught her son, 'embraced him, kissed him, and said, "Do not be frightened of me; I am your mother, and love you"';' with more to the same effect.

Their customs at the death and burial of their friends show how much they fear the dead, and especially their souls or ghosts. The dying are often dressed in their grave-clothes—that is to say, in their best garments—a little while before death. The legs, too, are often bent together, so that the feet come up under the back, and in this position they are sewed or swathed in skins. The object is, no doubt, that they may take up less space and need a smaller grave; and it is done during their life in order that the survivors may have to handle their corpses as little as possible. This dread of touching a dead body goes so far (as before-mentioned on page 137) that they will not help a man in danger—for example, a kaiak-man who is drowning—when they believe that he is at the point of death.

When they are finally dead, they are taken, if it be in a house, out through the window; if in a tent, through an opening cut in the skins of the back wall.[90]

---

[87] *Tartok* means properly 'dark.' Among the Eskimos of Southern Alaska, the same word, *taituk*, means 'mist.' In East Greenland *târtek* means 'black.' (Compare Rink: *Meddelelser om Grönland*, part 11, p. 152.)

[88] Rink: *Tales and Traditions of the Eskimo*, p. 44. In Scotland a singing in the ears is called 'the dead-bell,' and portends the death of a friend. Hogg: *Mountain Bard*, 3rd ed. p. 31.

[89] *Tredie Continuation, &c.*, p. 74.

[90] Holm, however, tells us (*Meddelelser om Grönland*, part 10, p. 105), that on the east

This corresponds remarkably with the common custom in our own country of carrying a body out through an opening in the wall made for the purpose.[91] The reason is, no doubt, the same in both cases—namely, that these openings can be entirely closed again, so that the spectre or soul cannot re-enter, as it might if the body were carried out by way of the passage or the door. It is not improbable that the Greenlanders may have borrowed the habit from the ancient Norwegian or Icelandic settlers in Greenland. It is mentioned in several sagas as having been the custom of the heathen Icelanders. In the Eyrbyggja Saga[92] it is said: 'Then he [Arnkel] let break down the wall behind him [the body of Thorolf], and brought him out thereby.' The clothes and other possessions of the deceased are also at once thrown out, that they may not make the survivors unclean. This recalls our death-bed burning, which is also a widespread custom among our kindred races in Europe.[93]

The survivors also carry their own possessions out of the house, that the smell of death may pass away from them. They are either brought in again at evening, or, as on the east coast, are left lying out for several days. The relatives of the dead man, on the east coast, go so far as to leave off wearing their old clothes, which they throw away.[94]

When the body is carried out, a woman sets fire to a piece of wood, and waves it backwards and forwards, saying: 'There is nothing more to be had here.' This is, no doubt, done with a view to showing the soul that everything belonging to it has been thrown out.

Bodies are either buried in the earth or thrown into the sea (if one of the dead man's ancestors has perished in a kaiak (?)). The possessions of the deceased—such as his kaiak, weapons, and clothes; or, in the case of a woman, her sewing materials, crooked knife, &c.—are laid on or beside the grave, or, if the body is thrown into the sea, they are laid somewhere upon the beach. This seems to be partly due to their fear of a dead person's property and unwillingness to use it; partly, too, as Hans Egede says, to the fact that the sight of these things and the consequent recollection of the dear departed would be apt to set them crying, and 'if they cry too much over the departed they believe that it makes him cold.'[95] This idea reminds one strongly of the second song of Helge Hundingsbane, where his widow Sigrun meets him wet and frozen, and wrapped in a cloud of hoar

---

coast the body is sometimes dragged out through the house-passage by means of a thong looped around the legs. In such cases, I take it, the dread of touching the body must have conquered the dread of taking it out through the passage, for if it is taken through the window it must be lifted and handled. By dragging it with the feet foremost and pointing outwards they probably think to hinder the soul from effecting a re-entrance.

[91] From information given me by Moltke Moe. Compare also Liebrecht, *Zur Volkskunde*, p. 372.

[92] Morris and Magnússon, *The Saga Library*, vol ii. 'The Ere-Dwellers,' p. 88.

[93] See Moltke Moe's paper in the *Norske Universitets-og Skoleannaler*, 1880, and the works there cited.

[94] Holm, *Meddelelser om Grönland*, part 10, p. 107.

[95] Hans Egede, *Det gamle Grönlands nye Perlustration*, p. 83.

frost, by reason of her weeping over him. ('Helge swims in the dew of sorrow.'[96]) Compare also the well-known Swedish-Danish folk-song of 'Aage and Else,' in which we read:

> 'For every time that in thy breast
> Thy heart is glad and light,
> Then all within my coffin seems
> With rose-leaves decked and dight.
>
> For every time that in thy breast
> Thy heart is sad and sore,
> Then all within my coffin seems
> To swim in red, red gore.'

But, beyond this, it was doubtless the belief of the Greenlanders that the deceased had need of his implements, partly for earthly excursions from the grave, partly also in the other world. They saw, indeed, that the implements rotted, but that only meant that their souls followed the soul of the deceased. Those who carry the body out, or have touched it or anything belonging to it, are for some time unclean, and must refrain from certain foods and occupations, which the angekoks prescribe; indeed, all those who live in the same house must observe the like precautions, partly to avoid injury to themselves, partly in order to place no hindrance in the way of the departed soul on its journey to the other world.

They must weep and mourn for a stated time over the deceased; and if they meet acquaintances or relatives whom they have not seen since the death took place, they must, even if it be a long while after, begin to weep and howl as soon as the newcomer enters the house. Such scenes of lamentation must often be exceedingly ludicrous, and are, in fact, the merest comedy, ending in a consolatory banquet. They have also many other mourning customs, which exercise a tolerably powerful influence upon their lives. Those, for example, who have carried out a body must do no work in iron for several years. Moreover, we must remember the before-mentioned dread of uttering the name of the deceased.

The great object of all this is no doubt, as the East Greenlanders said to Holm, 'to keep the dead from being angry;' whence we see what a powerful influence over this life they attribute to the departed. There is, therefore, nothing improbable in the theory that the whole belief in the tornat and tornarssuk may have developed from this fear. In process of time, however, other kinds of superstition have doubtless come to play a part in the matter.

The Greenlanders believe in a whole host of other supernatural beings. Of these I can only mention a few.

Marine animals are under the sway of a gigantic woman whom some call 'the nameless one,' others *Arnarkuagssâk*, which simply means 'the old woman.'

Her dwelling is under the sea, where she sits beside a lamp under which, as under all Greenland lamps, there is a saucer or stand to catch the dripping train-oil. In this saucer whole flocks of sea-birds are swimming, and out of it proceed

[96] See P. A. Gödecke's translation of the *Edda*, p. 170, and notes on p. 335.

all the sea animals, such as the seal, the walrus, and the narwhal. When certain impurities gather in her hair, she keeps the sea animals away from the coasts, or they remain away of their own accord, attracted by the impurities; and it is then the angekok's difficult duty to seek her out and appease or comb her. The way to her abode is perilous, and the angekok must have his tornak with him. First he passes through the lovely land of spirits in the under-world; then he comes to a great abyss, which he can cross only (by the help of the tornak) on a large wheel as smooth as ice, and whirling rapidly. Then he passes a boiling cauldron with live seals in it; then either through a dangerous picket of angry seals who stand erect and bite on every side, or else past a huge dog which stands outside the woman's house, and gives warning when a great angekok approaches. This dog takes only a few winks of sleep every now and then, and one must be ready to seize the opportunity; but this only the highest angekoks can manage. Here, again, the tornak must take the angekok by the hand; the entrance is wide enough, but the further way is narrow as a thread or the edge of a knife, and passes over a horrible abyss. At last they enter the house where the woman is sitting. She is said to have a hand as large as the tail-fin of a whale, and if she strikes you with it there is an end of you. According to some accounts, she tears her hair and perspires with fury over such a visit, so that the angekok, aided by his tornak, must fight with her in order to get her hair cleaned or combed; while others hold that she is accessible to persuasions and appeals. His task achieved, the return journey is comparatively easy for the angekok.[97] This myth reminds us strongly of the visits to the under-world or Hades which play so prominent a part in European legends, for example, in those of Dionysos, Orpheus, Heracles, and others (compare also Dante), and to which we have a parallel in our own mythology in Hermod's ride to Hel to bring back Balder. Similar legends are also found, however, among the Indians. From information given me by Moltke Moe, it seems scarcely doubtful that this Eskimo conception is coloured by, or even borrowed from, European legends. The smooth wheel,[98] for example, and the bridge which is narrow as a thread or a knife-edge, reappear, sometimes in the same words, in mediæval legends of journeys to the under world. In an old ballad of the north of England mention is made of 'the bridge of dread no wider than a thread.' Tundal sees in purgatory a narrow bridge over a horribly deep, dark, and malodorous valley, and so forth. The oldest appearance in legendary literature of this hell-bridge is in Pope Gregory the Great's Dialogues, dating from the year 594 (lib. iv. cap. 36).[99] But these mediæval conceptions, in their turn, are indubitably coloured by Oriental traditions. The Jews speak of the thread-like hell-bridge, and the Mahommedans believe that in the middle of hell all souls must pass over a bridge narrower than a hair, sharper than

---

[97] Paul Egede, *Continuation af Relationerne,* &c., p. 45; Hans Egede, *Grönlands nye Perlustration,* p. 118; Rink, *Tales and Traditions of the Eskimo,* pp. 40, 466.

[98] The Dakota Indians relate that on the way to Wanaratebe there is a wheel which rolls with frightful velocity along the bottom of the abyss below the mountain ridge mentioned on p. 239. To this wheel are bound those who have treated their parents despitefully. See Liebrecht, *Gervasius Otia Imperialia* (1856), p. 91, note.

[99] Reference communicated by Moltke Moe.

a sword, and darker than night.[100] According to the Avesta, the souls of the old Parsees, on the third night after death, had to cross the 'high Hara'—a mountain which surrounds the earth and reaches right to heaven—in order to arrive at the Tsjinvat-bridge which is guarded by two dogs. In the Pehlevi writings, this bridge is said to widen out to nearly a parasang when the souls of the pious pass over it, but it narrows in before the ungodly until they topple down into hell, which lies right under.[101]

An analogous conception is found (compare Sophus Bugge, *op. cit.*) in the old folk-song 'Draumekvædi,' as to the Gjallar-bridge on the way to the land of the dead. It hangs high in air so that one grows dizzy upon it ('Gjallarbrui, hon henge saa högt i vinde'), and in some variants of the song it is expressly stated to be narrow, whilst in others it is said to be 'both steep and broad.' In the Eddas we are told that Hermod, on the way to Hel, rode over the Gjallar-bridge, which was roofed with shining gold, and which thundered under his horse's hoofs not less than if five squadrons of dead men (that is to say 250) had been passing over it.

It seems probable that this belief of the Greenlanders in a narrow bridge or pass must be coloured by these European, or partly Oriental, conceptions, imparted to them by the ancient Scandinavians. At the same time there may also be something more original at the root of it. Thus we find among the Indians the notion of a snake-bridge, or a tree trunk swinging in the air, which leads over the river of the dead to the city of the dead.[102]

The notion of the huge dog who guards the entrance to the woman's house reminds us strongly of Hel's terrible dog Garm, with the bloody breast, who barks before the Gnipa-cave. For the rest, this notion of the dog in the other world is a common one. Among the Hindoos, two dogs watch the path to the abode of Jama,[103] and among the old Parsees, two dogs guard the Tsjinvat-bridge (see last page). The Indians station a huge and furious dog at the other end of the above-mentioned snake bridge.[104]

In European folk-tales, and especially in those of Scandinavia, we often meet with an old woman who bears rule over animals. She likes to be called 'Mother,' is fond of being scratched or washed, and is glad to get hold of a pair of shoes, a piece of tobacco, or the like. If the Ash-Lad meets her and does her any such service, she requites him with a 'motherly turn,' making her animals help him or giving him gifts. But besides this common theme which reappears in a majority of

[100] See Sophus Bugge, *Mythologiske Oplysninger til Draumekvædi*, in *Norsk Tidsskrift for Videnskab og Literatur*, 1854-55, p. 108-111; Grimm, *Mythologie*, p. 794; Liebrecht, *Gervasius Otia Imperialia*, p. 90. Compare also H. Hübschmann, *Die parsische Lehre vom Jenseits und jüngsten Gericht*, in *Jahrbücher für protestantische Theologie*, v. (Leipzig, 1879), p. 242.

[101] Compare H. Hübschmann, *op. cit.*, pp. 216, 218, 220, 222.

[102] Tylor, *Primitive Culture*, ii. 50. Compare, too, the Indians' conception of a mountain ridge as sharp as the sharpest knife (see p. 239). It is of course possible that the Indians may have got this idea from the Eskimos, or more probably, perhaps, from the Europeans after the discovery of America.

[103] Sophus Bugge, *op. cit.*, p. 114.

[104] Tylor, *op. cit.*, p. 50. Compare Knortz, *Aus dem Wigwam*, p. 142.

our folk-tales, we can also point to a particular story which is founded on similar conceptions. The Ash-Lad comes to the ogress with a whole company of animals, the stoat, the tree-bear (the squirrel), the hare, the fox, the wolf and the bear, to try to rescue his sister whom she has carried off. While he is eating, the ogress cries 'Scratch me! scratch me!' 'You must wait till I've finished,' says the boy; but his sister warns him that if he does not do it at once the ogress will tear him to pieces. Then he makes the animals scratch her, one after the other; but none of them content her until it comes to the turn of the bear, who claws her till her itch departs. In several variants, three brothers make the attempt one after the other, and she kills the first two of them.[105] Even at first sight this Scandinavian group of stories seems suspiciously like the Greenland legends, the scratching and washing especially reminding us strongly of the hair-combing; but when we also find that Arnarkuagssak is unknown to the Alaskan Eskimos, the connection seems to be clear. According to one Greenland legend she was the daughter of a powerful angekok who, being overtaken by a storm, threw her out of the woman-boat to save himself. She clung on to the gunwale, whereupon he, one by one, cut off her fingers and her hands. These were transformed into seals and whales, over which she obtained dominion; and when she sank to the bottom, she took up her abode there for good. Among the Eskimos of Baffin's Land the same legend is told of a woman named *Sedna*, who has, however, become a different being from Arnarkuagssak. The latter seems to be unknown on the Mackenzie river. 'If it should appear,' says Dr. Rink, 'that the Greenland myth is not known in Alaska either, we must conclude that it was invented during the course of the emigration to Greenland.'[106] It seems more natural, however, to conjecture, as I have done above, that it descends from the old Scandinavians.

On the whole, then, it seems probable that this Greenland divinity was originally a character in old Norwegian folk-lore, and that the description of the journey to her abode is descended from, or at least coloured by, European myths and legends, imported by the old Scandinavian settlers; but more original Eskimo elements may also be mixed up in it, having their origin in the west, and resembling the myths of the Indians.

The souls who go to the over-world have to pass the abode of a strange woman who dwells at the top of a high mountain. She is called *Erdlaversissok* (*i.e.* the disemboweller), and her properties are a trough and a bloody knife. She beats upon a drum, dances with her own shadow, and says nothing but 'My buttocks, &c.,' or else sings 'Ya, ha, ha, ha!' When she turns her back she displays huge hindquarters, from which dangles a lean sea-scorpion; and when she turns sideways her mouth is twisted utterly askew, so that her face becomes horizontally oblong. When she bends forwards she can lick her own hindquarters, and when she bends

[105] Communicated by Moltke Moe, from his unpublished collection of folk-tales. See also a tale reported from Flatdal in *Fedraheimen*, 1877, No. 18; a Hardanger tale (watered down) in Haukenæs's *Natur, Folkeliv og Folketro i Hardanger*, ii., 233. Danish variants in Kl. Berntsen, *Folke-Æventyr*, I. (Odense, 1873) p. 116; Et. Kristensen, *Jyska Folkeminder*, v. 271.

[106] Rink, *Meddelelser om Grönland*, part 11, p. 17. Compare Boas, *Petermann's Mittheilungen*, 1887, p. 303; Rink and Boas, 'Eskimo Tales and Songs,' in *Journal of American Folk-Lore*, 1889 (?), p. 127.

We may distinguish a third element in the people who originally dwelt upon this flat earth, in its displeasure with whom the Power above caused the earth to split and the water to rush forth. It seems scarcely doubtful that this conception is due to a direct intermixture of the Christian or Jewish legend of the Deluge, which might, of course, have passed from the west coast up along the east coast. Possibly, however, the notion of the flood may have been supplemented by touches from a very widespread legend in Europe, and especially in Scandinavia, as to how the subterranean or invisible people (*huldre-folk*) came into existence. The Lord one day paid a visit to Eve as she was busy washing her children. All those who were not yet washed she hurriedly hid in cellars and corners and under big vessels, and presented the others to the visitor. The Lord asked if these were all, and she answered 'Yes'; whereupon He replied, 'Then those which are "dulde" (hidden) shall remain "hulde" (concealed, invisible).' And from them the *huldre-folk* are sprung.[118] Be this as it may, the ignerssuit cannot but remind us of the subterranean people in our Scandinavian folk-lore.

Finally we have as a fourth element the glacier, which must belong exclusively to Greenland itself.[119]

Among other supernatural beings may be mentioned the different sorts of inland-folk who live in the interior of the country or upon the ice-fields. Some of these are called *tornit* (the plural of *tunek*) or *inorutsit*, or, upon the east coast, *timersit*. They are of human aspect, but of huge stature. Some say they are 4 metres (13 feet) in height, and others that they are as tall as a woman-boat is long, that is to say at least 10 metres (more than 32 feet). Their souls alone are as big as ordinary people. They live by hunting both land and sea animals. They can run exceedingly fast. On the sea they do not use kaiaks, but sit in the water 'with the fog for their kaiak.'[120] They can catch seals from the land (in great traps), and they can carry two huge saddlebacks or bladder-noses inland with them in a seal-skin bag upon their shoulders. As a rule they stand on a hostile footing towards men, but they are also open to friendly intercourse, and will sometimes even exchange wives with them.

Another class of inland-folk are the *igaligdlit* (the plural of *igalilik*), who go about with a whole kitchen on their backs. The pot alone is so huge that they can

[118] Communicated by Moltke Moe. Others relate that it was the ugly children whom Eve concealed, or that she was ashamed of having so many. (See Faye, *Norske Folkesagn*, 2nd ed. p. xxv.; Söegaard, *Fra Fjeldbygderne*, p. 102; *Dölen, 1862* (III.) No. 17; Storaker and Fuglestedt, *Folkesagn fra Lister og Mandals Amt*, p. 51; Finn Magnusen, *Eddalæren*, iii. p. 329; Grimm, *Deutsche Mythologie*, 4th ed. iii. 163, &c.) The legend is originally Jewish, and may be traced to the Rabbis; see, for example, Liebrecht on *Gervasius Tilberiensis Otia Imperialia*, p. 70.

[119] Paul Egede gives a somewhat different account of the ignerssuit's fall from human estate. They 'formerly dwelt upon earth, until the time of the great flood, which caused the earth to capsize, so that what had formerly been uppermost was now below.'—*Continuation af Relationerne*, p. 96.

[120] This suggests our Norwegian 'draug' which sails in a half boat (*i.e.* a boat split in two longitudinally); and it does not seem impossible that we may here trace the influence of the old Scandinavian settlers.

boil an entire seal in it; and it boils even as they carry it about. A third class are the *erkigdlit* (the plural of *erkilek*), who, according to some, are like men above and dogs below, but according to others have dogs' heads or dogs' noses. They are expert archers, and carry their arrows in quivers on their backs.[121] They are hostile to men. I may also mention the *isserkat* (the plural of *isserak*), who 'blink lengthwise'—which probably means that their eye-holes are perpendicular instead of horizontal.

As Rink has shown, there can be very little doubt that these inland-folk, who all play a prominent part in the Eskimo legends, were originally different races of Indians with whom the forefathers of the Greenlanders, while they still dwelt on the north coast of America, had dealings, sometimes amicable, but generally hostile. They brought with them to Greenland stories of these adventures, and they still laid the scene in the interior of the country, where the Indians in process of time became entirely mythical beings. The word *tunek* seems simply to mean Indian, and is so used to this day by the Eskimos of Labrador. By the Eskimo tribes on the west coast of Hudson's Bay and further west the word *erkigdlit* is applied to the Indians of the interior. The description of the tornit as large and swift applies well to the Indians, who are taller than the Eskimos, and have the upper hand of them by land. The fact that the erkigdlit are clever with the bow and carry their arrows in quivers—a custom not in use among the Greenlanders—also suggests the Indians. So, too, do the dogs' legs or dogs' faces attributed to them, these having no doubt arisen from the Indians' own belief that they are descended from a dog (see p. 271).[122] The isserkat, 'those who blink lengthwise,' may originally have been Indian races with remarkably oblique or otherwise peculiar eyes; such tribes are described by travellers. Here, then, we have supernatural or mythical beings who may be assumed to be of historical origin. The legends of wars with them have also, no doubt, a certain historical foundation. In the same way, probably, did the classical peoples come in contact with the mythical races of their legends.[123]

The *kivitut* (the plural of *kivitok*) are beings of a peculiar nature. They have at one time been ordinary men, who for some reason or other, often quite insignificant, have fallen out with their families or their companions, or have felt aggrieved by them, and have therefore turned their backs upon their fellows and fled to the mountains or into the interior. Here they henceforth live alone, feeding upon animals which they kill without ordinary weapons, simply by throwing stones at them, an art in which they become very skilful. While the kivitok has only been a short time away, it is still open to him to return to his fellows; but if he does not within a certain number of days obey the voice of his homeward longing, he loses the power of resuming his place among men. Some hold that a year is the allotted

---

[121] Paul Egede: *Efterretninger om Grönland*, p. 172.

[122] Legends of dog-men being widely spread over the world (they are found, for instance, among the Greeks), it is possible that the Eskimos may have received them from some other quarter, and applied them to the Indians, who, they knew, claimed descent from a dog.

[123] Compare Tobler: 'Ueber sagenhafte Völker des Altertums,' &c., in *Zeitschrift der Völkerpsychologie*, vol. xviii. (1888), p. 225.

period. He now acquires supernatural faculties; he becomes so swift of foot that he can leap from one mountain peak to another, he can catch reindeer without weapons, and whatever he aims at he hits. He grows to a great size, clothes himself in reindeer-skins, and, according to some, his face turns black and his hair white. Furthermore, he becomes omniscient or clairvoyant; he can hear the speech of men from any distance, and comes to understand the language of the animals. But he pays for all this in his inability to die, and he is always mournful, shedding tears of longing for humankind to which he can never return. He can, however, when opportunity offers, especially at night, make his way into houses or store-rooms to pick up something to eat, or perhaps a little tobacco. Those who have wronged him are always in danger of his vengeance.

The remarkable feature of this belief is that it probably has a certain foundation in fact. Suicide is almost unknown in Greenland, except in the case of a few old or hopelessly infirm people, who, finding themselves at death's door, sometimes throw themselves over a precipice into the sea (compare p. 170) in order to put an end to their sufferings and assure themselves burial. On the other hand, it now and then happens that someone or other, wounded, perhaps, by a single word from one of his kinsfolk, runs away to the mountains, and is lost for several days at least. I myself know Greenlanders who have done this; and authentic examples are given of people who have lived for years as kivitoks. About twenty-five years ago, on the island of Akugdlek in North Greenland, a cave was found which bore evidence of having been a human habitation for a considerable time. A well-trodden path led up to it, and within it was a hearth, a hole in the ground which had served as a store-room, a soft bed of moss, remains of dried fish, edible roots, &c. A few paces away, there was found a smaller cave with stones piled up against its mouth. In this the kivitok had buried himself when he found death approaching. There he lay, still in his seal-skin jacket; he had himself, from within, closed up the entrance to the sepulchre with a stone. The Greenlanders recognised him, and concluded that he must have lived there as a kivitok for two or three years. His reason for turning his back upon mankind is said to have been that, as a bad hunter, he was looked down upon and slighted by his kinsfolk; and, after the death of his little son, life became so hard for him that he fled.[124]

As Moltke Moe has pointed out to me, there is a remarkable resemblance between these kivitut and the *utilegumenn,* 'out-liers' so common in the Icelandic popular legends—criminals, that is to say, who have fled to the mountains and live in the wilderness far from mankind. The great part which these 'out-liers' play in the popular fantasy, and the mystic fear with which they are regarded, has caused them, from a very early period, to be in great measure confounded in common belief with trolls, huldre-folk, and other legendary creatures, in whose supernatural faculties they partake. They can see into the future, they know what is happening in distant places, they can conjure up mists and lead the traveller astray, and they possess superhuman strength.[125] Like the kivitok, they seek the

---

[124] See Hammer, *Meddelelser om Grönland,* part 8, p. 22; E. Skram in *Tilskueren,* October, 1885, p. 735. As to kivitut, see also Rink, *Tales and Traditions of the Eskimo.*

[125] See Arnasen, *Íslenzktar Þjóðsögur,* ii. 160-304, translation by Powell and Magnús-

abodes of men in order to pick up something to eat; they steal sheep, food, and clothes from the people of the settlements. The most characteristic feature of both the Greenland and the Iceland legends is that men, by being cut off from society, obtain supernatural power. The coincidence becomes still more striking when we observe that both in Greenland and in Iceland these legends form an *essential* part of living popular tradition and belief. Among other races (with the partial exception of Norwegians of the west coast, and especially of Nordland) similar ideas are scarcely to be found at all. The conclusion, then, is almost inevitable, that the belief in the kivitok is derived from the ancient Scandinavians, or rather from the Icelanders in particular.

I have still to mention, among the remarkable beings known to the Greenlanders, the *igdlokok*, who is like half a human being, with half a head, one eye, one arm, and one leg. Precisely similar beings are also to be found among the Greeks, the Mohammedans, the Zulus, and the Indians.[126]

As to the creation of the world, the Greenlanders had no definite opinion. The earth and the universe must either have come into existence of their own accord, or must have existed from all time and be destined so to endure.

Nor had they any clear idea as to the creation of man, or of the Eskimo race itself. Some were of opinion that the first man grew up out of the ground and mated with a mound of earth. It brought forth a girl, whom he took to wife.[127] This notion of growing up from the ground is quite common, occurring in Scandinavia and Iceland,[128] among other places. We say: 'He who strikes the earth with a stick beats his mother; he who strikes a stone beats his father'—an idea which closely corresponds with the Eskimo conception, in which, no doubt, the man should properly be represented as rising from a rock.

As to the origin of us Europeans, they have a legend which is not altogether flattering to our vanity. An Eskimo woman, with whom no husband would remain for any time, at last took a dog to mate, and was brought to bed of a mingled litter of human children and puppies. The puppies she placed on an old shoesole and pushed them out to sea, saying, 'Be off with you and become *kavdlunaks*' (*i.e.* Europeans). Therefore it is, say the Eskimos, that the kavdlunaks always live on the sea, and that their ships are shaped like a Greenland shoe, round before and behind. The human children she placed upon willow-leaves and despatched them in the opposite direction, so that they became inland-folk or Indians (*erkiligdlit* or *tornit*).[129] Precisely similar legends are to be found among the Eskimos of Baf-

son (London, 1866), pp. cxlvi, and 101-231. Maurer *Isländische Volkssagen*, p. 240; Carl Andersen, *Islandske Folkesagn*, 2nd ed., p. 258.

[126] P. Egede, *Efterretninger om Grönland*, p. 172; Tylor, *Primitive Culture*, i. 391; Tobler, *op. cit.*, p. 238; Liebrecht in *The Academy*, iii. (1872), 321.

[127] P. Egede, *Continuation af Relationerne*, p. 97; H. Egede, *Grönlands Perlustration*, p. 117.

[128] Compare Liebrecht, *Zur Volkskunde*, p. 332, and the authorities there cited. See also Moltke Moe in *Letterstedtske Tidsskrift*, 1879, pp. 277-281.

[129] H. Egede, *Grönlands Perlustration*, p. 117; P. Egede, *Continuation af Relationerne*, p. 47; Rink, *Tales and Traditions of the Eskimo*, p. 471; *Meddelelser om Grönland*, part 10, pp. 290,

finsland,[130] and also on the north coast of Alaska; though there they refer to the Indians alone, not to the Europeans. Analogous myths of descent from dogs (or wolves, or bears) occur among many races, Aryan as well as Mongolian or American.[131] They lie at the root of the mythology of many Indian tribes, who hold that the first woman took a dog to mate, and that they themselves are descended from this connection. It seems to me evident that the Eskimos have taken their legend from this source, and that they originally applied it to the Indians alone. When, subsequently, they fell in with another strange race (the Europeans), they extended it so as to account for them also. It is noteworthy that the shoe which turns into a ship occurs in the Baffinsland versions as well.

The Eskimos, according to some authorities, trace the origin of death to a woman who once said: 'Let people gradually die, or else there will be no room for them in the world.' Others believe that two of the first human beings quarrelled, the one saying 'Let there be day and night and let men die,' the other 'Let there be night alone, and let men live for ever;' and after a long quarrel the former gained the victory. Others, again, hold that there was a race between a snake and a louse as to which should first reach mankind; if the snake arrived first they should live for ever, if the louse arrived first they must die. The snake got a long start, but fell over a high precipice by the way, and had to make a long detour, so that the louse won the race and brought death with it.[132] These myths, by their very meaninglessness and incoherence, seem to show that they come from elsewhere, and are fragments of older beliefs whose original point and meaning is forgotten. If we look around in the world, we shall find remarkable analogies among the most distant races. The second myth (that of the quarrel) reappears in the Fiji Islands, where the moon wrangles with a rat, maintaining that men ought to die and come to life again as she herself does; while the rat maintains that they ought rather to die like rats—and he gets the best of it. Among the Indians it is two wolf-brothers, ancestors of the race, who quarrel. The younger says: 'When a man dies, let him come back the following day so that his friends may rejoice.' 'No,' says the elder, 'let the dead never return.' Then the younger kills the son of the elder, and that is the beginning of death.[133]

We find remarkable analogues in South Africa to the myth of the snake and the louse. On the Gold Coast, among the Zulus, and elsewhere, it is related that the first great Being sent an animal (a chameleon) to mankind with the message that they were to live and never die. But then the Being changed his mind, and sent after it another animal (the fleet-footed salamander) with the message that

342.

[130] Rink and Boas, *Journal of American Folklore* (1888?) p. 124.

[131] F. Liebrecht, *Zur Volkskunde*, 1879, pp. 17-25; J.C. Müller, *Geschichte der americanischen Urreligionen*, pp. 134, 65.

[132] P. Egede, *Continuation af Relationerne*, pp. 32, 80; *Efterretninger om Grönland*, pp. 127, 106. H. Egede, *Grönlands Perlustration*, p. 117.

[133] Tylor, *Primitive Culture*, i. 355; A. Lang, *La Mythologie* (Paris, 1886), pp. 204, 206; Smithsonian Institute, *Annual Report of the Bureau of Ethnology*, 1879-80, p. 45. The choice between day and night in the Greenland form of the myth may possibly be borrowed, directly or indirectly, from the biblical cosmogony.

they were to die; and as the latter arrived first, so it was. There are several forms of this myth. Among the Hottentots it was the moon who sent the message to mankind: 'You, like me, shall die and come to life again.' But the hare heard this, and ran ahead and said: 'You, like me, shall die and never come to life again.'[134] This myth, again, is remarkably similar to the Fiji legend quoted above; and thus we have a bridge between the second and third Greenland myth, which must accordingly be taken to be two variants of one original—an exceedingly ancient one, since it has spread so far.

The Eskimos trace to their fellow-countrymen the origin of almost everything in external nature. It was an old man hewing chips from a tree that brought into being the fishes and other marine animals. He rubbed the chips between his legs ('sudore testiculorum') and threw them into the water, upon which they turned into fishes. The Greenland shark, however, is of different origin: 'One day a woman was washing her hair in urine. A gust of wind carried away the cloth with which she was drying her hair, and it became a shark; wherefore the flesh of this fish still smells of urine.'[135]

The heavenly bodies were once ordinary Eskimos, living upon the earth, who, for one reason or another, have been translated to the skies. The sun was a fair woman, and the moon her brother, and they lived in the same house. She was visited every night by a man, but could not tell who it was. In order to find out, she blackened her hands with lamp-soot, and rubbed them upon his back. When the morning came, it turned out to be her brother, for his white reindeer-skin was all smudged; and hence come the spots on the moon. The sun seized a crooked knife, cut off one of her breasts, and threw it to him, crying: 'Since my whole body tastes so good to you, eat this.' Then she lighted a piece of lamp-moss and rushed out; the moon did likewise and ran after her, but his moss went out, and that is why he looks like a live cinder. He chased her up into the sky, and there they still are.[136] The moon's dwelling lies close to the road by which souls have to pass to the over-world; and in it is a room for his sister the sun. This myth seems to have come to the Eskimos from the westward. Among the North American Indians the sun and moon are brother and sister, and even so far away as among the Indians of the Amazon district we find the same myth, only that there the moon is a woman who visits her brother the sun in the darkness. He discovers her criminal passion by drawing his blackened hand over her face. (Compare also the myths from Australia and the Himalayas on the following page.) Among the Incas of Peru,

[134] Christaller in *Zeitschrift für afrikanischen Sprachen*, I. 1887-88, pp. 49-62. Compare also Bleek, *Reineke Fuchs in Afrika* (Weimar, 1870): Tylor, *op. cit.*, p. 355; A. Lang, *op. cit.*, p. 203.

[135] Hans Egede, *Grönlands Perlustration*, p. 117; P. Egede, *Continuation af Relationerne*, pp. 20, 60. As to washing in urine (see p. 29), I may remark that it seems to have been a custom of untold antiquity. We find allusions to it even in the sacred writings of the Parsees. Thus it is said (*Vendidad*, 8, 13) that corpse-bearers shall wash themselves with urine 'not of men or women, but of small animals or beasts of draught.'

[136] P. Egede, *Continuation af Relationerne*, p. 16; H. Egede, *Grönlands Perlustration*, p. 121; Rink, *Tales and Traditions of the Eskimo*, p. 236; Holm, *Meddelelser om Grönland*, part 10, p. 268.

the sun and moon were at the same time brother and sister and man and wife. (Compare also the Egyptians' Isis and Osiris.)[137] It is remarkable that among the Greenlanders the sun is conceived as being beautiful in front, but a naked skeleton behind.[138] This so strongly suggests our beautiful 'huldre,' who are hollow when seen from behind, that it seems as though the idea must be a European and especially a Scandinavian one, imported into Greenland by the old Norse settlers. According to the East Greenlanders, the reason why the sun has nothing but bare bones behind is that, when she is at her lowest point, that is to say on the shortest day, people cut her back with knives in order to make her rise again. The flesh is thus cut away, and only the bones remain.[139]

The moon has not yet turned over a new leaf, but still pays frequent visits to the earth in search of amorous adventures. Therefore, it behoves women to beware of him, not to go out alone in the moonlight, not to stand looking at his orb, and so forth. This erotic proclivity of the moon's seems to be of very ancient date. In Australia he is a tom-cat who, on account of an intrigue with the wife of another, was driven forth to wander for ever. Among the Khasias of the Himalayas, the moon every month commits the unpardonable sin of falling in love with his mother-in-law, who throws ashes in his face, thus causing the spots upon it.[140] According to a Slavonic legend, the moon was the sun's husband, who, on account of infidelity with the morning star, was cleft in twain.[141] Among the old Greeks and Romans the moon was of female sex, indeed, but the fair Luna was by no means exempt from amatory tendencies. Among the Eskimos, again, the moon is supposed to be the cause of cold weather. He produces snow by whittling a walrus-tusk, and strewing the shavings upon the earth, or else by blowing through a reed; and when he visits the earth, he always comes driving in a sledge over the winter ice. It is quite natural that such associations should attach to the moon, since it is in the ascendant during the night and in winter. As a frigid and austere influence, too, he is naturally enough regarded as a man; while further south, where heat is more dreaded than cold, it is the sun who is supposed to be of the sterner sex.

Thunder they believe to be produced by two old women fighting for a dry and stiff skin, and tugging each at her end of it; in the heat of the contest they upset their lamps, and thus cause the lightning. The origin of fogs they trace to a tornarssuk who drank so much that he burst.[142] As to the cause of rain, they have on the east coast another legend in addition to that already mentioned. Rain, according to this account, is produced by a being named Asiak, who dwells in the sky. In ancient days, after a long drought, the angekoks would set out for his

[137] A. Lang, *Custom and Myth*, p. 132; Tylor, *Primitive Culture* i. 288.

[138] Compare Rink, *Tales and Traditions of the Eskimo*, pp. 237, 440. Danish ed. suppl. p. 44. Liebrecht in *Germania*, vol. 18 (1873), p. 365.

[139] Holm, *Meddelelser om Grönland*, part 10, p. 142.

[140] This myth is so strikingly like the Greenland legend that there can scarcely be a doubt of their having sprung from the same source. Among the Khasias to love your mother-in-law is the direst sin, while among the Greenlanders it is worst to love your sister.

[141] Tylor, *Primitive Culture*, i. 354. See also A. Lang, *Myth Ritual, and Religion*, i. p. 128.

[142] P. Egede, *Efterretninger om Grönland*, pp. 150, 206.

abode to beg for rain. When they arrived, they would peep in, and would usually see his wife sitting on the edge of the sleeping-bench, while Asiak himself would be lying covered up close to the wall. On their imploring her aid, she would ultimately reply: 'Last night he wetted his rug a little, as he usually does;' whereupon she would take up the piece of bearskin on which he had been sitting, and would shake it, thus causing it to rain upon earth.[143] The very fact that the angekoks are represented as begging for rain, which is of no service whatever to a people of hunters and fishers like the Eskimos, seems to prove that this myth must have originated in other latitudes, where agriculture is practised. It is not impossible, as Holm conjectures, that Asiak may be identical with the rain-gods of several of the American aboriginal races—deities who lived on the tops of high mountains. The Mayas of Yucatan, it may be noted, called their rain-god Chac. But it is also possible that the whole myth may come from further west. Among primitive races, rain was very generally traced to a similar origin. In Kamtchatka we meet with the idea in its crudest form. When the modern Greek peasant indicates rain by the phrase κατουράει ὁ θεός, he is merely employing an image at least as old as Aristophanes, who makes one of his characters in 'The Clouds' (v. 373) remark that formerly when it rained he used to believe Zeus διὰ κοσκίνου οὐρεῖν. The same idea, more or less disguised, and generally with a touch of the jocose in it, reappears in many popular expressions current in Germany, Belgium, Norway, and elsewhere. They have all their root in a belief of primeval antiquity, which can also be traced among many other races—for example, among the old heathen Arabians, and even among the Jews.[144]

In their beliefs or superstitions the Eskimos used to be, and still are on the east coast, instructed by their priests or exorcisers, the angekoks (*angakok*, plural, *angakut*). These men are the wisest and ablest among them, but also, as a rule, the craftiest. They assert that they have the power of conversing with spirits, journeying both to the under-world and to the sky and other places unattainable to ordinary mortals, conjuring up the tornarssuk and other supernatural beings, obtaining revelations from them, and so forth. They influence and work upon their countrymen principally through their mystic exorcisms and séances, which occur as a rule in the winter, when they are living in houses. The lamps are extinguished, and skins are hung before the windows so that it is quite dark. The angekok himself sits upon the floor. By dint of making a horrible noise so that the whole house shakes, changing his voice, bellowing and shrieking, ventriloquising, groaning, moaning, and whining, beating on drums, bursting forth into diabolical shrieks of laughter, and all sorts of other tricks, he persuades his companions that he is visited by the various spirits he personates, and that it is they who make the disturbance.

---

[143] Holm, *Geografisk Tidsskrift* (Copenhagen, 1891), xi. 16. The idea that rain is due to the overflow of a lake in the over-world may possibly be traceable to more southern regions, where agriculture and artificial irrigation are practised, and where accordingly the mountain lakes have been dammed up. In the Greenland myth there is also mention of the lake being closed by a dam. (Compare Egede and Cranz.)

[144] See Schwartz, *Die poetischen Naturanschauungen*, i. pp. 138, 259; ii. p. 198; Schmidt, *Das Volksleben der Neugriechen*, i. p. 31; *Belgisch. Museum*, v. p. 215; Ign. Goldziher, *Der Mythos bei den Hebräern*, p. 88.

In order to become an angekok a long apprenticeship is naturally required, frequently as much as ten years. The neophyte must often and for long periods go into solitary retirement,[145] and rub a stone round upon another stone, following the sun, for several days on end, whereupon a spirit comes forth from the mountain. Then he must die of fright, but afterwards come to life again; and thus he gradually obtains the mastery of his tornat. He must not reveal that he is going through this probation until it is completed, but then he must make public announcement of the fact. If he is to be a regular tip-top[146] angekok, it is highly desirable that he should be seized and dragged to the seashore by a bear; then there comes a walrus, buries its tusks in his genital organs, drags him away to the horizon, and eats him up. Thereupon his bones set off homewards, and meet the shreds of flesh upon the way; they grow together again, and he is whole once more. Now he is at the head of his profession.

The influence of these angekoks of course depended upon their adroitness; but they do not seem to have been mere charlatans. It is probable that they themselves partly believed in their own arts, and were even convinced that they sometimes received actual revelations; although Egede is not inclined to believe that they had 'any real commerce or understanding with the devil.'

They can also cure diseases by reciting charms, give a man a new soul, and so forth. Among the diseases which they profess to cure are reckoned inability to catch seals, in a man, and, in a woman, inability to bear children. In the latter case, the East Greenland angekok, even to this day, has to journey to the moon, from which a child is thrown down to the woman, who becomes pregnant of it. After this laborious journey, the angekok has the right to lie with the woman.[147] This visit to the moon is, of course, connected with the aforesaid erotic proclivities of that luminary. Among the Indians, too, the moon seems to possess an influence over procreation.

In order that the angekok may heal diseases he must be well paid; otherwise his arts will be of no avail. It is of course not he himself that receives the gifts, but the tornak, for whom he merely acts as agent.

By reason of their connection with the supernatural world, the most esteemed angekoks have considerable authority over their countrymen, who are afraid of the evil results which may follow any act of disobedience. For it is in Greenland as it used to be here, with priests who were really masters of their craft—they were not only the servants of God, but knew 'the black book' as well, and had power over the devil. The angekoks, indeed, are for the most part well-disposed; but they may also work evil by robbing other people of their souls and giving them to their tornarssuk to eat, by sending their tornat to frighten the life out of their enemies, and so forth. Thus we find even among the Eskimos the beginnings of priestly rule.

For the most part, however, it is people of another class who are guilty of such

---

[145] This idea recurs in several parts of the world. Compare Christ's forty days' solitude in the wilderness.

[146] So in original (*Trans.*).

[147] Holm, *Meddelelser om Grönland*, part 10, p. 131.

misdeeds as killing others by magic, bewitching their weapons, and the like. These are the so-called *ilisitsoks*, who may be either male or female.[148] These wizards and witches are much hated. It used to be held that most evils, especially death and disease, were due to them; and if an old woman was suspected of being an ilisitsok she was remorselessly killed. This cannot surprise us, when we remember how our own ancestors, with the priests at their head, used to burn their witches. While the angekoks commune with the spirits in the presence of other people, the ilisitsoks' dealings with the supernatural powers are carried on in the deepest secrecy and always to noxious ends. They must be instructed in secrecy by an older ilisitsok and must pay dear for the teaching. It does not seem to be clear what supernatural powers they have dealings with; they are doubtless different from those known to the angekoks, and are purposely kept secret. In their diabolical arts they use many different properties, as for instance human bones, the flesh of corpses, skulls, snakes, spiders, water-beetles, and the like; but their most potent device consists in making *tupileks*. A tupilek is prepared in the deadliest secrecy of various animals' bones, skins, pieces of the anorak of the man who is to be injured or portions of the seals he has caught; all this being wrapped together and tied up in a skin. Finally, it is brought to life by dint of singing charms over it. Then the ilisitsok seats himself upon a bank of stones close to the mouth of a river. He turns his anorak back to front, draws his hood up over his face, and then dangles the tupilek between his legs. This makes it grow, and when it has attained its proper size it glides away into the water and disappears. It can transform itself into all sorts of animals and monsters, and is supposed to bring ruin and death upon the man against whom it is despatched; but if it fails in this, it turns against him who sent it forth.[149]

These tupileks remind us strongly of the widespread belief both in Norway and Iceland in *gand* or 'messengers,' and it seems scarcely doubtful that the Eskimos have borrowed this conception from our ancestors in Greenland. The 'gand' in Iceland is also a fabulous, magic creature, sent forth by wizards, with the power of transforming itself into every possible shape; and if it does not succeed in destroying the person against whom it is sent, it returns and kills the sender. It can, however, in Greenland, no less than in Iceland and Norway, be snapped up by other wizards or witches, and its evil influence thus averted.[150]

Rink sees in these ilisitsoks and their connection with the powers of evil a possible survival from an older or primæval faith in Greenland, which is persecuted

[148] Angekoks, too, might be of either sex, but women seem always to have been in the minority among them.

[149] Holm, *Meddelelser om Grönland*, part 10, p. 135; Rink, *Tales and Traditions of the Eskimo*, pp. 53, 151, 201, 461; N. Egede, *Tredie Continuation af Relationerne*, pp. 43, 48; P. Egede, *Efterretninger om Grönland*, p. 18, &c.

[150] Compare Carl Andersen, *Islandske Folkesagn og Eventyr*, 2nd edit. (1877) pp. 144-149. It is interesting to compare these Icelandic tales with the East Greenland legend related by Holm (*Meddelelser om Grönland*, part 10, p. 303), which is very similar in matter, though of course adapted to the conditions of life in Greenland. Analogous tales are also to be found in Norway, according to Moltke Moe, who has directed my attention to this remarkable similarity.

by the priests of the new faith, the angekoks.[151] Just so do we find that witchcraft among us consisted largely of remnants of the old heathenism and was, therefore, bitterly persecuted by the Christians. There seems to be much in favour of this ingenious conclusion of Rink's. It appears to me possible, however, that as the tupilek is descended from the ancient Scandinavians' belief in gand or 'messengers,' so the origin of the whole witch-lore may be found in the same quarter. There seem to be sufficient points of likeness to justify such a conjecture.[152] It is by no means improbable that precisely this belief in the power of the Evil One, the contract with Satan, the Black Book and so forth—in a word the whole belief in wizardry which lay, and to some extent still lies, at the very root of the superstitions of our race, even deeper, one might almost say, than the belief in God—might have been the first thing borrowed by the Eskimos in their dealings with our forefathers. This rapid and easy way of obtaining supernatural power must have been particularly attractive to them. So far as I have been able to learn, too, witchcraft does not play anything like such a prominent part among the more western Eskimos, if it is to be found at all (?).

I have still to speak of the Greenlanders' belief in amulets. They are used by almost everyone, and consist of particular objects, generally portions of animals or of human beings. Charms are sung or muttered over them, and they are given by parents to their children while they are still quite little; or young people are instructed by their elders how to find amulets for themselves. They are worn all through life, as a rule upon the body or among the clothes. The men, for example, often have them sewn into skin pouches made for the purpose, and worn upon the breast, while women often tie them into the top-knot of their hair. Others are placed in the house-roof or in the tent; or in the kaiak to prevent it from capsizing. One man as a rule will have several amulets. They are supposed to have power to protect one against witchcraft, and against injury from spirits, to be of assistance in times of danger, and to endow their possessor with certain peculiar faculties. Some amulets can even be used to disguise their possessors in the shape of animals, and thus remind us of the 'hamlöbing' (the putting on of falcon-skins, swan-skins, &c.) in our old mythology. If, for example, a man has a bird or a fish for his amulet, he may by calling upon it transform himself into a bird or a fish; or he may transform himself into a tree, seaweed, or the like, if his amulet consists of a piece of wood or of seaweed. The belief in amulets, as we all know, is spread over the whole world, and can be traced from the most primitive right up to the most highly developed races. Among the Eskimos it no doubt dates from a very early stage of development, and is the most primitive of their existing religious conceptions. The origin of this belief appears to me quite explicable. Sometimes,

---

[151] Rink, *Tales and Traditions of the Eskimos*, p. 42.

[152] One of the characteristics of the ilisitsoks, as well as of the angekoks, is that they breathe fire. In the mediæval legends, and even in more recent European folk-lore, this faculty was attributed to the Devil, and was often extended to those who had sold themselves to him. The Greenland fire-breathing is probably connected with this mediæval superstition. The ilisitsoks, moreover, when seen by the angekoks during their exorcisms, are observed to be black from the hands up to the elbows—a trait which may also have its origin in the popular European conception of the Devil and his host as black in colour.

of course, it may have arisen from a mere external accident, for example the observation of a series of fortunate events—that a man who is in possession of some particular object has always been lucky in his fishing, and so forth. But as a rule its source lies deeper. When, for example, a man sees that a bird, such as the falcon, cleaves the air with incredible ease and has extraordinary powers of attack with beak and claws, he is apt to attribute these powers to every part of the animal, and especially to the head, with the soul inhabiting it, to the beak, and to the claws. It is not at all unnatural that barren women, in order to have children, should take pieces of a European's shoesole and hang them round their necks. Seeing that Europeans are prolific, they think that through these shoesoles, on which our strength has rested, some part of it will 'pass into their garments and serve them to the like end.'[153] When a boy who spits blood, and whose family is consumptive, is given a seal-blood plug as an amulet (the plug which is used to stop the flow of blood from the wounds of a captured seal), and when this is sewn into the anorak upon his breast, the reason is surely clear enough. It is based upon the same belief in *sympathetic transference* which plays so great a part in the popular superstitions of all countries. The Eskimos often have for amulets portions of their forefathers' clothes or other possessions, as a rule of their grandfathers'. This has no doubt its origin in the belief that the souls of the dead can protect them, and that when they carry some portions of the dead man's possessions about with them, it is easier to come into rapport with him. Cases are also recorded of the carrying about of small male and female figures to serve as amulets.[154] The transition from this belief in amulets to fetish-worship, or rather idol- and image-worship, does not seem to me to be very difficult.

The Greenlanders also think they derive supernatural help from their charms. These are employed in sickness, in danger, against enemies, &c., and have about the same influence as the amulets. Even less than the amulets, however, have they any connection with spirits, and the method of their action is unknown—no one knows even the meaning of the words which are spoken. They are simply old formulas which have been handed down by means of sale from generation to generation. They have to be learned in secrecy, and must be paid for on the spot and at a very high rate, else they have no efficacy. They are uttered slowly in a subdued, mystic tone;[155] it seems as though they were connected to a certain extent with witchcraft. They remind us forcibly of our old witch-crones and their often meaningless formulas. It seems to me probable that they must be reminiscences of old customs, imported from outside, whose original signification has been lost. According to Rink, charms may also be learnt by listening to the song of birds.[156]

Besides these formulas, magic songs are also in use. The words of these, however, are comprehensible, and they may be sung in the hearing of others.

According to Rink, it is as a rule the deceased relations and ancestors of the person using the charm, and especially his grandparents, whose help is invoked

[153] Hans Egede, *Grönlands Perlustration*, p. 116.
[154] Compare Holm, *Meddelelser om Grönland*, part 10, p. 118.
[155] Holm, *Meddelelser om Grönland*, part. 10, p. 119.
[156] *Tales and Traditions of the Eskimo*, p. 51; Danish ed. suppl. p. 194.

in these formulas and in the songs. From Holm's account, on the other hand, we gather nothing of this sort. It seems to me not unreasonable, however, to suppose that they, and also the amulets, have often a certain connection with the dead, and may thus be the beginning of (or a survival from) a more developed ancestor-worship. When a boy is for the first time placed in a kaiak, the father, by means of magic songs, will invoke for him the protection of his deceased grandparents and great-grandparents.

Offerings to the supernatural powers are very infrequent among the Greenlanders. The most common form of offering is made to the inue of the sea, the so-called *kungusutarissat* (the plural of *kungusutariak*). They are fond of foxes' flesh and foxes' tails, which are, therefore, offered to them whenever a fox is caught, that they may make the fishing successful. In travelling, too, the Eskimos will make offerings to certain headlands, glaciers, and the like, which they regard as dangerous, in order to get past them unharmed. The offering is as a rule thrown overboard into the sea; it often consists of food, but may also take the form of beads or other things which they value.

Besides these religious ceremonies the Greenlanders have others, especially certain rules of life as to fasting, abstinence, and the like, which must be observed, for example, by women immediately before or after the birth of a child. It would, however, lead us too far to go in detail into these matters.

From this survey of the religious conceptions of the Greenlanders, it will doubtless appear that they are not so exempt from foreign influences as many have been inclined to think. We can trace in them admixtures from many quarters; we have found myths whose place of origin is certainly as distant as Central Asia; nay we have even found some which unquestionably bridge the distance between Greenland, South Africa, and the Fiji Islands.[157] The migrations of such myths presuppose immense periods of time. What is perhaps most interesting for us, however, is the traces which we find of our own forefathers' visits to Greenland. It is not only a few ruined buildings that bear witness to their presence; they have also left an unmistakable imprint on the spiritual life of the natives. I shall cite one or two more examples of remarkable resemblances to European, and especially Scandinavian, superstitions, which must in all probability have arisen from intercourse with our forefathers.

The Greenlanders believe that children born in secrecy, or murdered after birth, become dangerous spectres (*angiak*). Among other things, they are in the habit of seeking out a dog's skull, which they use as a kaiak, in order to persecute and kill their kinsfolk—either their mother's later-born children, or, it may be,

---

[157] As regards the greater part of these myths, the theory that they were invented independently in different parts of the world seems quite inadmissible; the coincidences are too numerous and too characteristic. Examples may be cited, indeed, of the same invention having been made independently by different races remotely situated from each other; but they are remarkably rare. On the other hand, it is surprising how certain tools, cultivated plants, and arts or accomplishments have been handed on from people to people over immense tracts of the earth. (Compare Peschel, *Abhandlungen zur Erd-und Völkerkunde*, 1877, i. p. 468).

their mother's brothers, who, by reproaching her for her misconduct, have led her to conceal the birth. Sometimes, too, they pursue people in the form of a feather, a mitten, &c.[158] This conception is very like the belief in what is called *utburden*, which is very widespread in Norway. These are children who, being born in concealment and killed, have not received a name. They cannot rest, but, in the form of visible or invisible ghosts, they pursue either the mother or people who pass by the place where they have been laid.[159] The resemblance between this Norwegian conception and the Greenland superstition is so great that there is every probability of its having been imported into Greenland by the old Scandinavians.[160]

Passing on to their fairy tales, we find many which resemble Norwegian and other European legends. For example we have in Norway an as yet unpublished tale[161] of three sisters who were bent upon getting married. The one said, 'I am minded to marry even if I got only a fox for a husband;' the second said she would marry if she got only a goat, and the third if she got only a squirrel. Thereupon there came a fox, a goat, and a squirrel, and took each his wife. Their father afterwards paid a visit to each of his sons-in-law. When he came to the squirrel's house, the squirrel bade his wife hang a pot over the fire, and then all three went out and came to a river, into which the squirrel dived and brought up a trout. When the man reached home he bade his wife put a pot on the fire and go out with him. On reaching a river, the man tried to dive as he had seen the squirrel do, but was drowned. In Greenland we find this story split into two. In the one it is two sisters who go down to the shore and wish, the one for an eagle, the other for a whale, as a husband; and these animals at once come and carry them off.[162] In the other we are told of a pair of old people who live alone with their daughter. One day there

---

[158] Glahn, *Nye Samling af det kongelige norske Videnskabelige Selskabs Skrifter*, i. 1784, p. 271. Rink, *Tales and Traditions of the Eskimo*, pp. 45, 391, 439; Kleinschmidt, *Den grönlandske Ordbog*, p. 33.

[159] See Moltke Moe's Introduction to Qvigstad and Sandberg: *Lappiske Eventyr og Folkesagn*, p. vii; *Nyrop, Mindre Afhandlinger udgivne af det philologisk-historiske Samfund*, Copenhagen, 1887, p. 193; Liebrecht, *Zur Volkskunde*, p. 319.

[160] I must not omit to note, however, that similar conceptions are to be found in different parts of the world. In Tahiti, Oromatus, the mightiest of spirits, is said to have come into existence in this way, and among the Polynesians generally the souls of children are regarded as being especially dangerous. (Compare F. Liebrecht, in *The Academy*, iii. 1872, p. 321.) One of my reasons for thinking that the Greenlanders may have borrowed their angiak from the Scandinavians is that, so far as I can ascertain, other Eskimo tribes have no such belief—at least it cannot be common among them. There is no mention of the angiak even among the legends collected by Holm on the east coast. On the other hand, there are several apparently more primitive myths of ordinary children who are turned into monsters. (Compare *Meddelelser om Grönland*, part 10, p. 287; Rink, *Tales and Traditions of the Eskimo*, p. 258; Danish ed. suppl. p. 125.) One of these, who on the east coast is the child of the moon by a human mother (*Meddelelser om Grönland*, part 10, p. 281), has on the west coast become an angiak. This is, no doubt, a late recasting of the legend—a theory which is borne out by the fact that variants occur on the west coast in which the angiak is an ordinary child.

[161] Communicated by Moltke Moe.

[162] Rink, *Tales and Traditions of the Eskimo*, p. 126; Holm, *Meddelelser om Grönland*, part 10, p. 276.

comes a big unknown man, who says that he lives near them to the southward, and asks for their daughter in marriage. He obtains her, and on leaving her home asks his father-in-law to come and pay them a visit. This the father-in-law does. When he enters the house, his daughter hangs a kettle over the fire and her husband goes out. The old man looks after him through the window, but sees only a cormorant which flies over the water, dives, and comes up with a sea-scorpion. Presently the son in-law comes in with the sea-scorpion, which he gives to his father-in-law to eat. On the old man's return home he asks his wife to hang the pot over the lamp, then rows with her a little way out from the land, and ties a stone round his neck and a long rope round his waist, saying to his wife: 'I will dive into the water, and when I tug at the rope you must haul me up again.' He jumps overboard and sinks, and when his wife hauls him up again he is drowned.[163] The resemblance between this story and the latter part of the Norwegian one is so great that there can scarcely be any doubt as to its origin. We must, however, take into account the possibility that it did not come through the old Scandinavians, but through Hans Egede and his people, or even later.

The following story resembles both Asiatic and European legends. A reindeer-hunter once saw a number of women bathing in a lake. He took away the clothes of the fairest of them, who had therefore to follow him home and become his wife, whilst the others rushed to the shore, put on their clothes, and were transformed into geese or mergansers and flew away. His wife bore him a son; but presently she set to work collecting feathers, by means of which she changed both herself and her son into birds, and flew away with him one fine day, when the man was out hunting. He set forth to search for them, and came upon a man who was cutting chips of wood which were transformed into fishes. This man placed him upon the tail of a big salmon which he made out of a chip, and told him to close his eyes, whereupon the fish brought him to his wife and son.[164] The American Eskimos have an altogether similar story. Among the Samoyedes it is related that a man went out on a journey and came upon an old woman who was felling birch trees. He helped her, and went with her to her tent, where he hid himself. Then in came seven girls, who talked to the old woman and went away again. She said to him: 'In the darkest part of yonder wood there is a lake; there the seven girls will bathe; take away the clothes of one of them'—and he did so. The remainder is quite different from the Greenland story, and there is nothing at all about their being changed into birds, though their home was in air or in the sky.[165] This story, whose likeness to the Greenland legend is remarked by Dr. Rink,[166] is not, however, so like it as an Icelandic story, in which we are told that a man was walking early one morning beside the sea and came to the mouth of a cave. He could hear sounds of dancing and merriment from inside the cave, and outside it lay a heap of seal-skins, one of which he took home with him. Later in the day he came again

---

[163] Rink, *Tales and Traditions of the Eskimo*, Danish ed. suppl. p. 119.

[164] P. Egede, *Continuation af Relationerne*, p. 19; *Efterretninger om Grönland*, p. 55; Rink, *Tales and Traditions of the Eskimo*, p. 145; *Meddelelser om Grönland*, part 11, p. 20, Suppl. p. 117.

[165] Castrén, *Ethnologiske Foreläsningar*, Helsingfors, 1857, p. 182.

[166] *Meddelelser om Grönland*, part 11, Suppl. p. 117.

to the mouth of the cave; there sat a fair young woman quite naked, and weeping. She was the seal who owned the skin. He gave her clothes, took her home with him, married her, and they had children. But one day when the man was out fishing his wife found the old seal-skin; the temptation was too strong for her, she said good-bye to her children, put on the skin and threw herself into the sea.[167] The Greenland story, for the rest, resembles the swan legends which are spread over almost the whole world, and of which we have several in Europe. That it cannot have been introduced into Greenland of recent years is proved by the fact that Paul Egede heard it there so long ago as 1735. The possibility that it may have been brought to Greenland by the old Scandinavians seems to me strengthened by the fact that swan legends and stories of a like nature do not seem to have been common in America. Powers, for example, in his book about the Indians of California, says that he can find no stories of this nature among them.[168]

If space permitted I could adduce several other remarkable coincidences between the folk-lore of Greenland and that of Europe, and especially of Scandinavia. It appears, then, that the intercourse between the old Scandinavians and the natives must have been greater than has generally been believed.[169]

---

[167] C. Andersen, *Islandske Folkesagn*, 1877, p. 205.

[168] The Iroquois, however, have a legend of seven boys who were transformed into birds and flew away from their parents. They have also a tale of a young man who goes out fishing and comes upon some boys who have put off their wings and are swimming. They give him a pair of wings which enable him to fly away with them; but they afterwards take his wings away from him and leave him helpless. Compare Rink, *Meddelelser om Grönland*, part 11, p. 21.

[169] It has hitherto been supposed that there are no traces of such intercourse except in the Eskimo legends (mentioned in Chapter I.), of their encounters with the old Scandinavians, and in the three following words: *nîsa* for nise (porpoise), *kuánek* for kvanne (angelica) and *kalâlek* (meaning Greenlander). The derivation of *nîsa* (old Norse nisa) and *kuánek* seems probable enough, though some doubt is thrown on the latter by the fact that in Labrador the word is applied to an eatable seaweed. *Kalâlek* was supposed to be the same as the Norwegian skrælling — the name given by our forefathers to the Eskimos, which in an Eskimo's mouth would sound something like kalalek. It is rather surprising, however, to find the same word among the Eskimos of Alaska in the form of *katlalik* or *kallaaluch*, meaning an angekok or chieftain (Rink, *Meddelelser om Grönland*, part 11, Suppl. p. 94; *Tales and Traditions of the Eskimo*, Danish ed. suppl. p. 200). It is possible, however, that the word may have been imported into Alaska from Greenland in modern times. Another thing which, as it seems to me, may possibly be a relic of the old Scandinavians, is the cross-bow which Holm found upon the east coast, and which was formerly in use on the west coast also. So far as I know, it is not found among the Indians.

CHAPTER XIV
THE INTRODUCTION OF CHRISTIANITY

All this superstition of which I have been speaking of course seems to us mere meaningless confusion, the extirpation of which must be an unmixed advantage. But if we place ourselves at their point of view, is it so much more meaningless for them than our Christian dogmas, which lead them into a world entirely foreign to them? In order to understand these dogmas, they had first to transpose them into their own key of thought, or, in other words, they had to make them more or less heathen before they could really grasp them at all. It is useless to imagine that a people can suddenly, at a word of command, begin to think in an entirely new manner. This transmutation has cost them much labour, and though they are still heathen at bottom and believe in their old legends, yet the new doctrine has introduced confusion into their ideas. This alone might tempt one to think that it would have been better to have let them preserve their own faith undisturbed. It gave them, with their comparatively meagre capacity for ideas, the easiest explanation of their surroundings; it peopled nature with the supernatural powers which they needed for consolation when reality became too hard and complex for them. And how characteristic these myths are of the Eskimos—for example, the conception of the region beyond the grave! Here there is neither silver nor gold, neither gorgeous raiment nor shining palaces, as in our stories; earthly riches have no value for the Eskimo. Nor are there lovely women, flowery gardens, and so forth. No; at most there is a mud hut, a little larger than his own, and in it sit the happy spirits eating rotten seals' heads, which lie in inexhaustible heaps under the benches; and around it there are splendid hunting-grounds, with quantities of game and much sunshine. In his eyes our Paradise of white-robed angels, where the blessed sit around upon chairs, seems a tedious and colourless existence which he does not understand, and which excites no longing in him. We can scarcely wonder at an angekok, who said to Niels Egede that he far preferred the tornarssuk's or 'Devil's house,' where he had often been; 'For in heaven there is no food to be had, but in hell there are seals and fishes in plenty.'

One would expect that the missionaries' victory[170] over heathendom would

[170] Missionary activity in Greenland, then a possession of the Norwegian crown, was commenced in 1721 by Hans Egede, who to that end set on foot a combined commercial and missionary company in Bergen. This mission was afterwards supported by the Danish-Norwegian Government, and after the separation of 1814, by which Denmark retained the Norwegian possessions of the Faroe Isles, Iceland, and Greenland, by the Danish Government alone. Ten years after Egede's arrival in the country, Count Zinsendorf, who had heard of his mission, despatched three Moravian brethren to Greenland. These also formed

be a very easy one among so peaceful and good-humoured a people as the Green-landers; but this can scarcely be said to have been the case. The natives had many objections to allege against the Christian assertions. For example, they could not understand that the sin which Adam and Eve committed 'could be so great and involve such melancholy consequences' as that the whole human race should be condemned on account of it. 'Since God knew all things, why did he permit the first man and woman to sin?' The idea of free-will seems to them, frankly speak-ing, mere rubbish, and, but for free-will, Adam's offspring would never have been corrupted, and the Son of God need not have suffered.

One girl was not at all contented with the answer she received to these ob-jections. 'She wanted to have them so answered that she could inwardly assent and feel that the answer was true, and that she could silence those who had so much to say against this part of our doctrine.' Similarly, they were of opinion that Adam and Eve must have been very foolish to think of chattering with a serpent, and 'that they must have been very fond of fruit since they would rather die and suffer pain than forego a few big berries.' Others thought that it was just like the kavdlunaks (Europeans); for 'these greedy people never have enough; they have, and they want to have, more than they require.' One angekok thought it was very unlucky that Christ, the great angekok, who could even bring the dead to life, was not born among the Eskimos; they would have loved him, and obeyed him, and not done like the foolish kavdlunaks. 'What madmen! to kill the man who could bring the dead to life!' When they saw that Christian Europeans quarrelled and fought, they had little faith in the Christian doctrines, and said: 'Perhaps, if we knew as much as they, we, too, would become inhuman.' And they thought that it was impossible to find well-behaved Europeans, 'unless they had been several years in Greenland and had there learnt *mores*.'

Some asked, since Christianity was so essential, why God had not instructed them in it sooner, for then their forefathers, too, could have gone to heaven. When Paul Egede answered that perhaps God had seen that they would not accept the Word, but rather despise it, and thereby become more guilty, an old man said that he had known many excellent people, and had himself had a pious father; and even if some of them might have despised the Word, 'still there were the women and children, who are all credulous.' When Paul Egede explained to them that worldly goods are 'trumpery,' altogether unworthy to go to heaven, someone an-swered: 'I did not know that these things were not worth thinking about; if it is so nice there, why are we so unwilling to leave the earth?'

When the Scriptures came to be translated, considerable objections presented themselves. Many even of the Christian Greenlanders thought that it would not be advisable for their unbelieving countrymen to be told, for example, of 'Jacob's slyness and treachery towards his father and brother, of the patriarchs' polygamy, and especially of Simeon's and Levi's matchless wickedness.' 'The story of Lot,'

a little congregation, and the German or Hernhutt mission has likewise obtained a footing. It has now a few stations in the Godthaab district, and one or two in the extreme south of the country. The peculiarity of these Hernhutt communities, so far as I could gather, is that in them the natives have sunk to an even greater depth of misery than elsewhere.

too, they thought unfortunate. 'A selection of what was most important would be best for this people.'[171]

The sacrament of the altar, of course, seemed in their eyes the most arrant witchcraft, and baptism likewise. One time, says Niels Egede, when they had seen some Europeans going through this ceremony, 'an angekok asked me why I was always denouncing those who practised witchcraft, when here was one of our own priests performing sorceries over us?' To which Egede found no better answer than that it was 'in accordance with Christ's command;' he did not think 'the dog had any right to know more.' Once, when the missionaries told a man 'that he should especially thank God who had given him many children,' he became very angry and answered, 'It is a great lie to say that God has given me children, for I made them myself. "Is it not so?" he said, turning to his wife.'

Their criticism of the doctrine and practice of the missionaries was sometimes so mordant that the intelligent and honest merchant Dalager has to admit that 'even the stupidest natives from far beyond the colony have often confronted me with such objections on these points as have made me groan, while the perspiration stood on my brow.'

Divine service seems at first to have bored them very much; they preferred to hear about Europe, and would ask many naïve questions: 'Whether the King was very big? Was he strong? Was he a great angekok? And had he caught many whales?' Paul Egede records that when they thought his father's sermons too long 'they went up to him and asked him if he was not soon going to stop. Then he had to measure off upon his arm how much of his discourse was left, whereupon they went back to their places and sat moving their hands down their arms every moment. When the preacher paused at the end of a paragraph, they made haste to move the hand right out to the finger-tips; but when he began again they cried "Ama" (that is, "Still more") and moved the hand back again half way up the arm. The singing was in my department, and when I began a new psalm, or sang for too long, they would often hold a wet seal-skin mitten over my mouth.'

The missionaries' treatment of the natives was not always of the gentlest. I may cite a couple of examples chosen at random from their own statements: 'I gave him to understand,' says Niels Egede, 'that if he would not let himself be persuaded by fair means, but despised the Word of God, he should receive the same treatment from me as other angekoks and liars had received (namely a thrashing).' 'When I had tried all I could by means of persuasion and exhortation, without avail, I had recourse to my usual method, flogged him soundly and turned him out of the house.'[172] A girl was beaten by her priest, 'because she could not believe that God was so cruel as he represented Him to be; he had said that all her forefathers were with Tornarssuk, and were to be tortured to all eternity, because they did not know God.' She tried to defend them by suggesting that they knew no better, whereupon he lost his temper; and when at last she said 'that it was horrible for her to learn that God was so terribly angry with those who sinned

---

[171] Compare Paul Egede, *Efterretninger om Grönland*, pp. 117, 162.
[172] Niels Egede, *Tredie Continuation af Relationerne*, pp. 32, 45.

that he could never forgive them, as even wicked men will sometimes do,' he gave her a beating.[173] It cannot but jar upon us to hear of such conduct on the part of our countrymen and Christian missionaries towards so peaceable a people; and it would scarcely make a better impression upon the natives themselves. We can only admire the good humour which prevented them from driving the missionaries out of their houses. In excuse for the missionaries, we must remember that they were born in Europe, and in a much ruder age than our own.

The conversion of the natives at first went but slowly and with difficulty; but they gradually discovered that the missionaries were in reality great angekoks, and that their ceremonies, such as baptism, their doctrines and formulas, the Christian books, and so forth, were magical appliances, potent for curing disease, protecting against want, and ensuring good fishery and other advantages; not to mention that conversion and a little appearance of contrition often bore immediate fruits in the shape of small rewards from the eager missionaries. Accordingly they said of them: 'They are good people, they gave us food when we believed and looked sorrowful.' A father whose son was dangerously ill, after having had recourse to various angekoks, took counsel with an old and experienced one 'as to whether he should not seek help from the priest at the Colony;' whereupon the old man calmly answered: 'You may do as you please; for I am of opinion that the Word of God and the words of skilful angekoks are equally powerful.' This gradually became the general opinion; and as it fortunately chanced in several cases that the Word of God seemed more effectual than that of the angekoks, it was natural that some should let themselves be baptised. The example once given, there were plenty to follow it, especially when distinguished hunters led the way.

But if the Greenlanders nominally went over to Christianity, they held, and still hold in a greater or less degree, to their old faith as well. It was at first very difficult to convince them of the falsity of the grotesque inventions of their angekoks. When they were reproached with their credulity they answered simply 'that they were not in the habit of lying and therefore believed all that people said to them.'

That they were not absolutely simple-minded, however, in their acceptance of all that the Europeans told them, seems clear from this, amongst other things, that when some Greenlanders could not get Niels Egede to swallow their assertion that 'they had killed a bear on Disco which was so big that it had ice on its back that never melted,' they said: 'We have believed what you tell us, but you will not believe what we tell you.'

To show what a little way below the surface Christianity has gone, and how some of them, at any rate, still understand baptism, I may mention that some years ago in North Greenland a catechist (a man who has received a theological education, and supplies the place of the clergyman in his absence) baptised not only his parishioners, but also his puppies in the name of the Father, the Son, &c. His wife was childless, and he took this means, as he thought, of setting matters right; and, sure enough, next year she bore a child.

The part of their old heathenism which now most haunts their fancy is, so far

------

[173] Paul Egede, *Efterretninger om Grönland*, p. 221.

as my experience goes, the belief in the kivitut or mountain-men (see above, p. 266). Of these they stand in great dread, and frequently think they see them. While we were at Godthaab several of them were seen. Whenever anything is stolen from one of their store-rooms it is of course the kivitut who have done it, and if a kaiak-man disappears, and his body is not found, he is at once supposed to have taken to the mountains, and become a kivitok. This belief seems of late years to have gained ground greatly. A catechist, in the 'Atuagagdliutit,' takes his countrymen to task on the subject, and exclaims: 'No, let us believe of those who perish on the treacherous sea that they rest their limbs upon the great burying-ground at the bottom of the ocean, and that their souls live in the joys of eternity.'

I had once an unpleasant proof of the ingrained nature of this superstitious terror. At Godthaab, late one evening, I went over to one of the Greenlanders' houses with a letter which was to be sent off early next morning with some kaiak-men from another place. When I entered, the whole house was in deep slumber; men and women side by side on the chief sleeping-bench like herrings on a thwart. Not to disturb them more than necessary, I wanted to awaken the only unmarried son of the house, Jacob, who lay alone on the window-bench. He and I were excellent friends, and saw each other daily. I shook him, and shouted 'Jacob' into his ear. He slept as heavily as ever, and I had to shake him long and violently before he at last opened his eyes a little and grunted. But when he saw me bending over him, his eyes grew glassy with terror, and he sat up, uttered a frightful shriek, and kicked and struck out at me. He went on shrieking more and more wildly, and fought his way backwards on the bench. All of those upon the main bench now sat up too and stared in blank affright at me, while poor I stood there in speechless astonishment at the hubbub I had created. At last I recovered my powers of speech, approached Jacob, held out my hands towards him, and spoke some reassuring words. But that only made him worse than ever. When I saw that words were of no avail, I stopped speaking, and began to laugh, whereupon the yells ceased as suddenly as they had begun, and Jacob became as red in the face as he had formerly been white, and muttered something in a shamefaced way about having dreamt of a kivitok that wanted to carry him off to the mountains. I gave him my letter, and withdrew as quickly as I could. The next day it was known over all the Colony that I had been a kivitok; for the neighbours had heard the yells.

CHAPTER XV

EUROPEANS AND NATIVES

The relation of the Europeans to the Greenlanders is in many respects unique, for the Eskimos have been treated more tenderly than any other primitive people which has been subjected to our experiments in civilisation. The Danish Government certainly deserves the highest respect for its action in this matter, and it were much to be desired that other States would follow the example here given them. Care for the true welfare of the natives has been largely operative in their policy, and there is scarcely another instance of a people of hunters which has come into such close contact with European civilisation and proselytism, and has held its own so well for so long a time.

We do not often meet with such enthusiasm as that which impelled our countryman Hans Egede and the first missionaries to seek out this at that time almost unknown land, and led them to endure so many hardships there. They did it with the best of motives, and thought that they were thereby advancing both the spiritual and temporal welfare of the Eskimo. If we compare this mission and the treatment of Greenland as a whole with the conduct of Europeans under similar circumstances in other parts of the world, we cannot but recognise the working of an unusually humane spirit; and as we examine the whole history of the government of Greenland down to our own day, we find ever new and gratifying examples of this spirit.

With all the good will in the world, however, civilised men cannot resist the tendency to look down upon a primitive people as essentially their inferiors. Even in the history of Greenland we find many proofs of this. We learn from his own writings that the devoted Hans Egede himself cherished no small contempt for the natives whom he held it his mission to christianise. He even relates how he often beat them, and had them flogged, or given the rope's end. On one occasion, learning from a small boy that an angekok, named Elik, had said that it would be an easy matter to root out the foreigners who had come to their country, he set off with seven armed men, fell upon the angekok, took him prisoner, and brought him to the colony. There 'he received some blows with the rope's end, and was put in irons.' In the evening the angekok's sons came to inquire about their father, and 'were permitted, at their own request, to pitch their tents in the colony.' After a few days the prisoner was set at liberty, and they went away. One might suppose that after such treatment the Greenlanders would bear ill-will to the foreigners; but their good-humour and hospitality are incomparable. As luck would have it, the following winter, Hans Egede's son, Paul, who had taken part in this high-handed proceeding, was driven by stress of weather to a place where he was surprised to find the angekok Elik. It was not particularly pleasant, as he himself confesses; but to his astonishment he was invited to take up his quarters with the angekok, who spread a reindeer-skin for him upon his own sleeping-bench. There Paul Egede had to remain for three days, and was entertained with the best of everything.[174] This is indeed 'To return good for evil' and 'To do good to them that hate you'; but Egede attributed it to the Greenlanders' willingness 'to put up with punishment when they feel they have deserved it.'

Hans Egede had also another habit, which does not show the greatest possible consideration towards the natives; he would now and then take children to his house, against their parents' wishes, and keep them there to learn the language from them. In this connection they made a song about him: 'There has come a strange man over the great sea from the West, who steals boys, and gives them thick soup with skin upon it (that is, porridge) to eat, and dried earth from his own land (that is, ship's biscuits).' When Paul Egede on one occasion offered a mother a present if she would let her son remain some time longer with him, she answered that children were not articles of commerce.

We can still find evidences in Greenland of how difficult it is for us to get rid of our ingrained contempt for all so-called aborigines. The motive of the Europeans for supporting colonies in the country is that they may be a blessing to it; it is, of course, exclusively for the sake of the mission and of the natives that trade is carried on. Nevertheless, the relation between the natives and the foreigners has come to rest on an entirely wrong basis. The foreigners are regarded both by themselves and by the Greenlanders as a higher race and the lords of the country, to whom all obedience is due; whereas, if they were really there for the sake of the natives, they ought rather to be their self-sacrificing servants. Half voluntarily, half involuntarily, the Europeans have themselves emphasised this relation, and have all along treated the natives as a subject race. We came to the country to preach Christianity; but how does this accord with our Christian doctrine of freedom and equality, and especially with the example of Christ himself?

As an instance of the extent to which this abuse has been carried I may mention that at several settlements in South Greenland the natives are forbidden to keep dogs, because the handful of European families who live there want to keep goats. This prohibition has, it is true, in many cases been determined upon in the local council (see p. 321); but it has been proposed by the Europeans, and as the Greenlanders, as I have said, always follow their lead, it was not difficult to get them to consent to it, against their own real wishes. I have heard them regretting bitterly that they should have been so foolish as to agree to such a prohibition. The most glaring injustice, however, is to be seen in the villages where the German missionaries reside, and where, for no other reason but that his own goats may live in peace, the reverend gentleman issues an ukase forbidding his flock to keep dogs.

I have spoken of this to many otherwise intelligent and kind-hearted residents in Greenland, but found them all of the opinion that since the dogs chased and

[174] P. Egede, *Efterretninger om Grönland*, p. 21; compare also p. 25.

worried the goats, it followed as a matter of course that they must be prohibited. On my objecting that the Europeans were few and the Greenlanders many, so that it was more reasonable that the latter should forbid the keeping of goats, they simply laughed in my face. It did not seem to occur to them that they themselves are the interlopers, and that the Eskimos have kept dogs from time immemorial. Nor did they see anything particularly wrong in the fact that the goats often tore the turf from the roof and walls of the Greenlanders' houses, injured their fish when it was hung up to dry, and so forth.

Another result of the different manner in which the rights of the Europeans and of the natives are regarded is to be found in the regulations concerning the sale of brandy. While it is illegal, as stated in Chapter V., to sell brandy to the natives of the country, the European residents are free to have as much of it as they please. This is unfortunate: for it can scarcely fail to annoy the natives to have it perpetually brought home to them that they are not held good enough to be entrusted with that which the meanest European may have at will. But this ordinance becomes still more hurtful from the fact that the Greenlanders who enter into the service of Europeans are allowed brandy every day, while others can obtain it if they sell something to the Europeans. That this may easily lead to the gravest abuses is clear enough, and we may be sure that it has actually done so. I pass over minor inconsistencies, such as the fact that certain individual natives of mixed descent and of social importance are allowed to order from Europe a stated quantity of brandy every year.

It was of course a clear necessity to forbid the sale of brandy in Greenland, on pain of greatly accelerating the extermination of the native race. But the only right and consistent thing to do would have been to make the prohibition apply to natives and Europeans alike. Many maintain, I am aware, that this would have been to inflict an unjust hardship upon the Europeans, who have all their lives been accustomed to this stimulant; and I know that this would have been specially the case with regard to people from Denmark, where brandy is drunk at almost every meal, even among the working classes, and where it is thus regarded as well-nigh a necessity of life. But notwithstanding this, I cannot but hold to my opinion that a general prohibition would have been the only right and advantageous thing for both parties. Such a demand cannot be called unjust; for if the prohibition is known beforehand, it is always open to any European to refrain from going to Greenland, and I have no fear but that, in any event, there would always be plenty of Europeans in the country.

But my demands would go still further. I hold that not only should the sale of brandy be prohibited, but also the sale of coffee, tobacco, and the other indubitably noxious, or at any rate valueless, products which we have introduced among the natives. It is certain that they had no desire for them; on the contrary, it took us a long time to make them acquire the taste for them. The East Greenlanders to this day do not like coffee. On the west coast, as before stated, we have been unhappily successful in begetting this taste, and coffee has contributed not a little to the decline of the race. But if the sale of coffee to the natives were forbidden, its importation for the use of Europeans should, of course, be forbidden as well. Many will call this fanaticism, but I cannot help it. My opinion is that if it be indeed for the sake of the natives that we have come to their country and undertaken to live there and teach them, we must prove this by our conduct, we must fulfil consistently the duties imposed upon us by such a responsible and difficult mission, and we must submit to the small deprivations it may involve. Such a work of self-sacrifice cannot be carried on without deprivations. The Apostles of the Lord have always regarded suffering as an essential part of their calling, and if we cannot endure it we are neither fitted for, nor worthy of, such a task, and ought to refrain from it altogether. If, on the other hand, we have come to Greenland not for the natives' sake but for our own, that is quite a different matter; but in that case let us call things by their right names, and not use big words such as civilisation and Christianity.

In order to remedy the state of lawlessness which arose from the disuse of the old customs through the influence of the missionaries, and from the fact that the meanest European felt himself entitled to look down upon and domineer over the natives, the enthusiastic energy of Dr. Kink has succeeded in introducing the so-called local councils (*forstanderskaber*), which consist partly of native members, chosen by the different villages or small districts. The intention was that in these councils all the internal affairs of the community should be regulated, the poor-rate should be determined, and, in general, law and order should be maintained. As the Greenlanders, however, did not themselves understand these matters, the pastor in every district was to act as chairman of the council, and the other European residents were to be members of it, and to advise and guide the native councillors. It now appears that the Europeans have gradually got into their hands the whole real authority, and that the others simply obey their wishes. It was a fine idea, and worthy of all recognition, that the natives should acquire the habit of self-government, and Dr. Rink's innovation marks a turning-point for the better in the history of the Greenlander. It suffers, however, from the disadvantage inseparable from all measures which the Europeans can devise for the benefit of the natives—to wit, that it has not arisen from among the people themselves who are to profit by it. The introduction of new social customs is nowhere to be effected in a moment; changes cannot be brought about by a single act of will, but must be the result of a long process of development in the people themselves. An institution imposed from without by foreigners must at least need a very long time to take root in the national life. Many Greenlanders now regard it as a distinction to serve as a councillor; but I have also known others, and these the most capable among them, who do not appreciate the honour, holding it of more importance to look to their hunting and to the support of their families than to travel long distances in order to attend meetings where, after all, with their exaggerated deference towards the Europeans, they can do nothing but follow their lead and agree to what measures they propose.

From what I have just said, and from many other passages in this book, the reader may perhaps be inclined to conclude that the Greenlanders are a people of no natural independence, and born for subjection. This, however, is quite a mistake. On the contrary, the Greenlander's love of freedom and independence has always been very marked. When the Europeans first came to the country, the natives held themselves at least their equals, and the idea of standing in a menial or subordinate position to another man, as they saw the Europeans do among themselves, seemed to them strange and degrading. It is true that the father of a family exercises a certain authority in his own household, and perhaps over all the families who live in the same house; but this authority is so mild and unobtrusive that it is scarcely felt. They have servants, too, in so far that women who have no parents or other relatives to provide for them are often received into the house of a hunter, to assist the mother, daughters, and daughters-in-law in the household work; but they stand on a footing of equality with them, and are thus servants in name rather than in reality. Male servants are entirely unknown. Consequently they could with difficulty reconcile themselves to the idea of going into service; and they still dislike above everything to be ordered about in a domineering fashion, even if their extreme peaceableness of disposition prevents them from protesting openly.

This love of freedom rendered it difficult at first for the Europeans to procure native servants. Gradually, however, European influence has demoralised the natives in this respect as well, so that even hunters now enter the service of the Company and sometimes feel a certain pride in so doing; for, among other things, they thus, as Danish 'officials,' are entitled to their snapsemik (dram) every morning.

Danish ladies can still bear witness to the fact that it is not so easy to avoid giving offence to the pride of their Greenland maid-servants. They are active and agreeable so long as they are well treated; but if a hard word is addressed to them, they will often disappear without ceremony and not come back again. If then the mistress is not prepared to eat the leek and beg pardon, she must look out for another handmaiden.

If the Greenlander sometimes impresses one as being of a servile disposition, I think the effect is due to his astounding patience and power of taking everything, even to the most open injustice, with imperturbable calmness. It must be this patience which Egede describes as 'the Greenlanders' inborn stupidity and cold-bloodedness, their lazy and brutish upbringing,' and so forth. I believe it is the hardship of their life that has taught them this apparently phlegmatic calmness. The very uncertainty of their hunting, for instance, often puts their patience to the severest tests; as, for example, when they strike a run of ill luck, and come home day after day with no booty to their hungry families. Egede least of all had any right to complain of this characteristic; since but for it, and their extreme peaceableness of disposition, they would certainly not have put up so amiably with the often violent proceedings of the first Europeans. I had many an opportunity of admiring their stoical patience—when, for example, I would see them in the morning standing by the hour in the passage of the Colonial Manager's house, or waiting in the snow outside his door, to speak to him or his assistant, who happened to be otherwise engaged. They had probably some little business to transact with them before starting for their homes, often many miles from the colony, and it might be of the greatest importance to them to get away as soon as possible in order to reach their destination betimes. If the weather happened to look threatening, every minute would be more than precious; but there they would stand waiting, as immovable as ever, and to all appearance as indifferent. If I asked them if they were going to make a start, they only answered, 'I don't know,' 'Perhaps, if the weather doesn't get worse,' or something to that effect; but I never once heard the smallest murmur of impatience.

The following occurrence, for which my informant vouches, affords an excellent illustration of this side of their character. An inspector at Godthaab once sent a woman-boat with its crew into the Ameralik fiord to mow grass for his goats. They remained a long time away, and no one could understand what had become of them. At last they returned; and when the inspector asked why they had been so long, they answered that when they got to the place the grass was too short, so that they had to settle down and wait until it grew.

With just the same patience do the Greenlanders await the ripening of their own ruin. They are a patient people.

CHAPTER XVI
WHAT HAVE WE ACHIEVED?

The purpose of our mission and of our work of civilisation in Greenland was, in the first place, to win honour for ourselves before God and man, and secure our own salvation in the other world; and, in the second place, to benefit the natives. But what have we done?

Let us first look at the purely material side. It might seem at first sight as if we ought to have been able to bring to a people like this, living practically in the Stone Age, many things that would aid them in their hard fight for existence. As a matter of fact, this has been by no means the case. The things that were of most importance for them, their weapons and their hunting implements, were in no way susceptible of improvement at our hands. It is true that we brought them iron, which is useful for harpoon-points and knives; but the Greenlanders were not entirely ignorant of it before, and, can, besides, get on quite well without it. They fitted their harpoons with points of hard ivory or stone, they made their knives of the same material, and caught, in those days, a great many more seals than they do now.

But have not our firearms been of great advantage to them? Quite the reverse. The rifle, for example, has enabled them to perpetrate terrible slaughter among the reindeer, merely for the sake of a small and momentary gain. This went so far, that on the narrow strip of naked, broken country which stretches along the west coast, no fewer than 16,000 reindeer were killed every year, only the skin, as a rule, being taken and sold to the Europeans, while the flesh was left behind to rot. Of course, this presently led to the almost total extermination of the animals, and hunting almost entirely ceased because, as it was explained, 'the reindeer had left the coast.' In former days, when they hunted with bow and arrow, they could kill all that they required, but the slaughter was never so great as seriously to diminish the numbers of the reindeer.

For marine hunting, too, the rifle has been the reverse of an advantage. When there are many seals in the fiord, they are frightened by the shots and set off to sea, whereas harpoon-hunting is carried on in silence. Moreover, it is, of course, easier to kill seals with the rifle than to harpoon them, and therefore the rifle has led to a decline in skill with the harpoon. And yet the harpoon remains of supreme impor-tance; for while the rifle hunter must stop at home in rough weather, the harpoon hunter can go out in all weathers and support his family. Harpoon hunting, too, is the more rational method, the wounded animal being almost always secured;

whereas of seals wounded by the rifle, at least as many escape and die to no purpose as are secured and brought home.

A FIORD LANDSCAPE ON THE EAST COAST (AT TINGMI-ARMIUT)

Nor has the shot-gun been of real service. In many districts it has tempted the inhabitants to devote themselves more to the easier bird-shooting than to seal-hunting, which is and must be the pursuit upon which depends the very existence of the Eskimo community; for the seal provides flesh, blubber, both for food and fuel, and skins for kaiaks, boats, tents, houses, clothes, boots, and so forth—nothing can replace it. Another evil is that, by help of the shot-gun, the Greenlanders are enabled to kill so many birds of certain species (for example, eider-ducks) that their numbers are yearly decreasing; and this will soon lead to great misery, for bird-hunting has now become the chief means of support of many families. At Godthaab, for example, the inhabitants live upon it during the greater part of the winter, there being few capable seal-hunters. In earlier times, the Eskimo killed birds with his throwing-dart. It, too, was an effective weapon, and the birds he wounded he secured; when he now sends his small shot scattering in among a flock of eider-duck, who can reckon how many are destroyed without doing any good to anyone?

No, we certainly cannot flatter ourselves that we have perfected his methods of hunting; we have only introduced disturbance into them, the full extent of whose ruinous results we cannot even yet foresee.

But worst of all is the irreparable injury which all our European commodities have done to him. We have, as I have shown, been so immoral as to let him acquire a taste for coffee, tobacco, bread, European stuffs and finery; and he has bartered away to us his indispensable seal-skins and blubber, to procure all these things which give him only a moment's doubtful enjoyment. In the meantime his woman-boat has gone to ruin for want of skins, his tent likewise, and even his kaiak, the essential condition of his existence, will often lie uncovered on the beach. The lamps in his house have often to be extinguished in the winter, because the autumn store of blubber has been sold to the Company. He himself must go on winter days clad in European rags instead of in the warm fur garments he used to have. He has grown poorer and poorer, the delightful summer journeys have for the most part had to be abandoned for want of woman-boats and tents, and all the year round he has now to live in confined houses where contagious diseases thrive and play worse havoc among the population than they ever did before. To show how great the decadence has been in certain districts, I may mention that at a place near Godthaab where a few years ago there were eleven woman-boats,[175] there was now only one, and that one belonged to the missionary.[176]

The statistics of population in Greenland during recent years may at first sight seem encouraging. For example, the number of natives on the west coast was, in 1855, 9,644, while in 1889 it was 10,177. But we must not lull our conscience to sleep with these figures; they are unfortunately deceptive, and the figures of the intervening years will show that the population fluctuates very greatly. In 1881 it was no more than 9,701, and in 1883 only 9,744 (thus showing an increase of only 100 since 1855). In 1885 it had risen to 9,914, and in 1888 to 10,221; but then it fell again in 1889 to 10,177. I have no later statistics. These figures, in which increase and decrease alternate, show that the state of things cannot be healthy. It ought not to be forgotten, too, that Hans Egede, a century and a half ago, estimated the population of the west coast at 30,000. This is probably a large over-estimate, but there is an enormous margin between 30,000 and 10,177. Assuredly this people is sailing with 'a corpse in the cargo.'[177]

Disease has of late years increased alarmingly. It is especially the Greenlanders' scourge, consumption, or more properly tuberculosis, which makes ever wider ravages. There can be few places in the world where so large a proportion of the population is attacked by it. It is not quite clear whether we imported this disease into Greenland, but most probably we did; and at any rate, as I have several times pointed out, our influence has in more ways than one tended strongly to promote the spread of this and other contagious diseases.[178] Tuberculosis is now so common that it is almost easier to number those who are not attacked by it than those

[175] That a man should have a woman-boat, which was formerly the general rule, is now regarded as a conclusive proof of exceptional wealth and capability; for he must of course catch many seals in order to have enough skins for it. Compare *ante* p. 85.

[176] It must be mentioned, however, that accidental circumstances, such as the removal of some good hunters to other places, had contributed in some measure to this great falling off.

[177] An allusion to the well-known nautical superstition. —TRANS.

[178] For instance, by causing the natives to wear worse clothes, and to live all the year round in their damp, insanitary houses, where the germs of disease find the best possible soil to flourish in, by introducing European articles of diet, and so forth.

who are. It is remarkable, however, what a power of resistance the natives show to this disease. They are sometimes so far gone in it while young as to spit blood copiously, and yet survive to a good age. I have even seen excellent hunters who had consumption, and who would one day lie abed spitting blood, and a few days later would be out at sea again. This power of resistance is probably due in part to the amount of fat they consume, and especially to the blubber which is admirably adapted to fortify them against the disease. It is proved, too, that people at the Colonies, who consequently live largely upon European fare, are most apt to succumb to it. As a rule, however, it reduces their strength all round, so that those attacked by it can do little for themselves; and it is clear that this must hamper the activities of so small a community. An epidemic disease such as smallpox, which we have of course also imported and thereby greatly thinned the population, is much to be preferred; for it kills its victims at once, and does not keep them lingering like this slow, sneaking poison.[179]

We see, then, that the result of our influence upon the Greenlanders' material circumstances has been a continuous decline from their former well-being and prosperity towards an almost hopeless poverty and weakness.

Many will admit this, but object that it was really to raise the level of their spiritual life and culture that we went to Greenland, and that this cannot be done save at the expense of their temporal welfare. Let us, then, look a little at this side of our activity. Many people think that a highly developed and civilised community can be fashioned at one stroke out of so unpromising material as a primitive race. This is a great mistake; human nature is not to be transformed at the good pleasure of individuals. It is, indeed, capable of modification; but the development always occurs slowly, like development in nature as a whole. We must not imagine, therefore, that we have the right, as we have done in Greenland and in other places, to swoop down upon a primitive race with our civilisation and impose it upon them. 'Try to fit a hand with five fingers into a glove with four,' says Spencer, 'and the difficulty is strikingly like the difficulty of implanting a complex or composite idea in a mind which has not a correspondingly composite faculty.'

The only change which can be brought about with any sort of rapidity among a primitive race is the change towards degeneration and ruin. Such a change, in the spiritual sphere, sets in as soon as we attempt to impose ethical conceptions upon a people at a stage of cultivation different from our own. This is precisely what we have achieved among the Eskimos. When, for example, in contempt of their own laws and ordinances, we have sought to impose upon them our conceptions of property, which are undeniably fitted for a more developed but less neighbour-loving community than that of Greenland, how can we expect to bring about anything but confusion and ruin? Their whole social scheme was arranged

---

[179] It is strange that the Greenlanders have in great measure escaped syphilis, which is usually one of the first gifts we confer upon those primitive people whom we select as subjects for our experiments in civilisation. It is found only in one place, Arsuk in South Greenland, where they try to isolate it. It is only of recent years that it has been introduced, but from what I hear it appears to have spread, and it seems probable that it will continue to do so, and in course of time affect the whole population.

to fit their primitive socialistic conceptions of property, and as their habits of life are irreconcilable with the new and foreign conception, degeneration is inevitable. And as with the idea of property, so is it with all the other ideas which we have sought to implant in them.

To take one more example: How baneful to them has been the introduction of money! Formerly they had no means of saving up work or accumulating riches; for the products of their labour did not last indefinitely, and therefore they gave away their superfluity. But then they learned the use of money; so that now, when they have more than they need for the moment, the temptation to sell the overplus to the Europeans, instead of giving it to their needy neighbours, is often too great for them; for with the money they thus acquire they can supply themselves with the much-coveted European commodities. Thus we Christians help more and more to destroy instead of to develop their old self-sacrificing love of their neighbours. And money does still more to undermine the Greenland community. Their ideas of inheritance were formerly very vague, for, as before-mentioned, the clothes and weapons of a dead man were consigned with him to the grave. Now, on the other hand, the introduction of money has enabled the survivors to sell the effects of the deceased, and they are no longer ashamed to accept as an inheritance what they can obtain in this way. This may seem an advantage; but, here, too, their old habit of mind is upset. Greed and covetousness—vices which they formerly abhorred above everything—have taken possession of them. Their minds are warped and enthralled by money.

Let us, however, look at another aspect of the case. Our true aim, I suppose, was, after all, to make them a cultivated people, and open up to them a wider range of spiritual interests. But even if we could actually attain this end, must it not necessarily be perilous in the highest degree to give a people like the Eskimos new interests which may divert them from the one thing needful—the duty of providing for themselves and their families. It is vaunted as a brilliant achievement that the majority of the natives of the west coast can now both read and write. Unfortunately for them, they can; for these arts are not to be learned for nothing, and they have indeed to pay dear for their acquirements. It is self-evident that an Eskimo cannot possibly devote his time to these branches of knowledge and nevertheless be as good a hunter as when he had only one interest in life, and learned nothing except hunting and the management of the kaiak.[180] We have direct evidence of the fact that skill with the kaiak has declined, in the many accidents which have happened of late years. Formerly, according to Rink, no more than fifteen or twenty deaths in kaiak-hunting occurred during the year; but in 1888 and 1889 there have been thirty-one fatal kaiak accidents each year.

The chief aim of all education must surely be to make the rising generation good and capable citizens of the community in which their lot is cast. But in what way does an Eskimo become a capable citizen of his little community? Since hunting and fishing are the sole means of supporting existence assigned by Nature to

---

[180] Just as I am sending this to press there appears Gejerstam's *Kulturkampen i Herjedalen*, in which the author argues, as I do, that our school teaching has been the ruin of the Lapps, by weakening their interest in the business of their lives.

this community, it follows that he can become a capable citizen only by acquiring the greatest possible skill in these pursuits. Of what profit, then, to the Eskimo, is his ability to read and write? He assuredly does not learn hunting by help of these arts. It is true that by means of the few books he possesses he may gain information as to other and better countries, unattainable conditions and alleviations, of which he before knew nothing; and thus he becomes discontented with his own lot, which was formerly the happiest he could conceive. And then, too, he can read the Bible—but does he understand very much of it? And would it not do him just as much good if the matter of it were related to him, as his old legends used to be? There can be no doubt that the advantage is dearly bought. We must bear well in mind that the Eskimo community lives upon the very verge of possible human existence, and that a concentrated exertion of all its energies is necessary to enable it to carry on the fight with inhospitable nature. A little more ballast and it must sink. This is what is already happening, and all the wisdom in the world is of no avail.

The upshot, then, of European activity in Greenland has been degeneration and decadence in every respect. And the only compensation we have made to the natives is the introduction of Christianity. In so far we have achieved a happy consummation, for, in name at least, all the Greenlanders of the west coast are now Christians. But the question seems to me to be forced upon us whether this Christianity, too, is not exceedingly dearly bought, and whether the most ardent believer ought not to have some doubts as to the blessings it has conferred upon this people, when he sees how it has cost them their whole worldly welfare?

What part of Christianity is most to be valued, its dogmas or its moral teaching? It seems to me that even the best Christian must admit that it is the latter which is of enduring value; for history can teach him how variable and uncertain the interpretation of the dogmas has always been. Of what value, then, have these dogmas, which he understands so imperfectly, been to the Eskimo? Can anyone seriously maintain that it is a matter of essential moment to a people what dogmas it professes to believe in? Must not the moral laws which it obeys always be the matter of primary concern? And the Eskimo morality was, as we have seen, in many respects at least as good as that of the Christian communities. So that the result of all our teaching has been that, in this respect too, the race has degenerated.

And lastly comes this question: Can an Eskimo who is nominally a Christian, but who cannot support his family, is in ill-health and is sinking into deeper and deeper misery, be held much more enviable than a heathen who lives in 'spiritual darkness,' but can support his family, is robust in body, and thoroughly contented with life? From the Eskimo standpoint at any rate, the answer cannot be doubtful. If he could see his true interest, the Eskimo would assuredly put up this fervent petition: God save me from my friends, my enemies I can deal with myself.

CHAPTER XVII
CONCLUSION

Let us cast a backward glance over the foregoing chapters, and mark what lesson they teach us.

They show us a people, highly gifted by nature, which used to live happily, and, in spite of its faults, stood at a high moral standpoint. But our civilisation, our missions, and our commercial products have reduced its material conditions, its morality, and its social order to a state of such melancholy decline that the whole race seems doomed to destruction.

And yet, as we have seen, it has been more kindly and considerately dealt with than any other people under similar conditions. Is not this a serious warning for us? And if we look around among other primitive peoples, do we not find that the result of their contact with European civilisation and Christianity has everywhere been the same?

What has become of the Indians? What of the once so haughty Mexicans, or the highly gifted Incas of Peru? Where are the aborigines of Tasmania and the native races of Australia? Soon there will not be a single one of them left to raise an accusing voice against the race which has brought them to destruction. And Africa? Yes, it, too, is to be Christianised; we have already begun to plunder it, and if the negroes are not more tenacious of life than the other races, they will doubtless go the same way when once Christianity comes upon them with all its colours flying. Yet we are in no way deterred, and are ever ready with high-sounding phrases about bringing to the poor savages the blessings of Christianity and civilisation.

If we look at the missions of to-day, do we not almost everywhere learn the same lesson? Take for instance a people like the Chinese, standing on a high level of civilisation, and therefore, one would suppose, all the better fitted to receive the new doctrine. One of 'the most enlightened mandarins in China, himself a Christian, and educated at European universities,' writes in the *North China Daily News* an article about the missionaries and their influence, in which, among other things, he says: 'Is it not an open secret that it is only the meanest, most helpless, most ignorant, necessitous, and disreputable among the Chinese who have been and are what the missionaries call "converted"?... I ask whether it cannot be proved that these converts—men who have thrown away the faith of their childhood, men who are forbidden by their teachers to show any sympathy, or indeed anything but contempt, for the memories and traditions of our ancient history—whether it cannot be proved that these men, as soon as they have had to relinquish the hope of worldly gain, have shown themselves to be worse than the worst of the common Chinese rabble? The missionaries are ready enough to tell their hearers that the mandarins are a parcel of idiots who believe in heavenly portents and all such nonsense, while the very next day they will probably be telling the same listeners that the sun and moon really stood still at the command of the Hebrew general, Joshua.' As to the alleged beneficence of the mission towards the natives in the way of relieving poverty and misery, the writer asks: 'Can it be shown that this assistance affords even the barest equivalent for the money which the Chinese Government has to pay for the protection of the missionaries? I believe that the interest alone of these immense sums would be sufficient to support a much larger staff of skilful European doctors and nurses.... Let it be shown what proportion of the millions which compassionate people in Europe and America subscribe for the China missions really goes to the relief of misery. Let it be shown how much goes to the support of the missionaries and their wives and children, to the building of their fine houses and sanatoriums, to postage and paper for their voluminous rose-coloured reports, to the expenses of their congresses, and many other things.... Is it not an open secret that the whole mission is nothing but a charitable foundation for the benefit of unemployed persons in Europe and America?' He further asks whether it is not notorious that the missionaries, 'with their high opinion of their own infallibility, are often intrusive and arrogant, and apt to mix themselves up, with self-imposed authority, in matters that do not concern them? If anyone doubts that the missionaries, taken as a whole, are inclined to these vices, let him study and note the tone and spirit of their own writings.'

This account of matters forcibly reminds us, in many particulars, of what we have just seen in Greenland. The main difference is that when the Chinese offer resistance to the missionaries who have come among them uninvited, they are not simply cuffed and flogged. Recognising the evils that threaten them, they 'beg the foreign powers, in the interests of China as well as of America and Europe, to recall the missionaries,' and having begged in vain, they then try to expel them by force; whereupon these gentlemen, who have come to preach the Gospel of Peace, call upon their Governments for protection, and are supported by gunboats and troops who direct a destructive fire of shells and grape-shot upon the natives, and secure for the pious missionaries a sanguinary compensation for the harm done to their goods and gear, as though it had never been written: 'Provide neither gold, nor silver, nor brass in your purses' (Matthew x. 9).

In all this we recognise the race which, when China sought to protect itself against the ruinous opium-poison, forced it, by means of a bloody war, to open its harbours to the noxious traffic, in order that Europeans might grow rich while the Chinese social fabric was being undermined—from first to last a piece of such shameless scoundrelism that no language has words adequate to describe it. The Eskimos, unfortunately, do not seem to be so far wrong in thinking the Europeans a corrupt and dishonourable race, which ought to come to Greenland in order to learn morals.

But do not the missions elsewhere produce better results? Scarcely. Statistics have recently been published as to crime in India, which cast grave doubts upon the benefits resulting from missionary enterprise. As to Africa I can find no statistics, but from all I can learn it appears that there, too, the results of the missions are nothing to boast of. African travellers are, I believe, unanimous in declaring that the native converts to Christianity are by no means those whom they prefer to take into their service or to rely upon in any way. And Norway, too, contributes its hundreds of thousands[181] yearly to the missions both in Africa and India! Have we so much superfluous wealth that we cannot employ this money to better advantage at home? The desire to help these poor savages whom we have never seen, and whose needs we do not know, is no doubt a noble aspiration; but I wonder whether it would not be nobler still to help the thousands of unfortunates whose necessities we have daily before our eyes? Since we are bent on doing good works, why not begin with those nearest to us? Then, when all at home were beyond the need of assistance, it would be time enough to look abroad and inquire whether there are not elsewhere others who need our help. 'Charity begins at home.'

I am by no means arguing that all missionary enterprise must necessarily be hurtful; but I am of opinion that in order to be really beneficent it must fulfil conditions which, in our time, are almost beyond attainment. In the first place, it demands such a number of noble, self-sacrificing, and altogether remarkable men as we cannot hope to find all at one time. One may come to the front, perhaps two or three, but there can be no steady supply of them. And then we must remember that so many evil influences follow in the wake of a mission, that the most ideal missionaries can neither hold them aloof nor repair the damage they do to the natives. So the result is always the same in the end.

Are we never, then, to open our eyes to what we are really doing? Ought not all true friends of humanity, from pole to pole, to raise a unanimous and crushing protest against all these abuses, against this self-righteous and scandalous treatment of our fellow-creatures of another faith and at another stage of civilisation?

The time will come when posterity will sternly condemn us, and these abuses, which we now hold consistent with the fundamental principles of Christianity, will be branded as profoundly immoral. Morality will then have so far developed that men will no longer consider themselves justified in swooping down upon the first primitive people that comes in their way, in order to satisfy their own religious vanity and to do 'good works' which shall minister to their self-complacency, but which may or may not be beneficial to the race in question. Then only competent and in every sense well-equipped people will take upon themselves to study the life and civilisation of another race in order to see whether it needs our assistance, and if so, in what way it can best be accorded; and if the result of the inquiry is to show that we can do them no good, they will be left alone. But before that time comes, most of such races, even of those which now survive, will have been swept away.

If we ask, in conclusion, whether there is no hope of salvation for the Eskimo community, everyone who knows the circumstances will be forced to admit that the only expedient would be for the Europeans gradually to withdraw from the country. Left to themselves, and freed from subversive foreign influences, the

[181] Crowns, the *krone* being equal to 1*s*. 1½*d*. — *Trans*.

Eskimos might possibly recover their old habits of life, and the race might yet be saved. But this possibility must doubtless be regarded as merely Utopian, at any rate for many a long day to come. In the first place, it would be a severe blow to the vanity of a European state to have to give up an experiment in civilisation which it has once begun, and which it has recorded in large letters to the credit side of its account in the other world; and in the second place it would be useless for the Danish colonies to withdraw unless the ships of other nations could be restrained from trading with the natives and importing European commodities, especially brandy.

NORTHERN LIGHTS—'THE DEAD AT PLAY'

But apart from their intercourse with us, another danger threatens the Eskimos: to wit, the alarming decrease in the number of seals. This is not due to their own fisheries, in which the 'take' is infinitesimal in comparison with the hundreds of thousands of newly born seal-whelps which the European and American sealers slaughter every year, especially upon the drift-ice off Newfoundland. Here it is again the white race which injures the Eskimo; but even if he knew of it, he would not have the power to set any limits to the abuse; his voice cannot make itself heard. Yet seal-hunting is an industry with which our society could very well dispense, while for the Eskimo the seal means life itself.

Thus we find this loveable people inevitably destined either to pass utterly away or to decline into the shadow of what it once was. But the Greenlander bears up cheerfully, and is perhaps happier than we are apt to be; he does not realise his own ruin, and does not hate us, but gives us a friendly welcome when we come to him.

Greenland was once an excellent source of revenue to the Danish Government; but that time is past. Now the Royal Greenland Company and the mission cost large sums every year, and the sums will grow ever larger. Is it to be expected that the Danish Government will keep this going for ever? Would it not be better and wiser for us first to recall our outposts, and then gradually to withdraw the colonies and hand over the warehouses and buildings to the natives? In my own opinion, the very best thing we could do in the end would be to pack up all the stores, put them and the traders on board the Company's nine ships, and set sail with the whole back to Denmark. This will have to be done sooner or later, but perhaps not until there are no natives left behind to inhabit the land. The lifeless numbness of the inland ice will extend to the margin of the sea, where only the mournful wail of the seagulls will be heard along the unpeopled shores. The sun will rise and set and waste its glory over a deserted land. Only once in a while will some storm-driven ship skirt the desolate coasts. But in the long winter nights the dead will dance in shimmering sheets of light over the eternal silence of the snow-fields.

THE END.

Lector House believes that a society develops through a two-fold approach of continuous learning and adaptation, which is derived from the study of classic literary works spread across the historic timeline of literature records. Therefore, we aim at reviving, repairing and redeveloping all those inaccessible or damaged but historically as well as culturally important literature across subjects so that the future generations may have an opportunity to study and learn from past works to embark upon a journey of creating a better future.

This book is a result of an effort made by Lector House towards making a contribution to the preservation and repair of original ancient works which might hold historical significance to the approach of continuous learning across subjects.

HAPPY READING & LEARNING!

LECTOR HOUSE LLP
E-MAIL: lectorpublishing@gmail.com